The Social Life of Justice

The Social Life of Justice

Nasar Meer

polity

First published in 2026 by Polity Press Ltd.

Polity Press Ltd.
65 Bridge Street
Cambridge CB2 1UR, UK

Polity Press Ltd.
111 River Street
Hoboken, NJ 07030, USA

ISBN-13: 978-1-5095-7364-6
ISBN-13: 978-1-5095-7365-3(pb)

A catalogue record for this book is available from the British Library.

Library of Congress Control Number: 2026934818

Typeset in 11.5 on 14pt Adobe Garamond
by Fakenham Prepress Solutions, Fakenham, Norfolk NR21 8NL
Printed and bound in Great Britain by Ashford Colour Ltd

For further information on Polity, visit our website:
politybooks.com

Contents

Acknowledgements

My first thanks are to my students, whose curiosity and engagement have shaped my thinking in this book, most recently those who attended my postgraduate module 'Perspectives on Justice' at the University of Glasgow, as well as to my generous colleagues more broadly. I particularly thank Les Back for his support and encouragement.

Earlier versions of chapters were presented and sharpened through discussion at various locations and events: the Center for Law, History and Culture, Gould School of Law, University of Southern California (16 April 2025); the Inaugural Amal Treacher Kabesh Annual Lecture, University of Nottingham (26 March 2025); a policy-practitioner workshop on Islamophobia co-organized with the Runnymede Trust at SOAS (10 April 2025); a joint keynote, 'Three Perspectives on Epistemic Disobedience', for IASH's 55th Anniversary at the University of Edinburgh (April 2025); a seminar with the Muslim Researchers' Network (28 October 2024); a keynote at the UNESCO RIELA Spring School, 'The Arts of Integrating' (7 October 2024); the British Academy Social and Cultural Infrastructure Policy Challenge Workshop on Tackling Disadvantage (23 September 2024); a keynote for the Institute for Research into Superdiversity (IRiS) Conference (6 September 2024); an invited address to the Foreign, Commonwealth & Development Office, EU Directorate (12 September 2023); contributions to the Scottish Institute for Policing Research – 'Race, Racism and Policing in Scotland: Challenges & Directions for Research' (25 January 2023) and SIPC 2023 (29 November 2023); the Royal Society of Edinburgh event marking the 75th anniversary of the Universal Declaration of Human Rights, Human Rights in Law and Life (7 December 2023); a presentation on 'Methodology and Migration in Cities of Hopes and Fears', University of Glasgow (11 October 2023); 'What's Race Got To Do with It? Critical Reflections on Researching and Teaching Social Policy', University of Edinburgh (9 October 2023); and the Royal Society of Edinburgh's Curious programme event, 'Surfacing Diasporas' (6 September 2023). I am indebted to the organizers and audiences at these meetings for their generous questions and suggestions, which have directly informed revisions to the argument and structure of the chapters. I am also grateful to Sophie Bennani-Taylor and my colleagues at the Centre on the Dynamics of Ethnicity (CoDE), Emma Hill, Hannah Haycox and Nissa Finney, for being able to draw on some of our project data in Chapter 4, including from the UKRI-funded 'The Impacts of the Pandemic on Ethnic and Racialised Groups in the UK'.

I owe ongoing thanks to my colleagues on the *Identities: Global Studies in Culture and Power* editorial team and the wider journal family, not least my co-editor Aaron Winter and our editorial and content officer Michaelagh Broadbent. The Stuart Hall Foundation remains a vital home for thinking in common, and I am grateful to colleagues there and to the scholars and fellows who make up its now formidable network, and who exemplify how scholarship and public life can meet. Sincere thanks also go to the reviewers of the proposal for this book for their constructive and generous feedback. As a journal and book series editor, I want to convey that this labour is seen and appreciated, along with that of the team at Polity, Jonathan Skerrett, Julia Davies, Shannon Kneis, Max Lee, Sarah Dancy and Rachel Moore, for their steady support and good judgment at each stage of the process. I am grateful to the Nuffield Foundation for their generous support for our team project 'Racial Equality since Devolution: Divergences, Outcomes and Frontiers'.

My daughter Aiisha has become an unexpected and incisive collaborator, and with her I have made sense of a multitude of authors and ideas. With characteristic succinctness, she has – inevitably – distilled the key problem as she sees it. And to Katherine, ever an intellectually demanding friend and a loving partner, I offer my deepest thanks.

This book is dedicated to my siblings Khadir, Malik, Khaliq, Khalda and Khadija, to all of whom I owe more than I can know.

Abbreviations

CaCHE	Collaborative Centre for Housing Evidence (UK)
CCC	Climate Change Committee (UK)
CCRA	climate change risk assessment (UK)
CEAS	Common European Asylum System
CJEU	Court of Justice of the European Union
CUKC	Citizen of the United Kingdom and Colonies
ECHR	European Convention on Human Rights
ECRE	European Council on Refugees and Exiles
EPRS	European Parliamentary Research Service (European Parliament)
EU	European Union
FOI	freedom of information (requests/disclosures)
HMICFRS	His Majesty's Inspectorate of Constabulary and Fire & Rescue Services (UK)
HMIP	His Majesty's Inspectorate of Prisons (UK)
ICC	International Criminal Court
ICIBI	Independent Chief Inspector of Borders and Immigration (UK)
IDMC	Internal Displacement Monitoring Centre
IHL	international humanitarian law

IHRL	international human rights law
IMF	International Monetary Fund
IOI	International Ombudsman Institute
IOM	International Organization for Migration
IPC	Integrated Food Security Phase Classification
IPCC	Intergovernmental Panel on Climate Change
ITU	International Telecommunication Union
MENA	Middle East and North Africa
NAO	National Audit Office (UK)
NAP	National Adaptation Programme (UK)
NBA	Nationality and Borders Act (2022)
NGO	nongovernmental organization
NRPF	no recourse to public funds (UK)
OCHA	Office for the Coordination of Humanitarian Affairs (UN)
OHCHR	Office of the High Commissioner for Human Rights (UN)
ONS	Office for National Statistics (UK)
PDNA	Post-Disaster Needs Assessment
PFS	Prepaid Financial Services
POST	Parliamentary Office of Science and Technology (UK)
TWAIL	third world approaches to international law
UDHR	Universal Declaration of Human Rights
UHI	urban heat island
UKHSA	UK Health Security Agency
UN	United Nations
UNDP	United Nations Development Programme
UNFCCC	United Nations Framework Convention on Climate Change
UNHCR	United Nations High Commissioner for Refugees
UNHRC	United Nations Human Rights Council
UNICEF	United Nations Children's Fund

UNRWA	United Nations Relief and Works Agency for Palestine Refugees in the Near East
USAID	US Agency for International Development
WHO	World Health Organisation
WWA	World Weather Attribution

Preface

I have been working on this book for some time, ever since I published *The Cruel Optimism of Racial Justice* in 2022. In the interim years, a palpable sense of uncertainty has come to characterize the public mood. Perhaps we've all felt it? A 'gnawing sensibility' (Goldberg, 2021: 4) that something we have produced or failed to stem is nearing. If nothing else, we've likely seen it expressed in news cycles that accelerate as our grip on the issues loosens, amid elections that arrive with a qualified optimism and disappointment thereafter; ceasefires that unravel as they are announced; rising prices that outstrip wages; and oddly warm summers joined later by unprecedented flooding. All of this mixes nerves about tomorrow with doubt about what's unfolding today. Maybe this is what a 'prelude to Disaster and the forerunner of Catastrophe' feels like (Césaire, 2000: 36), or, more optimistically, an 'interregnum' between a failing order with its 'morbid symptoms' (Gramsci, 1971: 276) and something better (if we can be organized enough to grasp it). Alas, this book cannot see round corners and, besides, social scientists aren't really in the futures business (not reliably, anyhow). The claims presented here are more modest, but, I hope, more useful in arguing that justice is how we stay truthful under pressure and build institutions that hold when reassurance is scarce. In this way, I treat justice in this book not as a final picture to be agreed in the abstract, but as a practice of design that reduces harms and shares benefits. Injustice, on this view, is not a fog that descends from nowhere; instead, it rises out of social dynamics, institutions and histories that decide who is seen and sorted, and who is heard or made to prove they are worth being listened to.

This book is written for more than one kind of reader. Some will come to it from a political theory vantage point, others from sociology, law or policy, and still others from the practical experience of watching institutions speak the language of justice while distributing its goods unevenly. That mixed audience has shaped the choices I have made on style. At times, the argument requires specialized terms, because these name real mechanisms in how categories travel, how institutions translate principle into procedure, and how harms become normal through routine. But I have tried to keep the conceptual apparatus in service of clarity about what justice does in social life, without allowing the prose to become a test of prior initiation. Where a technical concept is introduced, I define it as plainly as I can on first use, and return to that definition only when it helps the reader see a pattern more sharply.

My wager is that accessibility requires not that the argument is diluted, but that it is paced. If the writing sometimes slows down, it does so to keep visible the steps by which an idea becomes an arrangement, and an arrangement becomes a habit in how a policy label reshapes what can be claimed; how an evidential rule decides whose pain counts; how an administrative template can turn structural injury into a 'case' that is processed and closed. Justice in this sense is not only a value we affirm, but a practical vocabulary that loops back into the world through law, policy and professional judgment. The chapters that follow therefore aim to make that loop readable, so that the reader can track how justice is authored, limited and rebuilt under pressure.

Chapter 1 sets out the meaning of justice as a social practice answerable to evidence and institution. Chapter 2 reads the canonical archive as a living repertoire of moves that neutralize the 'social' in ideas that become arrangements, and proposes duties of design in place of tidy abstractions. Chapter 3 reframes the social contract as domination contracts, sexual and racial, and asks what it is that justice requires when we begin from subordination rather than symmetry, and with it revise categories and focus social action. Chapter 4 follows bordering as a renewal ceremony for domination contracts, and specifies how to convert benevolence into enforceable reciprocity. Chapter 5 develops an ethic of witnessing that refuses the rationing of grievability and shows how legality can be weaponized as innocence unless it is bound to redesign. Chapter 6 turns to climate, indicts adaptation without history and sets out a reparative programme that connects local and global contexts. The conclusion braids these ideas into a thesis that treats domination as baseline, widening law's lexicon from fault to design, tracking obligation along the paths of benefit and injury and building borders and memory as institutions of reciprocity rather than evasion. If our mood of uncertainty tempts aphorism or abstraction, *The Social Life of Justice* moves us the other way, towards social arrangements that can hold when reassurance is scarce.

1

Introduction: Justice in an Unjust World

One reason to write a book is the belief that sharing insight can help readers to better understand their world and, at times, even to change it. Scholarship on justice is an enduring example of this motivation. Namely, that, as a spur for social action, basis for legal principle and object of political dispute, ideas of justice give *reason* to our *intuition* that something is very wrong in a world where five men wield private fortunes larger than the annual economies of Norway, Denmark and Finland combined (roughly $1.35 trillion), but more than one-quarter of humanity lacks access to safe drinking water, one-third is without connection to the internet, and around one-tenth survive on less than the equivalent of $2.15 a day (IMF, 2024; World Bank, 2023; WHO, 2022; ITU, 2024). Rather than a concept for *the ages* therefore, justice is a concept for *our age.* On the one hand, granting access to an analytical vocabulary with which we can appeal to what is right, wrong, fair or otherwise; on the other, insisting we should *feel* it's more than an unfortunate contingency that an infant girl in a low-income country is thirty times more likely to die in delivery than her counterpart in a high-income country (WHO, 2024; 2025b).

The obvious question we face, however, is one that many readers may have asked themselves already – namely: 'What does justice mean in an unjust world?' It is a good question. For, accompanying the monopoly of power and runaway wealth that will further embed inequality for generations, we live amid advancing tides of political chauvinism that can be seen in the rise of populist parties in the democracies of Europe, the US, South America and India, intent on reversing hard-won progress on gender equality and protections for minorities. The apparent disregard for a patchwork of human rights and international humanitarian laws, meanwhile, stitched together over the past seventy-five years, further suggests that the moral arc of the universe, which the African American civil rights leader Martin Luther King believed ultimately tilts towards justice, is yet to take us with it.

If we add to this ledger the prospects of ecological catastrophe and the retreat from coordinated action tackling climate change, the hope for enlightened self-correction becomes a moot point given that we can only destroy the planet once. The horror of conventional warfare, in the meantime, offers ample evidence of our desire to dehumanize and destroy some of its inhabitants. As the United Nations Office of the High Commissioner for Human Rights (OHCHR) reports, in the three months following 7 October 2023, Israeli authorities detonated massive explosives equivalent to 'the energy of two nuclear bombs' on the Gaza Strip, one of the most densely populated urban areas in the world, and in which children made up half the total population (UNICEF, n.d.).[1] From the ground, US surgeons working with the medical charity Palestine American Bridge recounted in one interview: 'We're taking care of children in bits and pieces … There were some nights I spent more time putting little kids in body bags than I was doing actual surgery, and their body parts were still clothed in pyjamas' (BBC World at One, 3 July 2025). On witnessing cities razed to the ground, their collapsed buildings entombing inhabitants, we might respond to our question concerning what justice means 'only with a philosophical laugh' (Foucault, 1980: 121). As a gesture of critical distance to the absurdity of clinging to absent certainties, when the very conventions on which global justice had seemingly been erected are dismembered, strewn amid the body parts clothed in pyjamas, people of conscience may well wish to understand their world less well.

And yet, alongside the violence and grief, the world is still inhabited, still lived in, still capable of beauty and love, wisdom and care, cooperation and creation that demand of us a means to realize layered truths that acknowledge horror without letting it eclipse our ability to alter it. This is what the poet Zagajewski (2001) termed 'the mutilated world'. Recognizing historical trauma and human cruelty, the destruction of cities and the displacement of peoples means reckoning with brokenness without surrendering to despair. In this spirit, therefore, what follows is less a tour of ideals than a map of arrangements, tracking not just what our traditions say, but what they hide and what they license. It includes how each neutralizes 'the social' in different ways, and so reframes the familiar question (who wronged whom?) as the more difficult one of what arrangements produce which harms, and where duties to redesign them rest. It ends by asking for whom the imagined order of justice is used, preparing the pivot to a vocabulary that can name the concealed architecture doing the real work. For if the means to restrain atrocity no longer hold sway, the question is not only whether justice is possible, but how some losses come to count as losses at all. This is the point that Judith Butler (2004; 2009) has often reached in arguing that justice begins from the uneven social recognition of a life as a life, and where public grieving is not merely an after-effect of death, but the prior condition that makes some losses legible and others unseeable. For example, in *Frames of War*, Butler develops the claim that our shared 'ontological precariousness' (that all lives are vulnerable and dependent) is politically organized so that only certain losses 'count' within dominant media, legal and national frames (2009: 4, 23). Put starkly, our grasp of what is 'grievable' precedes and makes possible the recognition of a life itself; but where grievability does not attach, a life is not publicly registered as a life and its loss scarcely appears (ibid: 14–15). What matters for the argument that follows has long been recognized by postcolonial scholarship, perhaps neatly captured in Aimé Césaire's account of 'thingification' (2000: 42). Namely, how Europeans rendered those they colonized into 'things' and then counted them, if at all, as statistics. The very mechanism Butler calls a rationing of grievability was, for Césaire, the ordinary work of empire.

In different ways, both thinkers spotlight a kind of moral indifference that is shaped by the power to establish a moral vocabulary of public life, pre-sorting whose suffering can be named, deciding what counts as injury, loss and, ultimately, justice. Yet it is striking how this sentiment might easily take us back to a set of dialogues that rest at the foundation of Western thought on justice, and which also emerge from a moment when questions about justice and power felt anything but academic. Written around 380 BCE yet dramatized in the war-shadowed Athens of half a century earlier, Plato's *The Republic* turns a single evening's dinner into a searching debate on the meaning and worth of justice, pitting the philosopher Socrates against the rhetoric of sophists, the realism of soldiers and the ambitions of emerging politicians. In a memorable line from the dialogue's anti-hero Thrasymachus, we are told: 'The just is nothing else than the advantage of the stronger' (Plato, 1987: 338c).[2] Justice, in other words, amounts to a label pinned on whatever serves those who hold power, for every political regime, whether tyranny, aristocracy or democracy, 'enacts the laws with a view to its own advantage … and proclaims that the just for their subjects is that which is for their [the rulers] advantage' (339a). In this view, justice is nothing more than the compliance of the weak with the self-serving dictates of the powerful (cf. Annas, 1981; Reeve, 1988). No less important than institutionalized self-interest, however, the powerful also shape the moral vocabulary itself, meaning that power does not make what is right, it *is* right.

In the next chapter, we encounter the response from Socrates: that governance should be understood as an art or craft (*technē*), and, like any genuine art, it seeks to benefit its object rather than the practitioner (Plato, 1987; Bloom, 1991). The key point at this stage is the identification of moral vocabulary as a kind of fulcrum, which remains a fascinating and enduring observation returned to in subsequent chapters, including how what is *not* voiced jointly establishes knowledge and cements the conventions as that which *is* voiced. This concern more broadly runs throughout the book, no less so than current anxiety about naming injustice and the moral indifference this cultivates. For example, the distinguished cultural anthropologist Talal Asad, responding to an interview question on the difference between analysis and social action, has suggested:

> We simply don't have a language now to speak adequately of the changes in which we live and the threats we face. To develop such a language, one requires not only thought but also practical conditions for its development. But the time of danger is different from the time required to meet it practically. (Iqbal and Asad, 2017: 214)

We might take Asad to mean that the conceptual tools we currently use in our 'language' in the broadest sense (not just words, but also categories, frameworks, assumptions) are insufficient for the depth or complexity of the transformations and crises of our time. Recognizing this, however, is not the same as concluding that the world is changing faster than our ability to meaningfully interpret or narrate those changes. On the contrary, my argument in this book is that we do have a vocabulary if we are willing to grasp it in the social life of justice. Sometimes, the most consequential work is neither a complete theory nor the application of a settled principle, but the invention of terms that reorganize what can be perceived, contested and evidenced. A vocabulary in this sense can bring an experience into public consciousness and thereby alter what counts as an injury and what counts as a remedy. In that sense, the question is not whether we have language, but which language we allow to count, and this means looking to answers that rest neither in the promise of justice as a timeless ideal, nor in an assumption of progress. Rather, by extending an invitation to 'stay with the trouble' (Haraway, 2016) and forgo the reassurances of inevitable progress found in our conceptual language, *The Social Life of Justice* treats the topic as an unsettled social construct expressed in histories and institutions, yes, but also in the cultures and contemporary social relations of societies. Justice, in this sense, is both memorial and mobilizing since it keeps faith with the dead by refusing resignation and turns remembrance into commitments that reshape the conditions of life for those who remain. As Mary 'Mother' Jones once put it, we must 'pray for the dead, and fight like hell for the living' (Jones, 1969 [1925]: 41). The ethical upshot is not to mourn more loudly, but to refuse the hierarchy of what is 'grievable'.

Drawing on interdisciplinary perspectives, this book argues that addressing injustice therefore requires us to bear witness without numbing or forgetting, and not to presume that because today is not yesterday, our societies are 'gradually moving toward perfection – through incremental reforms' (Seamster and Ray, 2018: 316). This is key, because the focus on social dynamics can simultaneously lay bare the regressions of today as people navigate the hopeful certainties of continued progress towards a more just tomorrow. Indeed, it is arguable that every single account of justice ever written has needed some idea of the 'social' for justice to take place, or be hypothetically imagined as capable of taking place. Outside certain political theory traditions, however, social scientists rarely focus *directly* on questions of justice; yet we are deeply concerned with social justice, not only for practical reasons, but because we are committed to ideas about improving society and believe the social sciences have a role to play in this.

Still, and despite a colossal volume of work on justice, too often the very ideas about the nature of society that animate arguments about justice remain in the background or become overlaid with various qualifiers without diminishing assumptions of detached validity. Even while the contemporary justice canon is vast and internally diverse, this tendency is shared by different kinds of theorists, to varying degrees, who focus on principles for allocating benefits and burdens, while bracketing the very thing to be allocated: the concrete form and structure of the social world (Rawls, 1999 [1971]; Nozick, 1974; Sen, 1999; Pettit, 1997; Fraser, 2008; Mignolo, 2011; O'Neil, 2016). Judith Shklar (1990) can be read as an exception in this regard, precisely because she refuses the assumption that injustice is merely the absence of justice; rather, she insists that injustice has to be understood on its own terms, including in cases where officials or institutions fail to prevent foreseeable damage, a failure she names 'passive injustice' (1990: 3, 56). Even so, her work is still thinner on the social question that my argument puts centre stage, namely how institutions, histories and categorical power actively produce the 'goods' and 'bads' that later appear as objects of distributive reasoning. Specifically, Shklar leaves undeveloped the link between her evocative building blocks and an explanation of who is responsible, through what institutional processes and by what mechanisms responsibility is generated and assigned. My claim is not only that we mis-see injustice; it's that the social world is the formative medium of justice itself, and that requires more than a compelling sensibility. It requires analytic specification of how power and institutions make, stabilize and revise the terrain on which justice claims become possible in the first place.

The broader 'volume-variety paradox' means that, as the literature grows in size and variety, its grasp of the 'social' (sometimes expressed in terms of 'social ontology') remains thin, idealized or simply undefined. Put plainly, the problem is not that we lack theories of justice, but that we too often treat 'the social' as scenery; an assumed backdrop rather than the very medium through which justice is made or withheld. When the world is rendered as a neutral stage, injustice can be misread as a distributional glitch rather than the predictable output of institutions, histories and categories that organize life chances in advance. That is why this book keeps returning to the mundane machinery of justice – e.g., eligibility rules, evidential thresholds, administrative templates, contractual forms – alongside the big normative claims. The question is about how our dominant ways of reasoning have trained us to miss what justice is already doing. This explicit or implicit normativity overlooks what it means for societies to have histories, social structures and cultures of meaning that may (and have) been altered through appeals to justice, and which cannot stand apart from any idea of justice we can hold in our minds. Bridging this gap requires accounts of justice to *foreground* social and political institutions and power relations that fashion the material landscape of the very goods that theories of distribution seek to distribute. Yet, when we look to one of the most referenced authors on justice, John Rawls (1921–2002), writing a couple of millennia after *The Republic*, we are back to individuals tasked with deliberating on which principles could underpin a just society. Using a thought experiment to imagine how we might get there, the critical insight, according to Rawls, is that, without knowledge of their future position in society, individuals are more likely to prioritize fairness, since they could potentially occupy any social or economic position. As we discover in the next chapter, for Rawls, this 'veil of ignorance' is a key mechanism in ensuring that the principles of justice are not derived by self-serving motivations. As that chapter will also show, the device is an elegant trap in which abstracting from social dynamics turns structural injury into a distributive puzzle. Notwithstanding, the device serves as a cornerstone of contemporary frameworks of justice, subject to critique and so a point of departure, as well as providing ballast to overlook what it means for societies to have histories, social structures and cultures of meaning. Several unsatisfactory dialogues have unfolded between advocates of justice as distribution of material resources (redistribution) and approaches to justice as material resources being dependent on status and identity (recognition). Some writers, most notably Nancy Fraser and Axel Honneth (2003), tried to bring matters of equality together under the two registers, but have struggled because of how distributive justice has been configured in dominant theoretical traditions, namely in narrowing recognition to an idea of status – that is, what majority society thinks of a group, how *it* treats *them*, and without an understanding of what the cultural practice in question means (cf. Modood, 2024).

My point of departure for *The Social Life of Justice* is a refusal to treat the topic as discrete debates that can be solved within siloed literatures. The discussion therefore presses beyond the familiar critique of Rawlsian liberalism not simply by identifying its blind spots, but by staging a conversation in which 'canonical' reasoning is interrogated alongside critical traditions.[3] Whereas exemplary recent works, such as Ruha Benjamin's *Viral Justice* (2022) and Olúfẹ́mi O. Táíwò's *Reconsidering Reparations* (2022), treat justice as a distributed practice that scales up through small changes, and reframe climate justice as world-making redistribution, respectively, this book weaves environmental, racial, epistemic and gender justice into a coherent analytic of power and repair, integrating critiques of law, borders and datafied governance. Therefore, this is not a book against theory, but rather against the jurisdiction of 'ideal theory' as an inventory of possibilities – something that widens the chasm, as Charles Mills (1997) famously described, between discussions of justice and struggles for justice. Of course, all good concepts are promises, and justice no less so in being an ancient concern and contemporary topic in theoretical inquiry, a principle for political conduct and a force for social action. Recognizing this is to strike a balance between knowledge of the fundamentals and knowing how to disregard them, and this book invites readers to navigate justice as a contested and lived experience, focusing on questions of domination, knowledge, belonging, hope and the intersection of justice with pressing global issues such as climate change and migration.

The double hermeneutic of justice

This section establishes one piece of groundwork for everything that follows. It explains why I treat ideas about justice as part of social life rather than as commentary upon it. The claim is that concepts are not just descriptions; once they are taken up by institutions (by law, policy, professional practice, audit and education), they begin to organize what is thinkable and doable. That is why it matters that certain canonical ways of talking about justice still dominate syllabi and common sense, and endure as texts and habits of inference that travel. The assertion that prevailing theories of justice often evade its social life requires elaboration, and allows us to see the powerful legacy within Western thought that conceptualizes justice as an abstract ideal. This approach is epitomized by social contract theory, which variously fashions political legitimacy from the consent (or acquiescence) of a community's members. Although social contract theory is a product of modernity, the treatment of justice as an ideal is ancient, as we have noted, in going back to Plato's *Republic* and its account of Socratic dialogue on justice as the foundational virtue for both the individual soul and the city-state. The enduring influence of this tradition is evidenced by the canonical status of these texts. *The Republic* ranks as the second most assigned text in university curricula, while Thomas Hobbes, John Locke, Jean-Jacques Rousseau and, later,

John Rawls all consistently appear in the top quartiles (Open Syllabus, 2025).[4] This is striking, as these classics lack the rapid publication and citation cycles of modern economics or STEM fields. Their persistence points to a unique adoption across disciplinary boundaries: political theorists use Plato's tripartite soul to analyse civic stratification; criminologists model scenarios on Hobbes's 'state of nature'; policy analysts invoke Rousseau to frame citizen participation; and economists reinterpret Rawlsian principles in debates on global inequality (Putnam and Garrett, 2020; Sampson and Levy, 2022).[5] This broad, contemporary relevance across the humanities and social sciences signals more than mere resonance; it has a feedback loop in how ideas about justice shape institutions, and how institutions reshape the ideas we use. The 'double hermeneutic', then, is when concepts actively shape the social realities they seek to describe.

While there is not a 'best before' date on scholarship, the assumption is that our concepts, with all their depth and differentiation from everyday language, are challenged and revised in terms of their own coherence as well as in relation to the changing circumstance in which that insight is applied. But the task for social and political scientists is greater than may at first appear. For our analyses to be meaningful, they also must be reflexive, and this means that we also need to think about the intellectual frames through which we have come to understand what we name as justice and injustice. Meeting this challenge is important. Not doing so can overlook how, *through our concepts*, we sometimes help constitute, reinforce or ignore the things we claim only to study.

Two distinct but connected movements are captured by a 'double hermeneutic'. First, the interpretive labour of lay actors who already name and negotiate their worlds; second, the labour of social scientists who formalize those vernacular terms into analytic categories that subsequently re-enter public life via professional practice, policy and law. As Anthony Giddens insists, 'all actors are social theorists, and must be so to be social agents at all', and 'all social life is an active accomplishment' (1993: 14, 17), and this is why our descriptions are never observations from a distance, but interventions in the practice of the world. It is at the point of re-entry that concepts help make the very realities they purport to describe, and Giddens argues explicitly that 'the "findings" of social science do not remain insulated from the "subject-matter" to which they refer, but consistently re-enter and reshape it', and that this is not simply a matter of neutral 'feed-back mechanisms'; rather, 'the intrusion of concepts and knowledge-claims back into the universe of events they were coined to describe produces an essential erraticism' (ibid.: 18–19).

The relevant units here are not only grand theories of justice, but the mid-level categories that travel, such as 'risk', 'vulnerability', 'cohesion', 'hate crime', 'safeguarding', 'integration', 'adaptation', 'algorithm', etc. Once institutionalized, they organize attention and resources, invite particular forms of compliance and resistance, and thus alter the next round of research. The loop is real but asymmetrical, since state bureaucracies, platforms and professional associations function as privileged 're-entry points', amplifying some basic concepts and muting others. For that reason, Giddens also argues that sociologists have a distinctive duty of public address: 'in contrast to the situation in natural science, sociologists have a 'scientific', rather than only civic, obligation to present their ideas to a lay audience' (1993: 19). Treating justice as possessing this social life therefore commits this book to concept-work as method, because the 'double hermeneutic' is a live circuit of conceptual traffic.

Concepts, then, are not simply terms for phenomena, but structured ways of seeing, ordering and evaluating the world. It is sometimes said that concepts in the Platonic sense should 'carve at the joints' (Phaedrus 265d–266a, in Plato, 1989). By this, it is meant that the given properties that make up any concept should not be arbitrary but instead reflect the organization of repeated phenomena. The task of any researcher is to separate the segments at the appropriate points, just like a butcher carving up an animal at the 'joints' instead of randomly across the social field (or, indeed, carcass). This assessment begins to set a 'concept' apart from a 'term'. This doesn't mean that a term is without any analytical depth. On the contrary, as Cantwell Smith elaborates (1996: 16), a term too can come to be 'a significant index of how we think. Also, more actively, it is a significant factor in determining how we think.' The point is that, while both a term and a concept can offer interpretative order to our understanding of the social world, a *concept* offers us something weightier, something thicker. Inevitably, there is a much deeper theoretical argument that can help us to locate the place of a concept, one that is related to ways in which we can conceptualize language and text, and which remains unresolved in social scientific inquiry. This cannot properly be summarized here, but, briefly, we might point to a tradition of scholarship that is influenced by the later work of the philosopher Ludwig Wittgenstein (1953), and especially the idea that we should understand language as a coherent (though diverse) set of games that are governed by common rules. The rules bear resemblance to one another and emphasize the ways in which human agents 'are intentionally speaking according to their mentality and consciousness' (Garling, 2013: 18). Here, local context is important (e.g., in terms of the rules of the game), but in a way that is different from a second tradition, known as structuralism, which also views language as a system that can be studied according to the rules that are deemed to structure it. Owing much to the work on linguistics by Ferdinand Saussure (2006 [1916]), this tradition insists that 'words are not mere vocal labels or communicational adjuncts superimposed upon an already given order of things. They are collective products of social interaction, essential instruments through which human beings constitute and articulate their world' (Harris, 1988: ix). For people influenced by the first tradition, the focus tends to be on the 'players'; for those influenced by the second tradition, the prevailing focus is on the 'rules'. The challenge for a social scientific concept is that it has to be alive to both of these concerns. John Brewer once described the task as follows: 'What makes a concept sociologically significant is that the classification of empirical reality it institutes is one which succeeds in capturing … Unfortunately, this offers a range of possibilities. The word "concept" … is a blank cheque: its potential value depends on its use' (1982: 392).

This excellent observation is useful in a number of respects. First, it reminds us that even a theoretical concept, one that claims utility in helping to explain the social world, must bear some relationship to empirical phenomena. This need not be narrow, for it may take into consideration a variety of 'data', including biography. This is not to say that knowledge is relativistic, but that it is socially constructed and so there can be a politics to its appropriation. Second, it raises another question concerning the nature of the relationship between subjectivity and research. As Sumi Madhok has argued:

> Not only is there a need for concepts to describe and visualise different life-worlds but also for these different conceptual descriptions to intervene in and disrupt the normal and ordinary work of theory production that carries on thoughtlessly and wilfully ignorant of different life-worlds and their conceptual architectures. To put it differently, in the absence of concepts 'made to the measure of the world', the 'universal' concepts that are put to use in producing theoretical descriptions of the world are in fact, 'provincial', and reflect particular temporal, spatial, social and historical contexts. (2024: 9)

This sleight of hand does more than misdescribe reality; it reproduces hierarchy. When particular concepts masquerade as universals, they eclipse other sites of knowledge by relegating them to the status of the merely 'local', 'descriptive' or 'non-epistemic', and they narrow the field of imagination by rendering alternative modes of practice unthinkable. The consequences are visible across domains, not least human rights schemas centred on individuals, and they sideline relational personhood and collective membership. The point is that not meeting the standard implied requires concept-work as method through co-producing and translating categories with, not over, the worlds we study, alongside a comparative reflexivity about what each concept presupposes and obscures, and the institutional changes that allow the concepts that might emerge from this to count as theory. Only then do our descriptions intervene where needed, and our universals begin to earn their name.

A 'critical' approach?

Does this mean that this book takes a 'critical' approach? Yes and no. If the previous sections have signalled that justice does not hover above social life but circulates through it (its terms seized, reworded and redeployed by the powerful as well as by those who resist), then a 'critical' approach names the method equal to that fact. We cannot repair a damaged moral vocabulary by prescribing principles to a world to which those very principles will return and reshape conduct; we must work with the feedback loop itself. In that light, critique is not an external commentary, but a practice for redesigning the very categories that organize action, so that they disclose domination rather than naturalize it, and enable repair rather than obscure responsibility (cf. Iqbal and Asad, 2017: 214). This means moving past philosophical hubris that treats politics as a transmission belt for conclusions already settled elsewhere. Values are not external ornaments added to political life, but internal to it, and those values are clarified, contested and made answerable.

This is why the book distances itself from the jurisdiction of ideal theory in the Rawlsian sense (1999: 10), in which procedure secures impartiality partly by suspending exactly the kinds of structurally produced harms that are historically sedimented and power-laden. As we will see, if history is placed behind the veil domestically, entrenched hierarchies can be treated as noise relative to a clean choice of principles. If history is placed behind the veil internationally, empire, extraction, racialized domination and other long-run mechanisms shaping global inequality cannot appear as constitutive injustices that set the terms of what a fair international order would require.

For example, in *The Law of Peoples* (1999), Rawls frames his international argument as an extension of the liberal idea of the social contract, and he executes that extension by importing the central 'device of representation' developed for domestic justice in *A Theory of Justice* (1999 [1971]), namely the original position together with the veil of ignorance. The practical upshot is that structurally generated harms can be positioned as background conditions to be managed after principles are selected, rather than as constitutive injustices that should shape the selection of principles from the start. The architecture travels, but it is recalibrated with the same ideal-theoretic method operating across scales, from the basic structure of a domestic society to the basic structure of a society of peoples, and it does so by repeatedly bracketing knowledge of the very contingencies through which advantage and injury are historically produced (Rawls, 1982; 1993; 2005). This is an argument that I extend in this book by foregrounding the social ontology of justice: the infrastructures, organizations, power relations and material conditions that make goods possible in the first place. On this view, 'critical' does not mean anti-empirical or anti-theoretical. It names a style of inquiry that binds explanation to emancipation, diagnosing how practices and institutions work and orienting them to transformation. In place of a naivety of inevitability, as Tully (1999: 91) puts it, this book shares an ethos of reflective self-limitation and practical reason that entails several commitments that track the problems that have surfaced so far.

First, historicity over abstraction, because moral language is a battleground, not a neutral medium, and concepts must be treated as historical artefacts with users and effects. Across the contract tradition, the 'social' is variously neutralized – as danger (Hobbes), as pre-political property space (Locke), as a threat to unanimity (Rousseau), or as a background variable cleansed by thought experiment (Rawls). In each case, the mechanisms that reproduce domination are set aside as contingencies to be corrected after the fact rather than as the formative context that any credible theory of justice must face. This also applies to critiques, including parts of the decolonial lexicon, including Mignolo's promissory call for 'epistemic delinking' towards 'pluriversality as a universal project' (2005: 121). These brilliantly provincialize Euro-modern reason, yet risk relocating emancipation to the plane of knowledge, while under-specifying the institutions capable of disciplining capital, securing land or coordinating welfare (Tuck and Yang, 2012; see Meer, 2018b for an extended discussion).

Second, reflexivity about our own tools; since social scientific categories loop back into the world, they can entrench the very blind spots they aim to bring into view. The task is to build concepts that 'carve at the joints' of social life, not at the joints of our disciplinary habits, concepts thick enough to register how harms are produced across law, labour, care, data and border regimes (Phaedrus 265d–266a, in Plato, 1989; see also Cantwell Smith, 1996: 16). That means keeping faith with both sides of the language debate sketched earlier: attention to the 'players' (Wittgensteinian rule-following in use) and to the 'rules' (structuralist attention to the systems that shape sense), so that our categories neither float free of practice nor reduce practice to textual play (Wittgenstein, 1953; Harris, 1988: ix; Garling, 2013: 18).

Third, normativity without paternalism, for, while critical social science rejects the fiction of value-free description (Agger, 2006: 4), its normativity must be accountable to those most exposed to harm, not imposed over them. Hence the organizing questions concerning where justice is located, who gets to name it and which institutions turn claims into guarantees are joined to a methodological injunction to make concepts answerable to movements and to evidence. The point is not only to interpret the moral vocabulary of our time, but to change the conditions under which that vocabulary is authored and enforced (van Krieken et al., 2014: 5; Macey, 2000: 309). If 'might' so often is made into 'right', then a critical approach must work on the levers that translate words into worlds and the methods by which the social life of justice is rendered visible and *revisable*; this approach will guide the chapters that follow as they move from canonical arguments to the institutions and practices that sustain or subvert them.

There is also a personal reason to write this way. Like many readers, I have invested free labour in roles that I believed might make a difference, accepting trade-offs, strategic refusals and cumulative emotional work. I do so as a social scientist and as a Muslim who understands that my troubles cannot be solved as private troubles, but must be grasped as public issues, linked to the problems of history-making (Mills, 2000 [1959]: 226). The register of this book therefore matches its claim: a method that treats language as a site of struggle, history as constitutive rather than decorative, and institutions as the levers through which words become worlds. To 'stay with the trouble' here is not to dwell in melancholy, but to make the impasse analytically visible and practically revisable, so that optimism becomes a practice of design rather than a tether to scenes that wear us out (Berlant, 2011; Haraway, 2016).

Methods and materials

The chapters that follow try to keep normative claims answerable to records, while reading those records as products of power. The point is not to discard records, but to read them for both content and deployment: what they say, and how, where and by whom they are used. This is also why the book is wary of the contemporary institutional tendency to treat 'ethics' as a procedural overlay. In public life, ethical language is increasingly ubiquitous, but it often arrives as an instrument of closure in ethics as a set of rules to apply, a compliance hurdle to clear, or a list of 'values' displayed as self-certifying testimony to virtue. Even the vogue for deliberative consultation (e.g., citizen juries and participation exercises) can sometimes function as a displacement of judgment, as if the existence of process were itself sufficient to settle value conflict. Yet the central difficulty is usually prior to permissibility in what counts as ethical import, whose reasons are recognized as reasons, and how moral ambiguity is handled when it cannot be made to disappear. Read in this light, records perform and offer procedural cleanliness as a proxy for justice. That is why it matters to track how 'ethical' governance can collapse into the administrable forms that certify correctness while leaving underlying harm-design intact. The discussion of bordering and asylum accommodation work this method into the grain of specific institutions; inspection and audit materials (HMICFRS, HMIP, ICIBI, NAO), parliamentary briefings, case law and Home Office guidance are paired with testimonies from people housed in hotels and large site accommodation. Freedom of information disclosures help reconstruct subcontracting chains and compare stated oversight with everyday practice of curfews, door locking, food provision, mandatory reporting, the treatment of children. Primary accounts are anonymized and pseudonymized, and excerpts are selected under an ethics of witnessing that preserves specificity while minimizing risk. The archive itself is multi-scaler and, at the international level, includes analysis of 'institutional innocence' that treats classification systems (famine thresholds, IHL, compliance certifications) as administrative technologies. Documentary corpora from UN special procedures and humanitarian agencies are read alongside legal standards (Rome Statute; Geneva Conventions) and expert testimony to show how thresholds and templates can be operationalized to obscure intent, including where political override is documented (UNHRC, OHCHR, ICC).

A similar approach structures the chapters on displacement and recovery, and where national ledgers (post-disaster needs assessments, humanitarian situation reports, displacement estimates – e.g., Pakistan's 2022 'super-monsoon': PDNA/World Bank, OCHA, IDMC) are read against village-scale accounts of damaged irrigation, silted wells and debt cycles. Where the ledgers record numbers, local testimony supplies the language of loss and the sequencing of recovery, allowing the book to test whether resource flows track need or reproduce existing hierarchies. The evidential test is whether, taken together, the data reveal stable mechanisms that explain who recovers, who is left behind and why. The approach is repeated where climate and health are concerned, starting with official surveillance series that register excess mortality and heat-related deaths, anchored in meteorological baselines and rapid attribution studies that estimate the likelihood of such heat under anthropogenic warming (Met Office, WWA, ONS, UKHSA). To understand how hazard becomes harm, these series are read alongside urban (climate and building) physics work tracing the pathways through which heat is converted into risk. For example, the contribution of London's urban heat island during July 2022, or the systematic overheating associated with dwelling type and floor level (Simpson et al., 2024; Cole et al., 2024). The same pages then follow those mechanisms into the administrative domain (standards, enforcement, retrofit programmes, tenancy rights) showing how adaptation shifts from good advice to justiciable obligation (CaCHE, 2024; POST, 2024). The method here is movement across scales: from record temperatures, to population-level excess mortality, to neighbourhood and building-level mechanisms and, finally, to the levers by which institutions can be required to act. Across these domains, this book aims for evidential pluralism rather than maximalism; enough converging views to highlight injustice in contingency and design, and to locate the points at which ideals of justice become enforceable claims.

Chapter outline

Accepting that ideas about justice do not float above social life but loop back into it, Chapter 2 takes that loop seriously by asking where the language we use has come from, and how it has been adopted in our practices and institutions. Two moves in Chapter 2 directly pick up that thread. First, the return to *The Republic* – not to venerate it, but to treat it as a living archive of argumentative moves. From Thrasymachus' claim that those in power script the moral vocabulary, to Socrates' counter argument via the 'craft' and 'wages' approaches, which is not canon worship; rather, it is data about how justificatory concepts travel. Second, the section on law's 'operative lexicon' names how law overlooks structural harms, and so proposes widening the legally cognizable frame rather than abandoning law altogether, an example of theory re-tooling practice, not just describing it. This is also why the canon's continuing reach matters; ideas travel across disciplines and syllabi, and their blind spots travel too, not least in the social contract.

This is why we discuss Hobbes's (1996 [1651]) *Leviathan*, which locates justice in the centralized authority of a sovereign power that suppresses chaos and ensures civil peace. In the first of two further social contract thinkers, Locke's (1988 [1689]) *Two Treatises of Government* links justice to natural rights and the consent of the governed, a position that opens the way for liberal individualism and private property as a pillar of political legitimacy. Finally, Rousseau's *The Social Contract* (2010 [1762]) reimagines justice as the expression of the general will, seeking a collective sovereignty grounded in civic equality and participatory democracy. The most recent addition to the canon, Rawls's *A Theory of Justice* (1999 [1971]), reframes the social contract tradition by proposing 'justice as fairness', where principles of liberty and equality are chosen under conditions of impartiality. Reading Plato, Hobbes, Locke, Rousseau and Rawls as a transdisciplinary infrastructure of inference is the condition for changing what their inheritance licenses today. The argument thus moves from canon to contracts, from rules to the rule-making that stabilizes hierarchy, and from liability after the fact to duties of design before the harm.

Mindful that the reformulated question should be asked across the sites that give it force, in concepts that loop back into practice, in institutions that convert principle into routine, and in memories that either anaesthetize duty or bind it to redesign, Chapter 3 builds on the preceding discussion to show how the canonical arc of social contract formulations gains elegance, as they shed complexity and so really constitute domination contracts. In so doing, the chapter advances the case for justice to be reimagined not as a consensual abstraction, but as a terrain of contestation, shaped by memory, resistance and repair. It asks the reader to hold two moves together. Begin from domination rather than ideal symmetry and widen our legal-political vocabulary from backward-looking liability to the forward-looking design of institutions that predictably prevent harm. Reading Carole Pateman (1988), we see that modern citizenship was historically masculinized through a 'sexual contract' that relocated power to the household, allowing the public sphere to be presented as gender neutral while dependence persisted; the effect was to confer political personhood on men and codify women's subordination as ordinary order. Charles Mills (1997) complements and extends this by identifying a 'racial contract' that establishes a racial polity and juridical system designed to maintain white advantage, an arrangement that is not an aberration but the very substrate on which the social contract sits. Brought together, these insights license a non-ideal baseline for justice: start from group domination, take historical formation seriously (conquest, settlement, slavery, expropriation), and orient theory to rectification. The chapter closes by showing how these contracts travel into modern Britain through cases such as Windrush, where formal citizenship was laundered into rightlessness, and by foreshadowing the same logic at the border.

Chapter 4 carries forward the shift in focus to the sites where membership is withheld in bordering and asylum. The chapter reconstructs a regime of 'crisis ordinariness' in which inadmissibility, offshoring and externalization manufacture non-protection upstream of adjudication, while para-bureaucratic outsourcing produces intimate rightlessness as administrative common sense. It situates these moves within a wider European re-bordering, accelerated procedures, 'flexible solidarity' and the hardening of internal and external frontiers, showing how spectacle (shipwrecks) eclipses the submerged routines that make catastrophe predictable. It then follows two strands. First, the intimate administration of rightlessness in contingency estates such as Napier Barracks, delivered through outsourcing, where people are warehoused at scale, while the state's duties of care are distanced and diluted; the backlog, indefinite detention and hotelization of the system are not malfunctions, but routinized techniques. Second, via the spectacular and the submerged, from the Lampedusa shipwreck to everyday attrition, we watch how tragedies are narrated as accidents rather than sequences of decisions.

Against this grain, the chapter reads the parable of Omelas and the reality of Riace as ethical counter imaginaries, and argues, via a domination contract lens, that justice at the border requires converting discretionary benevolence into enforceable reciprocity, credible procedures, independent oversight and reception conditions as rights rather than favours. From Kenmure Street to sanctuary city practices, without lapsing into methodological localism, the upshot remains one of bordering as a renewal ceremony for domination contracts, one that converts the right to seek asylum into discretionary benevolence.

Chapter 5 scales out to 'global justice' and 'human rights', showing how institutional innocence is produced at planetary range. The critique of law's operative lexicon returns as an etiquette of impartiality that individualizes accountability where social orders have been collectively engineered. It shows how universalism can ventriloquize those it marginalizes, how legality can be weaponized as lawfare, and why witnessing must become both method and ethic, a refusal of frames that render some harms unspeakable and some lives ungrievable. Through the figure of Refaat Alareer and the politics of grief, it links first-person address to the redistribution of recognizability, drawing on accounts of grievability to insist that apprehension must precede adjudication. The chapter threads this analysis through the politics of memory, asking how remembrance softens obligations into consoling myth, but might also invite reflections that challenge us to struggle with harder memories. The discussion of famine and violence shows how technical thresholds and procedural etiquettes individualize catastrophe while shielding its authors; to hold elegy and institution together, the chapter argues, is to abandon innocence as a scholarly posture. The temptation at this point is to press the escape hatch marked 'global' and start again at altitude. But the air is no purer there. The habits that domesticate injustice locally reappear with new manners when the scale widens. The etiquette of impartiality can individualize what has been collectively engineered; universalism can ventriloquize as 'humanity' the priorities of a fraction. The method, however, travels. If domination is the baseline, then accounting must follow the path of benefit and injury.

Chapter 6 opens on a stark note: the climate crisis, far from being a great equalizer, is, rather, a great amplifier, relentlessly exploiting the fractures of social injustice that already divide us. It argues that our prevailing response (climate adaptation) has become a dangerous euphemism. In the hands of governments and policymakers, it has been stripped of its political teeth and repackaged as a series of technical, race-neutral adjustments: raising flood walls, planting urban trees, issuing public health warnings during heatwaves. This 'chameleonic' quality allows the concept to be adopted widely, but in the process it becomes a neutral mask, obscuring the brutal truth that vulnerability is not born of nature but engineered by society. To understand the racialized climate vulnerability in a place like the United Kingdom, the narrative first sweeps out to a global scale. It grounds the story in the unassailable arithmetic of injustice: the wealth and carbon-intensive development of the Global North were built on the colonial extraction of resources and labour from the Global South. Now, as the planet warms, the consequences are being disproportionately dumped back onto the very communities that were plundered, creating 'global sacrifice zones'. The chapter gives voice to the fierce critiques of Global South scholars and activists who have long decried this hypocrisy, whereby the nations responsible for the crisis dominate the negotiating tables and offer paltry, almost insulting sums for 'loss and damage' funds. This global hierarchy, the narrative insists, is the essential backdrop for understanding the domestic injustices that follow.

The chapter culminates in a damning indictment of this systemic blindness. The failure to mention race or ethnicity in hundreds of pages of official UK climate adaptation reports is framed not as an oversight, but as an active epistemic injustice. It is a refusal to see, to name, and thus to act. By wilfully ignoring racialized geography, policymakers allow their interventions to falter or, worse, backfire, transforming green gentrification projects into engines of displacement that further harm the communities they were meant to help. Ultimately, the chapter seeks a shift from a hollow, technical adaptation to a reparative one. This would require the courage to name race and colonialism as the root causes of vulnerability, to collect the data that makes disparities visible, and to centre the voices and agency of frontline communities in designing their own futures. The chapter leaves us with a challenging thought: a truly just adaptation isn't about helping people survive a broken system; it is about dismantling that system and building a new one that has learned, finally, to value every life equally.

The concluding chapter ends by calling for a turn from consensus abstractions to historically attentive frameworks that foreground memory, resistance and repair. It braids the claims of earlier chapters into a single foundation for action, insisting that concepts train perception, perception authorizes institutions, and institutions reproduce concepts, unless we interrupt the loop by making witnessing, repair and reparative adaptation the very criteria of a just order. It offers four instructions: treat domination as baseline; widen the legal lexicon from fault to design; re-tool contract language for non-ideal worlds so obligation tracks benefit and injury through time; and build borders and memory as a machinery of accountability, not an alibi. Justice, on this view, is the ongoing work of desubordination by design, answerable not in metaphors but in the institutions we are prepared to build tomorrow morning. We therefore leave principle where it is most comfortable and follow its work in the world: the way a moral vocabulary is trained to see some injuries and not others, to sort cases into micro-disputes while structure proceeds unremarked.

2

Where Is the Justice?

In February 1727, the *Edinburgh Evening Courant* carried a 'runaway' notice for 'Ann', an eighteen-year-old enslaved woman who had fled from captivity in Glasgow. She was described as wearing a brass collar engraved 'Gustavus Brown in Dalkeith his Negro, 1726', and a two guinea reward (about £250 pounds in today's money) was offered in the *Edinburgh Evening Courant* for her capture via named traders in Glasgow and Edinburgh (Historic Environment Scotland, 2018). The advertisement shows, unambiguously, that chattel slavery was being practised and publicly policed in Scotland, with newspapers mobilized to seek and return human 'property' (*Edinburgh Evening Courant,* 1727; Newman, 2018; University of Glasgow, n.d.). Brown, a locally born physician who trained in Edinburgh and later became a Maryland plantation owner in the USA, exemplifies the dense traffic between Scottish institutions and Atlantic slavery; the collar was very likely commissioned locally (Newman, 2023). Ann's ultimate fate is unknown; some accounts infer recapture and forced return, but surviving records do not confirm this (Historic Environment Scotland, 2018; Newman, 2018).

Beginning with this story clarifies what follows in this chapter, which argues that justice cannot be approached as an abstraction from history. In eighteenth-century Scotland, law, commerce and print culture already trained readers to recognize a woman as a commodity and to treat her flight as a breach to be remedied (cf. Spillers, 1987; Roberts, 1997). This episode therefore grounds the claim that canonical theories, and especially contractarian ones, must be read against the social orders they naturalized and the violences they rendered ordinary. This chapter begins from a premise that the 'canonical' concepts of justice are worth revisiting, not only to understand their internal logics, but also to uncover what they render invisible. For these reasons, alongside those established in Chapter 1, returning to the 'canon' is not an exercise in homage but a method of diagnosis, reading it as a living archive of argumentative moves that still instruct our institutions what to notice, what to ignore and how to name both, as well as common points of critical revision and departure returned to throughout this book. This might seem odd given the necessary (though provisional) mainstreaming of decolonial inquiry in social and political thought in recent years (Bhambra and Holmwood, 2021; Mignolo and Walsh, 2018; Ndlovu-Gatsheni, 2018). Indeed, this book relies upon such critique, but in ways that make a return to the original indispensable, for, in denying readers the chance to test the power of contemporary critiques, or later rescue attempts, is to overlook the details of the alleged wreckage and salvage operations. For example, and as already indicated, *The Republic* anticipates enduring tensions of justice, including in Thrasymachus' challenge as to whether justice can exist independently of power. As subsequent chapters will show, this question haunts global politics today, where legal norms often bend to economic and military might, and, when we encounter below Socrates' reply, we do not need to accept the conclusions as much as treat them as a live archive of argumentative moves where definitions are quietly trimmed, and examples are strategically chosen and still travel in judicial opinions, corporate charters and constitutional preambles.

In the case of *The Republic*, and given the enduring ways in which it attempted to define justice not simply as a personal virtue or a legal norm, but as the structural principle of a just society, this would seem especially valuable. Yet it is arguably the case that social contract thinkers haunt seemingly different contemporary critical literatures, notably in forms of abolitionist scholarship that re-specifies what the contract authorizes the state to do to its members (Davis, 2003: 6; McLeod, 2015: 1156). Namely, in asking whether criminal justice systems are the authorized means of securing the common good, or whether that authorization has to be withdrawn and reissued to non-carceral institutions that better realize equal protection. What this means, then, is that 'abolition' is not a leap outside the contract; it is, rather, a demand to reauthorize the state in line with the contract's own justificatory terms, in ways not dissimilar to the argument of Mills (1997: 9, 62–4) that we will come to concerning the modern social contract, which installs 'subpersonhood' for the racially subordinated. The point is that this seemingly external critique is a corrective from within the contract frame that says if legitimacy, equality and protection are the standards, then a racially restricted personhood and a curated ignorance cannot satisfy them. This is one illustration of how contemporary thinkers remain entangled in disputes over Hobbes's covenant of fear, Locke's compact on private property, Rousseau's suppression of civil society and Rawls's pivot from the stains of history, and the ways in which these conceal the architecture of modern social orders, the technologies that generate norms and the ways these stabilize hierarchy. At this stage, therefore, it is better to read critics and this 'canon' as being in a dialectic, including the arguments that will unfold from Mills's work that the social contract is *really* a racial contract, and Pateman's insistence that modern patriarchy is constituted *through* the social contract (Mills, 1997; 2007a; 2007b; Pateman, 1983; 1988; Pateman and Mills, 2007).

These are not only philosophical questions, but sociological concerns too, through which we can reach the question of how justice is multi-scaler in spanning international, institutional and interpersonal considerations. Especially relevant here are civil society and community-based organizations which have long been sites where these tensions are contested; functioning as, though not reducible to, spaces for articulating and mobilizing around claims of historical or accumulated injustice, whether racial, gendered, economic, or otherwise. One reason is that a concern with the social contract grants access to a deeper set of questions, including where justice resides. Is it vested in individuals or in communities, in states or in transnational orders? Does it flow from institutional design, or from collective memory, recognition and repair? As Mills has long maintained, 'the social contract, whether in its original or in its contemporary version, constitutes a powerful set of lenses for looking at society and the government' (1997: 3). Once we have surveyed the key scholarly efforts to conceptualize what justice is, and how it is made meaningful, this chapter allows for what follows: a shift from orthodox conceptions to more critical and historically attentive approaches. The next chapter, on domination contracts, will take it up from there, offering alternative formulations of justice that emerge not from abstraction but from contestation, and which go on to animate the remainder of this book.

Returning to *The Republic*

As the previous chapter sets out, the imprint *The Republic* has left on all discussions of justice that have followed, whether or not this is consciously recognized by authors, is unique in ways that make returning to it important. This includes the argument that, if we only knew what justice *is*, then not only could we practise it, but also the qualities defining justice in one context would mirror those in another. To illustrate this, Plato's account in *The Republic* records that Socrates suggested that justice for an individual can be understood by examining the nature of justice in the state, which serves as a larger and more visible framework with the same concerns. In this view, understanding the smaller by studying the larger, using the analogy of the state as a magnified version of the individual, means that, if one can be described as just, then so can the other.

In broad terms, Plato's concept of justice rests in ideas of alignment between reason, spirit (*thumos*) and desire, in which 'the individual is just in the same way the city is just: when each part of his soul performs its function' (*Republic*, 441d). If we recognize and set aside the gendered formulation for one moment (this will be taken up below and in the next chapter), we find that Plato distinguished between two facets of reason: a higher, theoretical kind that was eternal if not divine, and a practical faculty, unique to humans, that steers day-to-day conduct. The soul also houses spirit, the seat of emotions such as anger, pride, honour, ambition and appetite; because appetites are intrinsically unruly and spirit can lapse into irrationality, both need to be regulated by reason (Annas, 1981; Barney, 2006). As the previous chapter discussed, Socrates' first substantive antagonist is Thrasymachus, a travelling sophist and professional teacher of rhetoric and philosophy, someone who typically equips the sons of wealthy families with rhetorical skills necessary to succeed in public life (Ferrari, 2007). For Thrasymachus, and irrespective of whether a state is governed by a monarchy, oligarchy, aristocracy or democracy, those who hold power inherently constitute the stronger party. It is conventionally taught that, in three steps, Socrates neutralizes the argument from Thrasymachus, though, as we will see, there is also a view that the larger claim (that the powerful frame moral vocabulary) is only partially dented (Barney, 2006). The first step, often called the error argument (*Republic*, 339b–340b), strikes at Thrasymachus' definition of justice as 'the advantage of the stronger'. Rulers, Thrasymachus maintains, create laws explicitly designed to serve their own interests, compelling the governed to obey these laws under the guise of justice. Governing, Socrates counters, is fallible and so can misjudge what truly benefits rulers, and confuses 'what the stronger *thinks* to be to their advantage … it is not only just to do what is good for the stronger, but also its opposite, what is not good for him' (*Republic*, 339c). If a mistaken order is issued and people obey, their very obedience may well harm the ruler's interests. In that case, justice would require actions that are not to the advantage of the strong. We will see this in later chapters reflecting on how modern governance often reveals the problem Socrates identifies in Thrasymachus' definition; for example, restrictive policies designed to assert control or authority may result in economic decline, administrative crises or public backlash that damage the very interests they were meant to protect. Such failures would illustrate Socrates' claim that rulers, being fallible, may miscalculate their true advantage, and that blind obedience to flawed directives can undermine both ruler and ruled, such that, 'it is just to do things which are not good for the rulers and the stronger, when the rulers mistakenly give that which will harm them' (*Republic*, 339c–e). The question this raises, as in the case of the 'crisis ordinariness' of migration discussed in Chapter 4, is whether those governing are actually deemed responsible for policy failures (Meer, 2022a).

Socrates' second argument uses a craft analogy (*Republic*, 340b–341d), in that every genuine craft serves the good of its object: medicine heals bodies, navigation safeguards passengers, lecturers educate students, and so on. By the same token, the craft of governing must aim at the welfare of the governed, not the private gain of the leader, since they would otherwise fail in the very expertise that legitimizes authority. That is to say, officials are evaluated not by their personal or partisan benefit, but in how, for example, a government's budgeting process appeals to gains in population wellbeing in terms of such things as health, inequality reduction and environmental resilience.

The final step Socrates takes is the 'wages' argument (ibid., 346b–347e). Governing, he insists, is an onerous task that people undertake only for pay, for their ideas of what is good, or to avoid the penalty of being governed by their unqualified peers, since 'the chief penalty is to be governed by someone worse if a man will not himself hold office and rule' (ibid., 347b–d). If power naturally delivered self-enrichment, good people would not need such inducements; they would flock to office anyway. The need for external rewards shows that ruling, properly understood, is a service rendered for the benefit of others. Many competent individuals moreover avoid positions of authority because of the burdens of responsibility and public scrutiny, and the risk of personal harm or reputational damage.

Socrates wins the logical round as he pries open contradictions in Thrasymachus' slogans (Buenting, 2010), but he does not address the sociological argument on forging moral language as much as he establishes the relationship of justice to virtue, power and the unity therein. Thrasymachus' argument that the powerful frame the moral vocabulary of society remains deeply resonant. Whether through lobbying, media influence or the shaping of legal and economic norms, dominant groups often succeed in defining and entrenching what counts as 'fair', 'necessary' or 'just' in ways that preserve their own advantage. This is arguably one part of Thrasymachus' claim that justice is frequently equated with the interest of the stronger, and that the rhetoric of justice can serve as a veil for the pursuit of domination. As we will see, it follows that this also extends to the conditions in which moral indifference normalizes injustice, damages social ties and weakens the political system.[6]

Law's 'operative lexicon'

Another way of putting this is to say that *justice is greater than law*, in spite of the reach of what Ó'Cinnéide (2024: 38) calls law's 'operative lexicon'. Drawing upon Young (2011) in particular, this describes the very vocabulary that modern legal systems use to speak about responsibility and which too narrowly conceives injustice because:

> This lexicon is inevitably shaped by what law already regulates and the way it goes about such regulation. In turn, this shapes expectations as to what types of injustice law is expected to engage with, and how it performs this task. The grammatical structure of this operative lexicon – the form legal liability usually takes – thus inevitably exerts significant influence over how law frames responsibility for injustice. Types of framing that fit its existing form tend to be viewed as natural and appropriate: alternative modes of framing, not so much. (Ibid.)

That is to say, the lexicon side-steps the design choice and with at least three consequences. One, collective problems are atomized such that structural phenomena (e.g., gendered violence, racialized pay gaps, environmental degradation) are sliced into micro-cases against particular defendants, obscuring the larger social mechanisms at work. Two, established approaches are prized for predictability, while more holistic concerns with intersectional analysis are viewed with suspicion because they blur the crisp right or wrong boundary. Finally, since 'reasonableness' is set by prevailing social practice, progressive legislation and judicial creativity are hemmed in by deference to existing norms; public and private actors feel little pressure to move beyond business as usual unless a claimant can prove a rule was breached, and so the 'operative lexicon' of law defaults to the status quo, and as a result rarely reaches the systemic sources of injustice. The larger point is that these are not merely technical features of adjudication. They are design choices that distribute moral attention. When collective harms are sliced into micro-cases, when 'reasonableness' is indexed to prevailing practice and when intersectional mechanisms are treated as untidy, the result is that the status quo gets to appear as neutrality. In that sense, the lexicon does not just process claims; it trains a culture in what counts as a claim.

Émile Durkheim and Max Weber are useful here precisely because they both show (each in a different register) how easily justice can slide into the moralization of normality, or into procedural correctness that is mistaken for moral adequacy. This might seem obvious, since the starting point for any sociological analysis should be to refuse to treat legal categories as the horizon of what is just, yet this presumed starting point has not proven salutary and, on the contrary, the tendency to approach law as synonymous with justice has long been a problem of social inquiry. Durkheim provides an interesting illustration since, on the one hand, he looked beyond legalism in viewing justice as a moral condition of social life, not only a means of adjudication. For example, in *The Division of Labour in Society*, he insists that 'the moral consciousness of nations ... prefers a modicum of justice to all the industrial improvements in the world', a reminder that economic efficiency cannot substitute for right relations (1984 [1893]: 71). He goes further: 'Justice ... is the necessary accompaniment to every kind of solidarity. It is necessarily encountered everywhere men live a life in common' (ibid.: 135). On the other hand, Durkheim's own method treats morality 'as social facts', and the focus tilts from critique of the content of justice to a description of its social functions, in which prevailing norms are accepted because they maintain social integration. What counts as 'justice' is whatever helps reproduce order, even if that order embeds inequality. His posthumously published volume, *Professional Ethics and Civic Morals*, sharpens the point in his tendency to fold justice back into the moral order of exchange as already constituted. 'A just contract is not simply any contract that is freely consented to ... it is a contract by which things and services are exchanged at the true and normal value, in short, at the just value' (1992 [1950]: 211).

This is normatively tautological and thin on power, overlooking what fixes the 'true and normal value' when markets are structured by unequal bargaining power, cultural devaluation and institutional bias, the very phenomena law's operative lexicon tends not to detect. The risk that justice becomes functionalism by another route, through moralization of what is conventionally 'normal', is more obviously recognized in Weber's treatment of justice in his sociology of law and authority. In *Economy and Society*, he writes: 'Formally rational law is capable of the highest degree of calculability of legal means. It is bound to the logical consistency of the legal propositions, to the exclusion of all consideration of persons and to the strictest formalism. This formal justice is the specific characteristic of bureaucratic adjudication' (1978 [1922]: 657). This helps explain why a system optimized for predictability will prize rule conformity over redress of diffuse injustices, since the very features that make legality administrable (stable categories, evidentiary thresholds, tight causation) also make it systematically myopic about patterned disadvantage. Formal justice then does double duty in that it secures order and legitimates outcomes by certifying that the correct steps were followed, even when those outcomes reproduce unequal life chances. The critical weakness is not that Weber is wrong about the rationality of procedural regularity, but that his account leaves under-examined the particularistic politics of procedure itself. As this chapter will show, procedures encode background assumptions about who counts as a rights bearer, what injuries are intelligible as 'legal harms' and which remedies are thinkable. In practice, this means that legality can be both impeccably orderly and durably unjust, capable of processing claims with great internal coherence, while excluding, by design, claims that arise from segregation, labour market segmentation, environmental exposure or other structural mechanisms. Put differently, formal rationality is not neutral terrain; it is a technology of governance that sets the horizons of contestation. A richer approach would keep Weber's insight about the value of calculability and refuse to treat procedural correctness as a sufficient proxy for justice. It would surely ask questions about whether Weber's typology categorizes social relations and legal categories in ways that presuppose and stabilize, making some harms legally visible, and about which harms remain pervasive yet invisible and how the lexicon might be re-engineered through positive obligations, collective standing or duties of due diligence.[7]

The key implication is that any attempt to use law to remedy structural injustice must widen the operative lexicon. Legal responsibility must include upstream design, diffuse causal chains and cumulative disadvantage, and which means shifting emphasis from liability to the duties of institutions. Yet, taking justice to be greater than law does not mean abandoning law; it means re-tooling it while recognizing its limitations. Ó'Cinnéide (2024: 34) characterizes the belief that existing liability frames can 'do' structural injustice a kind of 'cruel optimism', placing confidence in a tool that was not made to build the house we need. In previous work, I too have used this concept, taken from Berlant (2011), to describe a harmful affective relationship to a desired object or outcome, where the very pursuit of that object actively works against the flourishing of the person or group who desires it (Meer, 2022a). Berlant's original account centres on a cultural logic at work in an increasingly unachievable postwar promise of the good life; a compelling and complex analysis that is developed with reference to art history, trauma theory and political studies. 'Optimism' in that argument is not the same as naivety or being 'co-opted' by state-agencies, and such like, but describes a sincere and, indeed, knowing attempt to 'repair … what may be constitutively broken' (2011: 227). In the present usage therefore, the optimism is 'cruel' because the object of desire is ultimately unachievable, or even damaging, within the prevailing system, yet the commitment to it persists, perpetuating a cycle of disappointment and harm. It is argued that social contract thinkers have, in different ways, left us with distorted accounts of the social life of justice, which have entrenched the operating lexicon of law. Specifically, and what is shown in this chapter, is that they tend to ignore or downplay the structural inequalities that shape social and political life, reflecting injustices that are neither incidental nor accidental, but historically entrenched and often reproduced through the very frameworks meant to secure justice.[8]

The social contract(s)

We might say that justice in the mainstream social contract tradition is a destination, for which the coordinates are ideas of individual self-interest, 'universal' (European) reason, sometimes general agreement and, chiefly, the need to defer to a political authority that, certainly for some, bypasses social contingencies. Nowhere is this stated as simply (or indeed dramatically) as in the formulation proposed in *Leviathan* (the title invoking a biblical sea creature with overwhelming power) by Thomas Hobbes (1996 [1651]). On the one hand, it's a misnomer to name Hobbes a social contract thinker, given that he draws a technical line between a 'contract' (where what you promise might be delivered on the spot) and a 'covenant' (where at least one party's promised performance lies in the future and therefore needs an enforcer). Unlike a contract that can be fulfilled immediately, the point of a covenant for Hobbes is also that it needs some assurance that it will actually be kept. On the other hand, *after* Hobbes, 'contract' became the catch-all-word for any binding agreement, and later political writers (not least Locke, Rousseau, also Rawls) adopted 'social contract' as their label and retroactively grouped Hobbes with them, even though his preferred technical term for the decisive political agreement is 'mutual covenant'. In this sense, and as Kymlicka (1991: 196; quoted in Pateman and Mills, 2007: 96) has put it, we might think of a 'contract device' which many different traditions have used' and which, following Pateman (1988: 1), is among 'the most famous and influential political story of modern times'.

There is then a vast number of introductions and commentaries on social contract thinkers, but, for the purposes of our opening discussion on Hobbes, the key is to note that justice for Hobbes was not an intrinsic virtue or a natural order, but a possibility allowed only through 'covenants' backed by a 'sovereign' power. The reason Hobbes anchors justice in a social order whose members authorize a sovereign (be it a monarch or an assembly) to govern is his certainty that, left to themselves, human beings are gripped by a 'perpetuall and restlesse desire of Power after power' (Hobbes, 1996 [1651]: 66). In the state of nature, we are told, even the weakest can conspire to kill the strongest, such that all are 'naturally equal in the faculties of body and mind' (ibid.: 86). As we will see, what is meant by a 'state of nature' is both a type of prehistoric society (which didn't exist), as well as a philosophical thought experiment: an imagined condition in which human beings live without formal government, law or institutions. All the social contract thinkers in some way appeal to a state of nature, and for Hobbes, one important path out of a state of nature is a common superior, a 'Leviathan', without which life becomes a 'warre of every man against every man', leaving existence 'solitary, poore, nasty, brutish, and short' (ibid.: 88–9). Our escape from this requires that individuals transfer power to, or authorize, one person or representative assembly to act in their name, for 'Covenants, without the Sword, are but Words, and of no strength' (ibid.: 117). This is what Hobbes means when he argues that justice appears only within political society, since 'the nature of justice consisteth in keeping of valid covenants' (ibid.: 101).

Justice, now defined as the keeping of valid covenants, relies on an effective adjudicator and enforcement apparatus. Any arrangement that fragments sovereignty returns society to the precipice of civil war, a 'Kingdome divided in it selfe' incapable of commanding the fear on which cooperation rests (Hobbes,

1996 [1651]: 225). Hobbes contends therefore that we face a stark choice: either to endure the terror of the state of nature or to establish a power strong enough to be feared; once established, that power must remain absolute in kind even if variable in form. The very civil society spaces where modern movements formulate claims of historical wrong are recast as threats. In this view, justice flows downward from legislation enacting the sovereign's will, not the other way around; it cannot emerge from communal practices of recognition or repair. Hobbes's insistence that 'justice … is a rule of reason by which we are forbidden to do anything destructive to our life' (ibid.: 91) further individualizes the concept that the fundamental wrong is breach of contract. Wrongs that operate through social structures (patriarchy, racial hierarchy, colonial extraction) find no conceptual foothold, for they are not broken promises. Indeed, nothing in that definition asks whether covenants are fair; substance yields to procedure. A slave society with impeccable contract law could, and did, qualify as perfectly just so long as slaveholders' rights were duly registered and enforced. Hobbes reinforces the displacement of distribution when he grants the sovereign discretion to 'assign … to every man a portion [of land], according as he … shall judge agreeable to equity and the common good' (ibid.: 173), because, since the initial distribution issues from will, subsequent hierarchy becomes legal by definition. As Ward (2022: 28) observes, Hobbes's sovereign is 'both the establisher and the original distributor of property', so inequality is reframed as an artefact of choice, not an injustice requiring redress. Social life, accordingly, is negative and residual, subjects are free wherever the sovereign has not spoken (ibid.: 150). People can resist commands that undermine their self-preservation, for protection is the very point of sovereignty, yet almost all other disobedience is unjust, since only the sovereign judges what threatens public safety. By anchoring normativity in sovereign will rather than in social practice, moreover, Hobbes converts justice into what power wills and obscures, severing justice from the social dynamics and history that generate enduring injustice.[9]

In some respects, Hobbes's authoritarianism is softened by John Locke, who anchors his vision of justice as a universal entitlement grounded in reason and supposed shared humanity, rather than in custom or law. In his *Two Treatises of Government* (1988 [1689]), literally naming the book's two distinct essays, the second treatise sets out Locke's account of the state of nature, natural rights to life, liberty, property and (of course) the social contract. The appeal of the latter, for Locke, is less about *fear* and more about *reason*, since the social contract allows individuals to form 'one body politic' so that 'every one of the members may be protected' (II §95: 331). The civil power this creates, however, holds authority 'only in trust' and exclusively 'for the good of the society' (II §131: 356). Even Parliament, for example, may not seize property without the owners' consent (II §138: 360), since justice rests in the faithful administration of laws *whose sole legitimate end* is the protection of life, liberty and property. In this respect, Locke's account embeds the safeguard that, whenever rulers exceed what they are permitted to do – e.g., by arbitrary taxation, suspension of laws or military coercion – that trust is 'dissolved', and people thereby regain their ultimate right to act and replace those rulers (people's 'appeal to Heaven') (II §149: 367; II §222: 430). The collective right of resistance is more than a safety valve; it affirms that legitimate authority is always conditional on securing pre-political rights.

What is especially notable here is that, while Locke's idea of justice combines a defence of individual rights and accountable government, it is anchored in a moral standard for judging arbitrary power which sees nothing wrong in its colonial and patriarchal foundations. His famous claim that, 'in the beginning, all the world was America' (II §49: 301), gives licence to the seizure of land from Indigenous peoples as well as the legal architectures of enslavement that shaped its Atlantic empire. British colonizers carried the same reasoning to Australia, but radicalized it further. When the First Fleet landed at Sydney Cove in 1788, imperial authorities declared the entire continent legally uninhabited, notwithstanding tens of thousands of years of Aboriginal occupation (Reynolds, 1987: 15–17). Henry Reynolds and Stuart Banner both show how this fiction licensed instant Crown radical title over the soil and erased Indigenous law from the record (Banner, 2005: 31–4). It endured until the High Court's landmark *Mabo v. Queensland (No 2)* decision in 1992, which repudiated *terra nullius* and recognized native title within Australian common law (High Court of Australia, 1992). For Pateman and Mills (2007), across both hemispheres, *terra nullius* functioned as the connective tissue of colonial legality. Put differently, the Lockean language of rights and property became globally plausible in ways that normalized the expropriation of Indigenous lands and the commodification of African labour. By fusing an ethic of agricultural 'improvement' with a Eurocentric test of political legitimacy, it rendered Indigenous homelands imaginatively vacant and juridically available. As the next chapter details, the concept's longevity (surviving in North American property doctrine and Australian land law well into the twentieth century) reminds us that the power of political narratives comes less in their empirical truth than in their capacity to organize authority, allocate land and naturalize dispossession.

David Armitage (2004) highlights how Locke himself served as secretary to the Lords Proprietors (1668–75) and helped prepare the *Fundamental Constitutions of Carolina* (1669), a settler scheme for a hierarchical slave plantation society. This is not a biographical contingency, for it reveals something deeper. Locke's theory of property in the social contract held that cultivation transformed commons into private estates (1988 [1689] II §27–32). The advocates for North American settler expansion applied his idea in portraying the continent as uninhabited bushland, ready for improvement under a notional 'husbandry right' grounded in Lockean accounts (Banner, 2005: 26).

Hence, it was argued that, since Indigenous nations possessed no 'civilized' polity (an argument that the US Chief Justice Marshall would eventually enshrine in *Johnson v. McIntosh* in 1823), the 'discovery' and occupation by Europeans were said to supersede any competing (or existing) claim. In effect, the US legal order was layered onto a landscape imagined as a pristine state of nature. As Parekh has described:

> Locke justified English colonialism in terms of his vision of the good life. Since Indians [first nations and native Americans] roamed freely over the land and did not enclose it, it was free, empty, vacant, wild, and could be taken over without their consent ... In Locke's view, the trouble with Indians was that they lacked the desire to accumulate wealth, engage in commerce and produce for an international market, and hence exploit the earth potential to the fullest. In this regard, English settlers were vastly superior and had a much better claim to the land. (2000: 37)

This is a key point in the unfolding argument that Locke's procedural justice secures property and liberty for some by ignoring the historical processes (conquest, enslavement, gendered dependency) through which others have been dispossessed. Given his striking opening statement, 'Man is born free and everywhere he is in chains', Jean-Jacques Rousseau's *The Social Contract* might have addressed Locke's shortcomings, especially where he focused on the political inequalities that the social contract tradition had accepted (Rousseau, 2010 [1762]: 5). Instead, he stakes everything on a singular, overarching claim: only a polity founded on a genuine pact of association, one that fuses each citizen's private will into an indivisible *volonté générale* (general will), can possess legitimate authority while simultaneously preserving individual freedom and enabling political equality. The task, therefore, is to devise 'a form of association' that defends 'the person and goods of each associate', while allowing each member to 'obey only himself' (ibid.: 10–11). Rousseau's solution is stark and uncompromising: the social contract demands that 'each of us puts his person and all his power in common under the supreme direction of the general will' (ibid.: 11). This total fusion is presented as the key to legitimacy: everyone surrenders everything (all natural rights and powers) to the collective entity; no individual retains a private advantage over another. The loss of natural independence is thus exchanged for political equality and a higher form of 'moral liberty' found only within the polity.

A key point here is that Rousseau distinguishes a 'general will' from the mere 'will of all', the aggregate of private preferences, and which might be manipulated (Munro, 2025). The general will, for Rousseau, by definition always aims at the common good. The obedience to laws implied by this collective self-legislation is his very essence of justice and underpinned his most notorious paradox: people who resist the general will may legitimately be 'forced to be free' (2010 [1762]: 13). Coercion, in this framework, serves only to recall the individual to the general will and is not to be conflated with government. Unlike Hobbes, and to some extent Locke too, government for Rousseau is not sovereign but a revocable 'commission' entrusted with the executive function of implementing the laws generated by the sovereign will. Whether monarchical, aristocratic, democratic or mixed, the form of government remains perpetually subordinate to the sovereign people and can be dismissed whenever it ceases to faithfully execute the general will.

Admirers highlight Rousseau's profound insight into the moral necessity of citizens, recognizing themselves in the laws that bind them (Bertram, 2004), and also his distinction between the true common good and the simple aggregation of private, potentially conflicting, interests (Munro, 2025). Yet, central to Rousseau's anxiety is the threat of fragmentation to the general will. As a consequence, he too is profoundly distrustful of civil society associations, the 'smaller societies' existing between the individual and the state, warning that 'when particular interests start to make themselves felt and the smaller societies begin to influence the larger one, the general will falters' (2010 [1762]: 58–9). These 'partial societies' express the 'will of all', not the general will, and their influence distorts the common good by prioritizing factional advantage.

Rousseau's remedy, unsurprisingly, is not the encouragement of pluralism, but its severe limitation, and his ideal seems to be direct, unmediated participation of individual citizens within the sovereign assembly, ensuring that their will aligns purely with the common interest. Like Hobbes, Rousseau fears division above all; like Locke, he idealizes a kind of consensus. But he pushes further towards unity by marginalizing the spaces where dissent traditionally forms. The stark paradox, moreover, of being forced to be free brackets the concrete, historical inequalities (of wealth, status, gender, race and power) that individuals inevitably bring into any real or imagined social contract. As Dagger (1981: 367) has argued, if citizens enter the contract with vastly unequal resources, capacities or social positions, the application of a 'uniform discipline' mandated by the general will weighs unevenly. Berlin's (1969: 23) critique distilled this danger with the observation that a concept of positive liberty (freedom to realize one's 'true' self or will) mutates into 'a verbal disguise for brutal tyranny' whenever the state arrogates to itself the authority to *define* and *enforce* an individual's 'real' will against their expressed preferences. In his effort to protect the 'general will' by suppressing civil society, Rousseau sidelines the community groups and organizations that have historically been essential in the fight against injustice.

Paths to and from Rawls

Even as the scholarship forged by Hobbes, Locke and Rousseau over the centuries does not stand outside the history in which their work was formed, so the same can be said of subsequent approaches to the social contract. Having 'lain dormant since the eighteenth century', the most formidable return to 'the contractarian imagination' is also the most referenced modern work in the study of justice (Freeman, 2007: 15).[10] This is John Rawls's *A Theory of Justice* (1999 [1971]), which both inherits and refashions the idea of the social contract described by Hobbes, Locke and Rousseau, and in ways that saw 'social contract theory … spectacularly revived' (Pateman and Mills, 2007: 98). Rawls himself openly places himself in the lineage he is refurbishing, writing that 'justice as fairness is an example of what I have called a contract theory' (1999 [1971]: 36). In his iteration, however, *right* goes before *utility*, freedom is inviolable and the priority is no longer obedience, natural right or civic fraternity, but instead a demonstrably *impartial* agreement: 'Justice is the first virtue of social institutions, as truth is of systems of thought; moreover, each person possesses an inviolability founded on justice that even the welfare of society as a whole cannot override' (ibid.: 3).

Rawls's chosen method is to imagine outwards from the state of nature (or 'original position') to an initial choice situation in which nothing counts as authoritative until each participant can accept it as reasonable. 'Justice as fairness begins … with one of the most general of all choices which persons might make together, namely, with the choice of the first principles of a conception of justice' (1999 [1971]: 15). Like Hobbes's pre-political war of all against all, Locke's moralized state of nature and Rousseau's moment of total alienation, this original position allows for a thought experiment in which rational agents, stripped of their identities, must decide the rules that will regulate every future criticism and reform of institutions. This is Rawls's famous 'veil of ignorance', where 'no-one knows *his* place in society, *his* class position or social status' (ibid.: 102, my emphasis). Behind that veil, the parties, though perfectly rational, are denied knowledge of wealth, gender, creed or race, and are therefore obliged to deliberate on the basis of general considerations alone. The neutrality that Hobbes pursued through the fear of violent death, Locke through the sanctity of procedural law and Rousseau through the cultivation of civic fraternity is here achieved *epistemically*: people must devise principles that could govern any social position because they do not *know* whether these principles will advantage or disadvantage them. Justice thus becomes the product of practical reason operating under self-imposed constraints, not the discovery of existing injustice:

> Among the essential features of this situation is that no one knows his place in society, his class position or social status, nor does any one know his fortune in the distribution of natural assets and abilities, his intelligence, strength, and the like ... The principles of justice are chosen behind a veil of ignorance ... Since all are similarly situated and no one is able to design principles to favour his particular condition, the principles of justice are the result of a fair agreement or bargain. (Ibid.: 102)

Deliberation under these conditions converges, Rawls argues, on two principles. The first holds that 'each person is to have an equal right to the most extensive scheme of equal basic liberties compatible with a similar scheme of liberties for others' (ibid.: 53). The second requires that 'social and economic inequalities are to be arranged so that they are both (a) reasonably expected to be to everyone's advantage and (b) attached to offices and positions open to all' (ibid.). Clause (a) gives birth to the 'difference principle', requiring any unequal distribution of income, wealth or authority to be allowed if it raises the life prospects of those worst off; clause (b) entrenches a demanding conception of fair equality of opportunity. Critically, the principles stand in 'lexical' order, meaning that 'liberty can be restricted only for the sake of liberty' (ibid.: 214). In resurrecting the Socratic argument that *right* has priority over *might*, Rawls argues that basic liberties cannot be sacrificed for efficiency, nor can equal opportunity be traded away to maximize aggregate wealth:

> No one deserves his greater natural capacity nor merits a more favourable starting place in society … Instead, the basic structure can be arranged so that these contingencies work for the good of the least fortunate … The social system is not an unchangeable order beyond human control but a pattern of human action … In justice as fairness men agree to avail themselves of the accidents of nature and social circumstance only when doing so is for the common benefit. (Ibid.: 76–7)[11]

Placed against the historical conversation, therefore, Rawls is both heir and innovator. He retains Hobbes's artificial standpoint, Locke's moral equality and Rousseau's insistence that legitimate law must be self-imposed, yet removes their dependence on fear, natural property rights or civic sentiment. The social contract becomes pure procedure, independent of any substantive conception of the good, yet capable of issuing concrete distributive directives. Directive is the right word because Rawls *emphasizes* that, under the right conditions, justice as fairness is *meant* to guide real politics, not haunt books; indeed, he outlines a sequence in which the principles shape, first, the constitution, then ordinary legislation, then administrative adjudication and, finally, the day-to-day judgments of citizens (1999 [1971]: 171–6). Each stage permits a wider range of empirical knowledge than the previous one, but remains accountable to the original contract. In this way, the theory treats justice as an architectural property of the 'basic structure of society', and 'the way in which the major social institutions distribute fundamental rights and duties and determine the division of advantages from social cooperation' (ibid.: 6).

More than half a century after its first appearance, Rawls's *A Theory of Justice* has become, rather than the last word, an inescapable starting point of the contemporary conversation. Its strength is to expose the arbitrariness of inherited hierarchies, its creative naivety expressed in the hope that rational individuals, when made ignorant of their contingencies, would organize for the benefit of the vulnerable. Its limitation is to imagine that the stains of history can be laundered simply by being set aside. The original position, after all, seeks to formalize omission: injustice may be re-described as the outcome of a fair bargain because the background of oppression has been scrubbed from view. The difference principle, while generous to the least advantaged, permits hierarchies and runaway wealth, to say nothing of the motivational criticism that citizens cannot internalize the demanding ethos of the second principle without a thick ethical culture in the already existing society.

Where is the 'social' in 'the social contract'

The problem that Rawls unintentionally amplifies is that all four contractarians truncate the social field that precedes, sustains and sometimes subverts the political authority that is meant to arbitrate justice. In this chapter's final section, therefore, we will consider how Hobbes, Locke, Rousseau and Rawls evade a sufficient idea of the social in the social contract. We can see this in how Hobbes defines society negatively (as the cessation of war), thereby sidelining historically established practices of cooperation, mutual aid and norm generation conventions that predate his covenant. He denies natural sociability, yet makes the social the decisive artefact of politics in the construction of the 'great Leviathan', an artificial person whose unity consists in representation, so that outside this artefact there is 'no society … no law; where no law, no injustice' (1996 [1651]: chs. 13, 16–17; Skinner, 1996: 1–2). His idea of the social therefore appears as a mass of bodies to be represented and regulated rather than as a web of people and shared meaning. Locke widens the moral horizon with natural right and rules, yet retains a thin social ontology: his labour-mixing story presumes an individualism in an ostensibly empty nature, ignoring household and communal labour and encouraging the violence of gendered and colonial accumulation (Locke, 1988 [1689]: §27; Pateman, 1988; Arneil, 1996; Mills, 1997). Thus, his vocabulary of consent masks the collective dimensions of production and resistance that suffuse societies with patriarchal and imperial dynamics.

Rousseau radicalizes popular sovereignty through the *volonté générale*, but he distrusts 'partial societies', treating civil society associations as distortions rather than as schools of solidarity, dissent and claims-making, and structural inequalities appear as impediments to unanimity rather than as constitutive features requiring political recognition (Rousseau, 1994 [1755]; Young, 1990). The paradox is familiar in suppressing plurality to secure unity, so reproducing domination in the name of an undifferentiated collective (Berlin, 1969). Lastly, Rawls appears to reinstate the social by making justice a part of the basic structure, yet the veil of ignorance intentionally abstracts from race, class and gender so completely that domination is treated as a contingency (sometimes to be compensated) rather than as a formative context that shapes capacities and expectations. His appeal to public reason thus further privileges individual justification, while under-theorizing the social relations through which people acquire the very faculties of judgment and solidarity.

Across this arc, then, what falls from view is the social as constitutive ground of political normativity, the arena in which recognition, redistribution and representation are forged through ongoing practices of cooperation and contestation (Taylor, 1985; 1994; Modood, 2024). This is apparent in these contractarians' understanding of the formation of solidarities, their disinterest in the structuring of domination and their hostility to the role of civil association revising the social norms of justice. For without an account of how solidarities emerge, of how domination is reproduced through everyday interaction and of how civil associations renew the moral language of public life, contract theorists replicate the very injustices they claim to adjudicate. A more adequate approach must therefore braid sociological insight into normative theorizing, for justice is more than a function of authorized rules; it is a living practice sustained within (and often against) the social structures that those rules presuppose. As we will come to see, for some, including Mills, on that reorientation, contract reasoning does not disappear; it is resituated, and its elegant architectures are tested and revised by the thick, plural and conflictual social life that gives justice both its urgency and its possibility.

These arguments stand even in the face of sympathetic 'revisionist' views, which maintain that Hobbes, Locke and Rousseau are chiefly theorists of authority, legitimacy and freedom, with justice being only derivative. For example, Michael Oakeshott's influential introduction to *Leviathan* maintains that, since 'no valid law can, strictly speaking, be "unjust"', we should view Hobbes as an analyst of civil association rather than as a moralist of justice (1975: 45). Quentin Skinner's (1996) contextualist history reinforces this reading by arguing that Hobbes's central preoccupation is political obligation under sovereign power, not the articulation of a distributive ideal, a point made differently in Tuck's (1989: 164) view that the point of sovereignty is to secure peace rather than justice. Related views can be found on Locke and Rousseau. On the former, Dunn (1968: 68–87) long held that to read the *Two Treatises* as a justice treatise is to misrecognize a polemical intervention about consent, resistance and obligation, framed theologically and politically, something shared in Laslett's introduction (Locke 1988 [1689]: 45–67), and also Waldron's (2002) commentary, which argues that the *Two Treatises* are centrally about the grounds of legitimate political power. On Rousseau, meanwhile, Judith Shklar (1969: 184–97) insists that *The Social Contract* offers a theory of civic membership via the general will, rather than a freestanding doctrine of justice, something reiterated by others pointing more to a concern with freedom (Riley, 1986: 122; Cohen, 2010: 23; Bertram, 2004: 62–3).

The challenge these accounts face is that which is laid out in the substantive discussion of this chapter, and which shows how Hobbes, Locke and Rousseau all embed a normative account of justice through (and sometimes under) their accounts of authority and freedom, including in what is *owed* and is *owned* within those projects – e.g., a juridical justice of covenant keeping and peace in Hobbes; a rights-based justice (with reparative and, at times, distributive implications) in Locke; a civic egalitarian justice of general, equal laws in Rousseau (see also Hampton, 1986; Lloyd, 2009: 24, 30–2; Simmons, 1992: 307–52; Ward, 2021: 517, 527, 530). It is true that these three classic thinkers are not Rawlsian architects of an egalitarian 'basic structure' with explicit distributive principles, but each seeks to ground justice in universal reason and general agreement, and they all undoubtedly furnish justice frameworks that later theorists (not least Rawls) recast and systematize. Consistent with the stated objective in Chapter 1, therefore, this chapter has treated them as a living archive of argumentative moves, including their bypassing of the thick social realities (of race, gender, class and empire) that constitute injustice in practice. Paradoxically, the commentators on the canon reinforce this point. For, in ranking authority and freedom ahead of justice, these contemporary writers deny what their arguments nonetheless presuppose, namely that justice talk relies on an antecedent and necessary picture of the social. Without some account of the social world that contracts are meant to organize, justice has no purchase and the contract has no content. So, it is this chasm, between the imagined neutrality of contract and the historical weight of injustice, that the next chapter on domination contracts begins to close up. For, if the current chapter has shown how a language of justice can win its arguments while losing the world, the next step is to read the canon for what it authorizes. Chapter 3 thus names this concealed architecture as sexual, racial and settler contracts by making a deliberate pivot from 'Who wronged whom?' to 'Which arrangements predictably produce which harms, and who must redesign them?'.

3

Justice and Domination Contracts

In April 2025, the United States Naval Academy released a list of 381 books it had removed from its Nimitz Library, a list whose subject headings map what authorities would prefer students not to think about: race, gender, colonization, citizenship and democracy. The list spans critical histories and handbooks, children's non-fiction on antiracism, and scholarship flagged under 'Racism in education – United States/Great Britain', making the cull less a tidy up than an organized programme of forgetting (*New York Times*, 2025). This climate is no more than background noise for a chapter on justice; it is a symptom of the conceptual problem identified in Chapter 2, when power is repackaged as neutrality.

As previously argued, dominant theories too often treat justice as a matter of allocating benefits and burdens, while bracketing the social world (the institutions, histories and material infrastructures) that give those benefits meaning. When libraries and curricula remove the very literatures that disclose how domination is made ordinary, they reinstate that bracket, narrowing the intellectual commons precisely where it had widened and illustrating what contract traditions prefer to forget. Chapter 1 traced how law's operative lexicon atomizes structure into cases; here, we follow the logic upstream to the contracts that tell officials how to sort persons, claims and memories. To begin from domination does not abandon normativity; it earns it by taking account of the durable pattern of laws, institutions and social dynamics that frame individual choice.

For that reason, this chapter does not simply seek to pluralize the social contract tradition; rather, it tests the tradition's claim to be a shared language of justice by examining what its architecture hides – namely, that if concepts train us to understand the world, they may also prompt us to sideline truth and, in doing so, strike quiet bargains with injustice. The previous chapter considered the formative ways of anchoring justice in elaborations of the social contract, which rely on a theory of society that is inadequate for their stated aims. Specifically, either by rendering the 'social' to a dangerous surplus of power (Hobbes), to a pre-political stage for proprietary individualism (Locke), or to a threat to unanimity (Rousseau), or by treating the social as a background variable in a thought experiment (Rawls). We also navigated between slightly different priorities within the social contract. For Hobbes, it means, first, that people come together to create a political body and, second, that they agree to keep the promises that make this arrangement stable. For Locke, this involves separating the idea of forming a political society from the moral rules that exist before it. For Rousseau, it is about creating political authority by transforming people into citizens who share a moral commitment to the common good. And for Rawls, it concerns the shared ideas and values needed for principles of justice established via his thought experiment. Having worked through key arguments expressed in the primary materials of these authors, this chapter turns the lens back to what is left out of these accounts and which will be unfolded in the rest of this book.

The argument here is not simply that today's world would look very different had yesterday's promises been kept. It is, instead, that ideas of the 'social' in the social contract were such that they are better conceived as a 'domination contract'. This is the concept advanced by Charles Mills, who explicitly builds on and extends Carole Pateman's feminist rereading of social contract scholarship, using examples drawn from global politics, legal systems and economic structures. Even though these two key thinkers have a shared interest in what the domination contract signals, it is worth keeping in mind that there is significant disagreement as well as agreement between them. While Pateman rejects the very idea of a 'recovering' approach to the social contract for progressive purposes, Mills argues in favour of a 'revisionist' approach that can rework it in the interests of justice. As we will see, such an ambition cannot escape either disputes in historical events or the genealogy of thought that has come to narrate the story of the social contract. The point is to grasp why such disputes are as much present-centred and future-oriented as they are historical. In other words, if we understand the social contract as a domination contract, we can see not only how the 'contract generates norms', but also how 'stipulations about how to apply these norms … themselves reinforce domination, and so which need to be interrogated by those seeking to end their subordination by the contract' (Pateman and Mills, 2007: 109). Once we establish this, we are much closer to answering why injustice pervades despite stated commitments to the contrary. For example, and as we will encounter in the next chapter, the 'crisis ordinariness' that currently surrounds approaches to asylum and migration reflects how the social contract is reproduced and represented as a contest between undesirable individuals and the weight of a nation. The profound impact of the most desperate people carrying the weight of moral blame, in being characterized as a strain on resources, is one of many enduring legacies. So, if the classical texts establish how an order of justice might be imagined, the next move is to ask for whom that order was built, for it looks very different if we take domination as seriously as we do harmony.

At this point (and given that each author's ideas are now well established), an entirely reasonable concern is that revisiting them risks a rehearsal of established arguments. Yet, while it is true that a great deal of literature draws on Pateman and Mills, respectively, it is surprisingly sparse concerning the social contract tradition, at least in a sustained way. Engagement in the topic is typically in the form of a staging post for a new signature approach, rather than a deep delve into the implications of each author's treatment of the social contract today. For example, Nancy Fraser builds on feminist and antiracist critiques that expose the claimed 'neutrality' of contractarianism as ideological. She then relocates the normative centre of her own account to parity of participation, and, in her work on the public sphere, she advances the idea of 'counterpublics' as key arenas of contestation (Fraser, 1990; 2001; 2008; 2013). Importantly, she also presents 'parity of participation' as a concept through which we can adjudicate justice claims without relying on a shared conception of the good (Fraser, 2001). This too, however, can remain abstract unless it is paired with thicker institutional specification, and can drift back towards a form of ideal theory.

Elsewhere, Linda Martín Alcoff (2015) and Robbie Shilliam (2018) foreground the racialzed construction of personhood. But their interventions are mainly diagnostic critiques of whiteness and welfare moralities, rather than attempts to offer a redesigned institutional language in the way Pateman and Mills do. This highlights the limits of critique, especially given the divergence between Pateman's account of the domination core of contract and Mills's explicitly revisionist, non-ideal project. Much of the secondary literature ends up taking sides, either abandoning contractarianism as ideologically compromised or recovering it as a tool for rectification (cf. Farris, 2017; Taiwo, 2022; Sen, 2009). In this chapter, and in the book more broadly, the disagreement is used methodologically in showing how the contract becomes a design vocabulary for allocating upstream responsibility where harms are predictable, which is much closer to the spirit and internal logic of Pateman and Mills's (2007) original argument.

Who would sign a domination contract?

One of the stated assumptions in the introductory chapter of this book is that addressing injustice involves knowledge of the supposed fundamentals and learning how to disregard them, not least by inviting readers to navigate justice as contested. The idea of a domination contract does precisely this by naming the background architecture in which some groups are made into full political persons and others are positioned as partial, conditional or disposable, often under the rhetoric of neutrality and consent. Simply put, this is the idea that modern societies are organized to create an implicit pact that institutionalizes the domination of some groups over others by structuring rights, authority and personhood to privilege some groups, rather than to create a free and equal social contract promised in the various approaches surveyed in Chapter 2. The domination contract is a versatile idea that spans time and space. From the principle of 'coverture' in nineteenth-century Britain, which made a wife's legal status merge into that of her husband (Pateman, 1985), to the ways in which US states removed the franchise from voters with criminal records, disproportionately curtailing Black people's political participation, the legacies and patterns that originated in these examples persist today in plain sight, in the latter case leaving around four million people disenfranchised as of 2024 (Uggen et al., 2024). They are, moreover, not restricted to the Global North, as illustrated by the Indian Government's *Citizenship Amendment Act 2019*, which fast-tracks citizenship for non-Muslim migrants, and which reorders rights by membership of the majority religion (Gazette of India, 2019; see also Government of India, 2024).

The precise origin of the concept might be traced to Pateman's feminist rereading of social contract traditions, which, in her view, assume and therefore hide an earlier 'sexual contract' in which men's citizenship status is constituted by subordinating women. In her words, a 'contract always generates political right in the form of relations of domination and subordination' (1988: 8). While Pateman did not coin the term 'the domination contract', her work is undoubtedly a key precursor. As Mills stresses: 'Pateman is developing a strand of contract theory classically, if very schematically, initiated by Rousseau and that can be generalized to race and class as well as gender … I call this the domination contract' (Pateman and Mills, 2007: 101).

Despite Mills's comment linking Pateman to Rousseau, and to which we will return below, we could say that Pateman's intervention into contractarian discourse begins with a blunt reversal of the theories of Rousseau, as well as of Hobbes and Locke (Pateman, 1983; 1985; 1988; Pateman and Mills, 2007). While their origin myths of the social contract state that 'each man is born free', Pateman insists that 'the sexual contract is a story of subjection' (1988: 10), so that the narrative of free, equal individuals founding political society is only 'half the story'. From Hobbes to Rawls, Pateman argues, the social contract relies on a structuring rule that she first described in an earlier work, *The Problem of Political Obligation* (1985). In this, she critiques Rousseau's characterization in particular as 'fraudulent contract', since it is a pact that 'gives "all to one side" and is based on inequality; its function is to maintain and foster that inequality by legitimising political regulation by the liberal state' (1985: 148–50). The idea of the social contract, in short, is a legitimating ideology for domination.

In *The Sexual Contract*, Pateman extends the charge, arguing that, because citizenship was imagined as male, women had to 'contract into fraternal patriarchy if civil society is to be convincingly portrayed as an order of civil freedom' (1988: 180). Her argument is that sexual subordination is not an embarrassing hangover, but the very mechanism by which the social contract understands the idea of the social. As she puts it, 'civil freedom is a masculine attribute and depends upon patriarchal right' (ibid.: 2). From the outset, therefore, the founding pact is 'a sexual as well as a social contract', which instituted 'the law of male sex-right' as a basic political entitlement rather than as a custom of yesteryear (ibid.: 2). This is why Pateman reframes modern patriarchy not as father rule, but as fraternity secured through a spatial and conceptual division that renders women's subordination politically invisible:

> A crucial portion of the story is missing. The true origin political right is overlooked in this interpretation; no stories are told about its genesis ... Paternal right is only one, and not the original, dimension of patriarchal power. A man's power as a father comes after he has exercised the patriarchal right of a man (a husband) over a woman (wife). The contract theorists had no wish to challenge the original patriarchal right in their onslaught on paternal right. Instead, they incorporated conjugal right into their theories and, in so doing, transformed the law of male sex-right into its modern contractual form. Patriarchy ceased to be paternal long ago. Modern civil society is not structured by kinship and the power of fathers; in the modern world, women subordinated to men *as men*, or to men as a fraternity. The original contract takes place after the political defeat of the father creates modern *fraternal patriarchy*. (ibid.: 3)

Social contract traditions can thus proclaim gender-neutral citizenship, while preserving the substance of patriarchal authority, for, in relocating power to the household, sex-right is 'deemed non-political because it is deemed private' (ibid.: 90). No less significantly, 'women are not party to the original contract ... women are the *subject* of the contract' (ibid.: 6, my emphasis). That founding structure is then reproduced in 'the contracts of everyday life', which 'create what I shall call civil mastery and civil subordination' (ibid.: 7). The marriage contract exemplifies this logic, for, uniquely among civil contracts, it codifies an 'explicit commitment to obey' (ibid.: 181–2). Read this way, women are required to contract into fraternal patriarchy so that civil society can be 'convincingly portrayed as an order of civil freedom', a formulation Pateman develops when setting out how women's 'consent' to marriage stabilizes the appearance of universal, gender-neutral personhood even as it institutionalizes dependency (ibid.: 180–1; see also p. 227). What presents itself as a universal pact among equals thereby confers political personhood on men, while consigning women to marital and economic subordination.

Fundamentally, Pateman underlines that the public/private dividing line does not limit sex-right to the home; it organizes *both* domains. The 'private, womanly sphere (natural)' and the 'public, masculine sphere (civil)' take their meaning from one another, and, since 'men pass back and forth between the private and public spheres', the writ of male sex-right runs in both (1988: 22–4). In this light, the social contract's canon's promise of abstract equality is not accidentally compromised by a past custom. Rather, sexual subordination is the very mechanism through which 'civil freedom' is produced and maintained. By shunting power into the household, however, social contract scholarship can announce gender-neutral citizenship while preserving patriarchal authority. In other words, what the social contract story presents as a universal pact among equals is instead something that confers political personhood on men, while consigning women to marital and economic dependency.

This analysis, and the sexual contract thesis that Pateman (1988) advanced more broadly, prompted Mills to attribute to her the inspiration for the term 'domination contract', insisting that 'Pateman's peculiar use of the contract idea revives a strand of contract theory so marginalized and ignored that it does not even have a name ... what I have called elsewhere the "domination contract"' (Pateman and Mills, 2007: 101). Pateman herself welcomes this, but, in the joint introduction to *Contract and Domination* (2007), she and Mills also write that the intellectual genealogy of domination contract critique is cumulative. In important ways, especially for Mills (as hinted above), it was Rousseau who supplied the first glimpse of contractual domination, especially in his class analysis, which established 'a clear precedent … in the Western contract tradition for the idea of an exclusionary manipulative contract deployed by the powerful to subordinate others in society under the pretext of including them as equals' (Pateman and Mills, 2007: 105). It was Pateman, however, who demonstrated how sexual subordination is smuggled into the very heart of the social contract, to which Mills's earlier work, succinctly entitled *The Racial Contract* (1997), located a similar role for a racial covenant. Indeed, and with Hobbesian directness, Mills's opening sentence in that work, 'White supremacy is the unnamed political system that has made the modern world what it is today' (ibid.: 1), sets out his own stall for a critique of social contract scholars through his idea of a 'racial contract', which he described as follows:

> The Racial Contract establishes a racial polity, a racial state, and a racial juridical system, where the status of whites and nonwhites is clearly demarcated, whether by law or custom. And the purpose of this state, by contrast with the neutral state of classic contractarianism, is, inter alia, specifically to maintain and reproduce this racial order, securing the privileges and advantages of the full white citizens and maintaining the sub-ordination of nonwhites. (Ibid.: 14)

Like Patemen, Mills does not treat this pact as a local aberration; rather, 'the Racial Contract underwrites the modern social contract' and is therefore logically and chronologically antecedent to it (ibid.: 62). For example, the Lockean language of rights and property could become globally plausible only because earlier Europeans had already normalized the expropriation of

Indigenous lands and the commodification of African labour. What classical theory hails as rational impartiality is, in Mills's phrase, a 'racial epistemology' that occludes anything contradicting white self-image: 'The peculiar contract to which I am referring, though based on the social contract tradition that has been central to Western political theory, is not a contract between everybody ("we the people" but between just the people who count, the people who really are people ("we the white people")' (ibid.: 3).

We can see that, read alongside Pateman, Mills's argument contributes to a layered architecture of domination when the rights of men rest on a sexual contract that secures patriarchal right over women, and on a racial contract that secures imperial right over colonized peoples. As Pateman puts it:

> Political theorists ask their readers to imagine what society would be like if it were empty of the institutions of a modern state and if individuals lacked civil characteristics. Each political theorist draws the picture of the natural condition that is required to justify his particular account of civil society and government. The modern state is justified because it keeps the inconveniences or war of the state of nature at bay, whether it is the state of Leviathan or Locke's 'umpire'. But even as an heuristic device, 'the state of nature' is not completely disconnected from the real world, from the English Civil War or 1688. (Pateman and Mills, 2007: 66)

While Pateman may have had in mind John Rawls's previously discussed veil of ignorance, the significance is surely wider in pointing to a recurring manoeuvre in canonical political theory, namely the invitation to overlook the social so that political obligation can be rebuilt from first principles. The crucial claim is that this is never an innocent exercise. Each theorist draws the picture of a pre-political world that will do the justificatory work their preferred settlement requires. In this respect, the state of nature is less a discovery than a crafted baseline, a narrative device that turns a particular political architecture into the answer to a problem that the theorist has already framed.

Intersectional injustice

When Hobbes insists that covenants without the sword are but words, Locke that property precedes government, and Rousseau that sovereignty must be indivisible, we should ask where the sword was nonetheless brandished, recognize that property was first accumulated without the consent of its inhabitants and then laboured with plantation slavery, and that the general will was first defined in the context of enslaved bodies deemed incapable of citizenship. Several Black feminists had previously drawn attention to these intersections. This includes Angela Davis's argument that gender and race are indispensable for reproductive labour, since the labour that sustained waged and unwaged work was rendered invisible in social contract scholarship, which had nothing to say about 'the work of giving birth to, raising, disciplining, and servicing the worker for production' (Davis, 1981: 133). Combined with Black women's organized resistance and struggles over sexual violence, not only under slavery, but also during the eras of Reconstruction, Jim Crow and twentieth-century labour and reproductive politics, Davis's critique spans material considerations and epistemological concerns, often challenging canonical universal stories about women's suffrage that are modelled on white middle-class feminism.

One of the most detailed historical elaborations in this vein comes in Dorothy Roberts's study *Killing the Black Body: Race, Reproduction, and the Meaning of Liberty* (1997), which charts how slavery converted Black women's 'reproductive capacity' into a legally protected component of slaveholders' property, meaning that 'property' was reproduced through the womb.

This is because Black women were compelled to serve simultaneously as *producers* and *reproducers*, with slave plantations seeking to maximize both roles. As Roberts puts it, 'every aspect of slave women's reproductive lives was dictated by the economic interests of their white slave masters' (1997: 25). This was not incidental, but was, rather, encouraged by legal entitlements that made children follow the condition of the mother, such that courts 'deemed any child who resulted from the rape [of a slave woman] to be a slave', refusing to recognize the rape as a crime and thereby converting sexual violence into a mechanism of asset-creation (ibid.: 29). In this domination contract, the law assumed prenatal interests in the 'increase' of enslaved women (future children could be willed, transferred and litigated before birth), entrenching a regime in which ownership preceded and pre-empted motherhood (ibid.: 34). This architecture of property therefore severed maternal bonds by authorizing the routine sale and forced separation of families at slave auction, where children might be stolen from their mother and sold on the spot, making kinship precarious because the legal and economic systems deemed it a tradable asset in the slaveowner's favour.

A related argument made by Hortense Spillers reads plantation slavery through the so-called private realm of sexuality and kinship. She details how a legal and economic regime was fashioned through sexual and racial terror, producing a lasting 'grammar' through which race, gender and property have been organized (1997: 67–8). Amongst a number of contemporary writers who argue that intimacy must be understood in view of this history, Christina Sharpe theorizes sovereignty's 'afterlife of property', arguing that 'Black lives are still imperilled and devalued by a racial calculus and a political arithmetic that were entrenched centuries ago' (2016: 22). Indeed, if the traditional social contract, reread as a domination contract, already revealed how norms and their applications secure hierarchy, Black feminist critique shows how those norms are, at once, differentially reproduced across the intimate, the cultural and the institutional, and so they both converge with and sharpen the domination contract view by insisting that race, gender and class are not additive 'axes', but interlocked relations that organize power. Among the things these yield, therefore, are practical sites of action, for example, in building counterpower where people actually live, across households, schools and workplaces.

A further point of convergence between the domination contract critique and Black feminist critique comes in how Patricia Hill Collins, for example, identifies the way in which a 'matrix of domination is organized via four interrelated domains of power, namely, the structural, disciplinary, hegemonic, and interpersonal' (2000: 292–3). Domination contract critique shares this view by highlighting different sights of inquiry and by responding to the different formulations of the social contract. Hence, Mills (1997) distinguishes distinct but interconnected strands of the social contract seen in its political, moral and epistemological features. The *political* contract is the most visible layer, where the structures of law and governance are designed to protect the privileges of the historically dominant groups. The *moral* contract defines who is considered fully human and deserving of moral consideration. It establishes the norms, values and interests of the dominant group as the standard for society, while sidelining or dehumanizing subordinated groups. This moral framework can obscure the harms done to these groups, rendering their suffering invisible or justified within society's ethical ideals. Finally, the *epistemological* contract shapes how knowledge is produced and who is recognized as a credible source. It determines what counts as valid evidence and which historical narratives are preserved or erased. Mills (1997) refers to this as a 'cognitive model' that supports an agreement to misinterpret the world and sustains a structured ignorance. Recognizing these differences is akin to holding different pieces of a jigsaw, in that all the parts are required to make up the picture. This means that even political systems are justified by moral frameworks that prioritize the values of dominant groups, and both are sustained by epistemic norms that obscure or deny the realities of racial and gendered inequalities:

> In part, then, the political contract simply *codifies* a morality that already exists, writing it down and filling in the details, so we don't have to rely on a divinely implanted moral sense, or conscience, whose perceptions may on occasion be distorted by self-interest. What is right and wrong, just and unjust, in society will largely be determined by what is right and wrong, just and unjust, in the state of nature. The character of this objective moral foundation is therefore obviously crucial. (1997: 15)

Together, Mills, Pateman, Spillers, Roberts and Collins show the need to challenge not only the political institutions that uphold injustice, but also the moral and epistemic foundations that legitimize and reproduce it. It is perhaps odd then that, far from rejecting contract theory, Mills insists that 'contract theory has a radical potential barely tapped' (Pateman and Mills, 2007: 24), and that its apparatus can expose rather than conceal structures of race, class and gender. Pateman herself remains sceptical, yet their exchange signals productive tension: should the social contract vocabulary be abandoned as hopelessly patriarchal, or reclaimed? For Mills, the key challenge is to address the idealizations and 'the misleading framework of assumptions' (ibid.) by recognizing some key social realities that conventional theory screens out.

First is *group ontology*, which argues that modern societies are structured by group domination, so the units of analysis cannot be treated as an abstract aggregate of individuals. Our accounts of justice must therefore start from the patterned relations between groups, rather than a population of interchangeable persons (Pateman and Mills, 2007: 23). Second is *historical realism*, meaning that in place of the timeless ideal presented in the social contract, we should reach for a record of how polities were actually made through 'conquest, settlement, slavery and expropriation' (ibid.: 24). Third is a *non-ideal orientation* for our models of justice in order to map injustices that guide rectification, rather than imagining these away (cf. Meer, 2022a). The pursuit of justice is messy, and, ultimately, Mills argues that 'more is gained by complicating the contract idea than is lost by the relinquishment of simplicity' (Pateman and Mills, 2007: 26). Once domination is taken as a baseline rather than an aberration, the guiding question of contractarian analysis flips. Instead of asking how free and equal actors might design a just order, the task becomes to show how already subordinated groups can dismantle the institutions and ideologies that reproduce their disadvantage.

Nations and empire

One of the impediments to this ambition is an inability to overcome the epistemological ignorance that pervades the imagination of membership and belonging. This is in no small part a reflection of the historical understanding whereby race is minimized within a 'narrative contract' (Kaviraj, 1993) between the nation-state and its narrators. If the 'state of nature' and 'original contract' are world-making ideas that underpinned colonization, then the question is less about whether nations can be separated from empire than about how imperial formations were constitutive of nation-making in Europe and its settler offshoots. Even if this means 'unmasking the complicity of history-writing in patrolling the borders of national identity' (Burton, 1997: 240), we can minimally agree on the need to think about racism both in its relationship to nationalism and in relation to nationalist historiography (Gilroy, 1990: 114). No less than Locke, discussed earlier, and in seeking a purer polity defined by direct identification with the whole, we might point to how Rousseau evacuates the 'impure history from which political life is made' (Brown, 2001: 4) and, with it, makes room for the messy, conflictual processes through which subordinated groups challenge power and redefine the common good. Indeed, and as Wendy Brown has shown, Rousseau's vision of the social contract makes no mention of colonized peoples, Indigenous populations or the trans-Atlantic slave trade. As John Christman has argued, this omission is not incidental, but structural. Eighteenth-century Geneva, Rousseau's idealized model *Republic*, thrived on global trade, including commodities produced by enslaved Africans; yet 'Rousseau never engages in a protracted description or condemnation of it [slavery]', and Indigenous peoples, enslaved Africans and colonized subjects never enter his calculus (Christman, 2022: 1463). By constructing a social ontology of abstract individuals stripped of race, gender and property, Rousseau renders invisible the systems of domination (chattel slavery, colonial extraction) sustaining the European societies contemplating his contract. The abstraction allows domination to persist beneath the ideal of unanimous self-rule by failing to account for how power operates between societies, and how the 'freedom' of contracting citizens may be predicated on the unfreedom of others excluded from the compact. Among others, Christman argues that this silence has profound philosophical implications, exposing the limits of a theory that cannot grasp the material foundations and global entanglements of the national community.

From here, a preliminary but often unstated question arises: why remake national projects at all? In debates about social welfare in the Global North, there is, at present, no getting away from the centrality of the national. This does not dismiss cosmopolitan critiques or bottom-up collectivisms (Bhattacharyya, 2015) that cultivate a 'shared fate' (Williams, 2003: 208). Rather, it notes that the meta-membership underwriting modern welfare states (the legal-political boundary that decides who counts for redistribution, care and voice) cannot be grasped through cosmopolitan or purely local framings alone.

The very institutions that allocate welfare are historically the lineal descendants of national projects entangled with empire. Burton's (1997: 234) provocation is apposite: 'Who can afford to be sanguine about (or oblivious to) needing the nation?' Groups that mobilize to reimagine national projects are often those for whom exclusion has entailed 'material dispossession and political disenfranchisement' (ibid.). Nor are interior and exterior racial injustices 'aberrant offshoots' (Stoler, 1995: 54) of nation-state formation; rather, they reflect a 'reciprocity of determination' between race-making and nation-making (Balibar and Wallerstein, 1991: 2). Hence the familiar claim that ideas of 'race' and 'nation' operate simultaneously as categories of inclusion and exclusion (Miles, 1987: 27), repeatedly reifying contingent boundaries as if they were natural divisions. The settler contract demonstrates this mechanism in maximal form: by re-describing populated homelands as 'empty' and peoples as 'uncivil', it converts colonial signification into legal title and political membership.

Yet, so much canonical theorizing of nations and nationalism has sidelined domination contracts, to the extent that European imperialism is often treated as incidental, as if 'the core or essence of nationalism' had long since been 'laid out' (Gellner, 2008: 42) and race were inconsequential. The integrative argument here resists these assumptions, since the national and the imperial were mutually constitutive, and the institutions that allocate belonging (and thus the social contract) are indicative of that history. One result, however, is that nationalism studies and race scholarship have proceeded in parallel. As Saidiya Hartman insists, this has not been a concern of historians; across the Global North, 'black lives are still imperilled and devalued by a racial calculus and a political arithmetic that were entrenched centuries ago' (2007: 6). The afterlife of skewed life chances, curtailed access to health and education, premature death, incarceration and impoverishment all flows from the very systems that built the modern world. Even Eric Hobsbawm's (1968) analysis of industrial capitalism, nationalism and imperialism does little to advance Eric Williams's earlier account of how the 'commercial capitalism of the eighteenth century developed the wealth of Europe by means of slavery and monopoly' (1944: 210), priming the nineteenth-century industrial capitalism that became central to standard narratives of nationalism.

Viewed against the period of 'classical modernity' (Berman, 1982) following the French Revolution, colonization and imperial extraction from the Global South were keystones of European nation-state formation. The notion that Spanish, Portuguese, German, French and Belgian empires annexed human beings, resources and knowledge across continents without underpinning nation-building can only be sustained by omission. Imperialism both preceded and proceeded from 'classical modernity', so setting it apart from European nation-making forecloses the possibility that a 'long imperial hegemony, and the intimacy of the relationship between capitalist development at home and colonial conquest overseas, laid the trace of an active racism' (Hall, 1980: 338).

At least two thoughts emerge directly from this integrated view. First, prevailing accounts of nation-state formation have overlooked imperialism and colonialism, not least 'the exterminatory dimension of nation-building' (Moses, 2002: 34). Second, this occlusion hides how 'reciprocally, colonialism subsequently came to furnish a racialized mythology that could be displaced back onto stigmatized minorities within Europe itself' (Wolfe, 2016: 11). These insights matter not only for historical accuracy, but also for diagnosing injustice today, particularly for remedies in which 'rectifying past wrongs in present circumstances includes future-oriented considerations about improving the situation that resulted from them' (McCarthy, 2004: 769). Read in this light, remaking the nation does not equate to nostalgic retreat but is a means of contesting the social contract by rebuilding meta-membership. This involves reopening foundational narratives and facing, rather than bracketing, their entanglements of nation and empire, so that the political fictions that naturalized dispossession can be named, refused and replaced.

At this point, the argument re-converges on the present-day concerns about the national welfare state, which remains the principal institutional site where the 'trace' is either reproduced through exclusionary meta-membership, or reworked through projects of inclusive belonging (Meer, 2022b). To read nationhood *only* as a flattening process of domination overlooks the challenges and revisions advanced by racialized minorities, who seek to reopen founding narratives by insisting on the recognition of racial histories and by pressing claims to remake membership. Indeed, and because the form and content of nationhood organize access to security, welfare and voice, the pursuit of racial justice cannot vacate the national terrain; it must engage and recast it.

Windrush then and now

Approaching justice through an account of domination contracts allow us to fuse race, gender and class into a single device for non-ideal theory, and to map 'the non-ideal unjust society we already have and want to get rid of' (Pateman and Mills, 2007: 22). This begins with a recognition of the ways in which prevailing thought has, across time, simultaneously idealized justice and intellectually buttressed injustice. Read in this light, Hobbes's covenant appears as a contract of fear that licenses domination, Locke's compact doubles as a settler contract of dispossession, Rousseau's pact functions as a class contract of usurpation and the modern liberal democratic bargain operates as a racial-sexual compact that normalizes white and male privilege. At the same time, Rawls is not exempt from the charge. His original position serves as an ideal-theoretic filter that brackets the history of white supremacy and patriarchy by restricting choice to a family of 'well-ordered societies', and his methodology displaces the very legacies of conquest, slavery and empire that structure our basic institutions. As Mills notes, Rawls has little to say about race and never squarely confronts how liberal orders were historically built through racial exploitation, which risks laundering status quo advantage through abstraction (Mills, 2009: 161–84; 2017: 139–60). Hence, the Rawlsian compact functions as a racial-sexual liberal bargain that normalizes white and male privilege, showing the need for a non-ideal redrafting (one that forces choosers behind a suitably revised veil to reckon with the history of domination) to convert the framework into a programme for rectificatory justice (Pateman and Mills, 2007: 22–3; Mills, 2017: 139–60). The analytical impact discredits single-axis approaches by revealing how axes of power interlock; the practical implication is to coordinate campaigns for reparations, feminist reforms and economic redistribution under a single conceptual flag. In short, the domination contract does double work as both a unifying framework for intersectional critique and a normative engine for policy design (Pateman and Mills, 2007: 22–6).

Let us reflect on these points to understand the treatment of Paulette Wilson, Hubert Howard, Ivan Anglin and Nathaniel and his daughter Veronica, for their stories offer a profound illustration of the domination contract's enduring logic. Each were among the many Black and Brown people who arrived from the Caribbean (principally, but from elsewhere too) as Citizens of the United Kingdom and Colonies (CUKCs) between 1948 and 1973, legally entitled to all the rights of full British citizenship, yet who were systematically stripped of this status in what became known as the Windrush scandal (Perry, 2018).

Paulette Wilson arrived in the UK aged 10 in 1968. Nearly fifty years later, in 2017, she was told she was in the country illegally. She was arrested twice, prevented from working as a cook in the House of Commons, detained for a week, and taken to Heathrow for deportation to Jamaica, a country she had not seen since childhood (Committee on Home Affairs,

2018). Hubert Howard, who arrived from Jamaica aged 3 in 1960, was in full-time work until 2012. When he tried to renew his passport, he was told he had 'overstayed'. He was then sacked from his job and was also denied cancer treatment (de Noronha, 2020). Ivan Anglin, returning from his sister's funeral in Jamaica in 1998, was given forty-eight hours by immigration officials to pack up thirty-five years of life in the UK and was returned to Heathrow for deportation. Exiled for twenty years, he missed the births of his grandchildren and the death of his only son (Gentleman, 2019). In 2001, Nathaniel went on holiday to Jamaica with his daughter Veronica, only to be barred from re-entry because the travel documents he had held for forty-five years were suddenly deemed insufficient. He died in Jamaica nine years later, unable to afford treatment for prostate cancer, while Veronica took career breaks to care for him (Williams, 2020).

These stories force us to connect the longue durée of imperial membership to the present calculus of belonging. To dismiss this scandal as a mere bureaucratic blunder is to profoundly misrecognize its nature. It is true that many of those affected had moved as CUKCs before their birth countries had gained independence and, for various reasons, may not have possessed formal documentation. Indeed, the UK Home Office never systematically issued such paperwork, making the full scale of those affected difficult to ascertain. The National Audit Office (2018) estimated that 500,000 people might struggle to document their lawful status through no fault of their own. Those who see a policy error point to legislation like the 2002 Nationality, Immigration and Asylum Act, which expanded powers to deprive people of citizenship, a mission vigorously pursued through the 'hostile environment' policy framework of the 2014 and 2016 Immigration Acts (Meer, 2018b). Yet, as the cases show, the pattern of domination long predates this legislation.

What appears as 'documentation failure' is better read as the downstream effect of a polity that converted descent into entitlement and erased labouring histories from the ledger of citizenship. As Mondon and Winter (2020) show, the authoritarian vocabulary of the far right is often curated by institutions that imagine themselves as neutral arbiters, translating exceptionalism into everyday common sense through editorial routines, policy briefings and platforming decisions. To explain these outcomes in any depth requires us to place them in the larger historical pattern that constituted them, to see them not as private troubles but as public issues of justice, as symptoms of the *domination contract.* This requires an epistemic disobedience that brings into view the knowledge, events and people who disappeared down one of George Orwell's 'memory holes', an attempt to give the impression that the postcolonial present is unrelated to colonial expansion (Orwell, 1949). The legal architecture that enabled Windrush was not an aberration, but a recalibration of the racial contract. The 1948 British Nationality Act transformed imperial 'British subjects' into Citizens of the United Kingdom and Colonies.

Yet, a postimperial story of exclusion can be traced through subsequent legislation, including the Commonwealth Immigrants Acts of 1962 and 1968, and the 1971 Immigration Act, which partly enshrined a citizenship based on ethnic descent through a 'patriality' clause. This meant that 'new' Commonwealth citizens (from the West Indies, South Asia and East Africa) were less likely to qualify for entry than 'old' Commonwealth citizens (from Australia or Canada) (Paul, 1997). The 1981 Nationality Act finalized this exclusion by creating a tiered system of citizenship that ultimately withdrew the right to settlement from most Commonwealth citizens. Through this legislative evolution, 'populations that would, historically, have been part of the body politic were placed beyond it as the ground so cruelly shifted under their feet' (Meer, 2022a: 112). The UK is not unique here; European nation-states have seldom recognized their formation through imperial systems built on racism (Wekker, 2016). But Britain is among the few nations that simultaneously celebrates and deports the very communities who, after the Second World War, helped rebuild the society that the bodies of their forebears first made wealthy. The key point is that the Windrush scandal would not have been plausible without an underlying *epistemological contract* (Mills, 1997) that rationalized it. Nation-states have imported an imperial mode of governance that relies on race-making, rendering certain populations invisible within the moral and political calculus of citizenship. This raises an uncomfortable question in justice literature: if you do not dissent from an orthodoxy that you did not establish but have done nothing to alter, are you responsible for maintaining it?

This epistemic failure is mirrored in academia, with notably few scholars in the field of nations and nationalism having had much to say on the role of empire in contemporary racism or in the formation of the nation-state itself (Meer, 2022b). Despite being an interdisciplinary field invested in historical analysis, much of the literature that does exist (with some exceptions) has treated European imperialism as incidental to European nation-state formation, echoing John Seeley's quip that the British Empire was acquired 'in a fit of absence of mind' (1883: 12), and offering an intellectual example of what Gloria Wekker (2016) calls 'white innocence'. Minimally, the charge remains that it has seen too little in the racial histories of nation-state formation. This is self-evidently a problem because, as this chapter has argued, empire has been *constitutive* of nation-state formation; in Britain, this legacy 'came home' long before the Windrush scandal docked at Tilbury. The missed opportunity to engage with this constitutes a profound frustration in critical race scholarship. It stems from a necessary belief in the possibility of changing what is constitutively broken, the very work that a non-ideal theory of justice demands. This endeavour is captured in James Baldwin's enduring insight: 'Not everything that is faced can be changed, but nothing can be changed until it is faced' (1962: 12). To face the domination contract is the first step towards dismantling it.

The Windrush scandal offers a devastatingly clear case study of the racial domination contract in its full, intersectional dimensions: the political (laws stripping citizenship), the moral (devaluing Black lives and contributions), and the epistemological (erasing colonial history and creating 'memory holes'). Critics of conventional memorialization argue that its seeming inefficacy stems from a tendency to encourage a form of abjection, where identification is narrowly focused on either victims or resistors (LaCapra, 2001). This process allows for a comfortable self-distancing from those rendered as malefic perpetrators, effectively eviscerating memory's critical force for rethinking one's own complicity in present structures (Rothberg, 2009). The call to remembrance issued by past generations demands something far greater than an egoism that simply confirms who we are and what we already know. It requires the very epistemic disobedience that challenges the 'cognitive model' that Mills (1997) identifies, the agreement to misinterpret the world that underpins the racial and sexual contracts. Therefore, a warranted scepticism towards the progressive prospect of historical memory is not a conclusion, but a starting point. It is welcome if it prevents a return to hortatory injunctions that take memory's critical potential for granted, but injudicious if it leads to a wholesale dismissal of remembrance's social and political importance (Brown, 2001). The task, aligned with Mills's (2007b) non-ideal orientation, is to realize that practices of remembrance can be accomplished in different ways with radically different consequences. Will they be employed, as they so commonly are, to reinforce the state-oriented commemorations that enact social cohesion on terms set by the domination contract (Anderson, 1991; Nora, 1989)? Or can they be recalibrated as tools of critical, intersectional analysis that expose the interlocking domains of power, as Collins (2000) outlines?

The Windrush story exemplifies this choice, and this chapter has argued that the pursuit of justice requires a radical dismantling of the frameworks that present domination as neutrality.

From bracketing disruptive histories in a naval library to banishing entire populations from the body politic in the Windrush scandal, we see the enduring logic of the domination contract at work. The theoretical critiques of Pateman and Mills provide the essential tools for this task, revealing how the classical social contract tradition is not a neutral foundation of justice, but a political, moral and epistemological system designed to institutionalize the power of some groups over others, whether through the sexual contract of patriarchy, the racial contract of white supremacy or the settler contract of colonial expropriation. The stories of Paulette Wilson, Hubert Howard, Ivan Anglin and Nathaniel are not anomalies; they are the predictable outcome of a polity built on these intersectional contracts. Their experiences force an epistemic disobedience, a refusal to accept the state's 'memory hole' and a demand to face the unvarnished history that the domination contract seeks to erase. As we turn to the 'crisis ordinariness' of asylum and migration in the next chapter, we carry this framework with us.

The asylum and migration regimes analysed in the next chapter should therefore be read as contemporary theatres where domination contracts are renewed: the 'crisis ordinariness' of bordering sets vulnerable individuals against a nation imagined as already exhausted, while reproducing hierarchies of value that were installed in earlier contracts. Carrying this theme forward keeps analysis anchored to the lived distribution of power and orients remedies that lean towards dismantling the contracts that organize it. Windrush teaches that domination contracts both found status and teach its application. The border is where that lesson is examined. Offshoring, inadmissibility and externalization are not administrative quirks but design choices that keep the 'contract' from forming at all, converting rights into discretionary benevolence. Chapter 4 therefore moves from architecture to site: to the places where crisis is made ordinary and where the promise of protection is routed through routines that naturalize moral indifference as common sense.

4

Legislation and Policy, Bordering as Design

Before dawn on 3 October 2013, a fishing boat carrying more than 500 people journeying from Libya and bound for mainland Italy caught fire within sight of the island of Lampedusa in the Mediterranean Sea, located between Tunisia and Sicily (BBC News, 2013). The boat's fuel had ignited, panic spread and the vessel capsized, killing at least 366 people before sinking to rest on the seabed (UNHCR, 2013; 2023). In the days that followed, specialist divers entered the forward compartments of the sunken vessel and began removing people. Among those who had drowned and were brought to shore, to be laid out in long rows inside the island's airport hangar, was a young Eritrean mother found with a newborn still connected by the umbilical cord. Italian coverage published that day added clinical details, noting the mother's age as 'just under twenty' and the infant's markedly premature appearance (La Repubblica, 2013), findings that were consistent with a delivery triggered under acute stress during the fire and capsize (Amnesty International, 2015). Officials reportedly discussed how to register the infant, before placing both together in one coffin, with Lampedusa's chief physician publicly confirming that he chose not to sever the cord before burial (de Bellis, 2023). In the absence of sustained forensic strategies and international coordination, many of the people who died that day remained unnamed (Olivieri et al., 2018), an anonymity that is less an accident of the sea than an artefact of policy design.

To call the Lampedusa drownings 'a shipwreck' collapses a chain of choices – including visa regimes that foreclose regular routes, carrier sanctions that criminalize transport, the withdrawal or contestation of search and rescue, fragmented identification protocols and the outsourcing of reception to actors insulated from public law – all into one single naturalized event. Yet each link in the chain is authored somewhere: in ministries, in intergovernmental compacts, in contracting frameworks and standard operating procedures. The dead are thus not lost to waves; they are lost to categories that fail to recognize them, to institutions that decline to name them and to archives that struggle or refuse to remember them. For if contracts are the grammar, bordering is the prose, the everyday sentences in which status is spoken, withheld or revoked. Read sociologically, the border a repertoire of techniques (risk-scoring, admissibility filters, 'safe third country' designations, temporal queues and infrastructural choices) that convert political priorities into moral technologies. It is at the border that queues ration hope, thresholds police credibility, para-bureaucratic supply chains disperse responsibility – until it becomes difficult to locate the hand that harms. In this register, tragedy is not the negation of order but one of its foreseeable outputs. Those who drowned were not orphans of fate; they were the victims of decisions.

This chapter moves from naming how contracts generate and apply norms of domination to tracking how, through approaches to asylum and migration, those same moves are routinized as policy design used in bordering societies. More than a decade on, the Lampedusa tragedy has proved to be a prism rather than an isolated catastrophe, through which we can see how a contractarian imaginary organizes membership and protection for insiders, while filtering outsiders at the threshold. The imaginary teaches administrators what counts as a claim, how much uncertainty to tolerate, and when to allow a 'we' to expand. It licenses a style of governance that narrates preventable harms as regrettable by-products of order rather than as the predictable consequences of rule-making. Seeing that is the precondition of redesign. The task is not simply to condemn the shipwreck, but to rewrite the prose and replace technologies that manufacture non-protection with arrangements that make reciprocity enforceable, to move identification from discretionary grace to obligation and to ensure that the language of membership cannot be deployed to render lives unnameable, and therefore uncounted, at sea.

Desperate designs

People do not choose clandestine journeys to Europe as a preference; they are driven to them by a mix of urgent need and closed doors. Conflicts, persecution, authoritarian rule and conscription, along with economic collapse, food insecurity and climate-related shocks: these are all factors that push people to move. Many also try to reunite with family in places where language, community and prospects make survival plausible (UNHCR, 2025a). Yet formal routes that might meet these needs are vanishingly small or practically unreachable. As we will come to, policies of externalization and deterrence, pushbacks at land and sea borders, deals with transit states, and curtailed or contested search and rescue do not halt movement; they reroute it through longer, riskier and more exploitative channels, expanding the market for smugglers (EPRS, 2025; European Union Agency for Fundamental Rights, 2024; Heller and Pezzani, 2016; Amnesty International, 2025b). The resulting journeys are deadly; IOM's Missing Migrants Project continues to record high rates of deaths and disappearances on

Mediterranean and Atlantic routes (IOM, 2025a; 2025b). In short, clandestine travel is less a personal choice than a policy outcome. When safe, affordable and predictable pathways are absent, people still move, only by far more dangerous means. Read against the wider pattern of deaths on migration routes, the Mediterranean remains the single deadliest migration crossing. IOM's decade review records 28,854 deaths and disappearances on the Mediterranean between 2014 and 2023, with 3,105 in 2023 alone (the highest annual toll on that sea since 2017) (IOM, 2024: 7). Within this grim aggregate, children are among the first victims. UNICEF estimates that approximately 3,500 children died or disappeared on the Central Mediterranean between 2015 and 2024, the equivalent of roughly one child every day over that period (UNICEF, 2025: 2).[12]

This chapter argues that the social contract is the foundation of status and also teaches administrators how to apply status in practice; once that double movement becomes evident, bordering reads as a technology for deciding who even has the right to form a reciprocal relation with the state. If we recall, Hobbes frames this enforcement as precontractual, staging the border as the sovereign's test of capacity before any reciprocal duties can be recognized (1996 [1651]: 102). Locke converts the state's later claim to territory into the retrospective vindication of individual appropriation, an imaginary of settlement that informs who counts as a 'rightful' member and who arrives as a trespasser (1988 [1689], II §49: 124). Rousseau then fuses political belonging to enclosure, making property the hinge on which membership turns (1994 [1755]: 28). Rawls translates this into a late-modern register: peoples may limit entry to preserve their basic structure, albeit subject to duties of assistance (Rawls, 1999 [1971]: 45n.48). The endurance of these notions is an insight into why asylum is habitually treated as an exception at the gate; protection is offered where it can be made compatible with insiders' sovereignty over territory, institutions and resources, and often via procedural hurdles that keep the 'contract' from forming at all (inadmissibility, 'safe third country' rules, offshoring). Borders appear not as neutral gates but as the contract's proving ground, the place where norms generated by the domination contract are applied to stabilize hierarchy. What the social contract names, in other words, the border performs as an activity of natural sorting.

In practice, that boundary does more work than we care to concede, since it decides who is owed what by convention, performance hierarchy through nationality and racialization under the cover of neutrality. Pateman's (1988) sexual contract critique, meanwhile, alerts us to how 'private' dependence is imported into 'public' status through spousal thresholds, tied visas and insufficient attention to gender-based violence. In this book's terms, if justice is to be more than rhetoric at the gate, the task is societal, aimed at altering approaches that normalize moral indifference, while keeping protection discretionary concerning which foreseeable harms are narrated as regrettable by product of order rather than the outcome of design choices. As such, this chapter moves from naming how contracts generate and apply norms of domination to tracking how, through approaches to asylum and migration, those same moves are routinized as policy design used in bordering societies. The pages that follow pursue that redesign brief in law, administration and lived experience.

'Sovereign control'

Since the early 2000s, Europe's approach to inward migration generally, and especially to asylum, has been reshaped by a pronounced re-bordering and turn to ethno-nationalism (GLIMER Project, 2025). While the early 2000s were defined by the construction of common minimum standards, the first and second phases of the Common European Asylum System (CEAS), the period since 2015 has seen national political pressures – fuelled by far right gains and mainstream parties' attempts to outflank them – that have normalized intensified bordering at and within Europe's frontiers, even as the EU has simultaneously sought to bind states into tighter common rules (European Commission, 2024a; 2024b). The 2024 Pact on Migration and Asylum (European Parliament and Council, 2024a; 2024b; 2024c; 2024d; 2024e) epitomizes this dual movement; it centralizes and accelerates procedures while giving member states 'flexible solidarity' options that accommodate national preferences (European Commission, 2024a). The politics driving this shift are unmistakable. The 2024 European Parliament elections delivered a clear rightward drift and notable advances for nationalist parties, pushing centrist actors to harden border rhetoric and practice (Reuters, 2024b). In several member states the reintroduction or extension of internal checks has become a salient political signal of 'sovereign control', notwithstanding legal limits and the costs to free movement within the EU.[13]

It is at the external frontier, however, that bordering has become more materially visible. The literature of bordering can sometimes be allegorical, capturing a variety of concerns that lead to and from the function of literal borders, yet there's no avoiding the fact that Europe has seen an extraordinary proliferation of walls and fences. European Parliament researchers (Dumbrava, 2022) estimate that, since the late 2010s, the aggregate length of border fences inside the EU/Schengen area (and at its external borders) grew from roughly 315 kilometres in 2014 to about 2,048 kilometres by 2022. The external border fencing alone covered about 1,522 kilometres, with most built after 2015 (EPRS, 2024). This literal re-bordering has been politically popular with governments facing nationalist competition, and it has been accompanied by sustained efforts (led by a coalition of Schengen states) to secure EU co-financing for hard infrastructure (Statewatch, 2023).

The major motivation for re-bordering, however, is externalization, and a suite of third country arrangements that keep asylum seekers away from EU territory; this is illustrated by the 2016 EU–Turkey Statement, which marks the consolidation of a transactional policy of 'externalization' by which the EU sought to curb arrivals not by expanding protection on its own territory, but by contracting neighbouring states to police Europe's borders. The EU–Turkey Statement supplied the operational template: people arriving irregularly on the Greek islands could be returned to Turkey, while the EU financed Turkey's enforcement and reception capacities (European Parliament, n.d.). Using the same blueprint, the EU extended the activities to Tunisia in 2023 and, a year later, to Egypt in a €7.4 billion 'Strategic and Comprehensive Partnership' on land and sea bordering (European Commission, 2023; 2024c; Stanicek, 2024). Human rights bodies and the European Ombudsman have warned that the Tunisia deal lacked transparency and credible safeguards, associating EU funds with practices that included collective expulsions into desert areas (Amnesty International, 2023; Khawaja, 2025). National experiments have pushed further still and include Italy's 2023–4 scheme to transfer certain applicants to Albanian-run centres, which has faced sustained legal challenge; in August 2025 the CJEU delivered a judgment seen as striking at aspects of the model (Amnesty International, 2025a). These policies speak to a politics in which 'control at a distance' answers domestic nationalist demands, while shifting protection responsibilities outward (IOI, 2024).[14]

Among the objections is that these policies breach the principles of non-refoulement, which is the simple rule that no one should be sent (directly or indirectly) to a place where they face a real risk of serious harm – e.g., persecution, torture, inhuman treatment. In Europe that duty doesn't just come from the Refugee Convention; it's also baked into human rights law (ECHR) and the EU Charter, which means it applies to everyone, not only to recognized refugees (Meer et al., 2021). Always, however, the duty travels with the state. If authorities control a boat on the high seas or outsource border work to another country, the obligation still holds. The Strasbourg court made that point crystal clear in *Hirsi Jamaa v. Italy*: intercepting people at sea and returning them to Libya without real safeguards violated the Convention. That precedent underlines a wider point: namely, control at a distance does not put people's rights at a distance. There are however exceptions that are revealing in their function, illustrated by unanimous activation of the Temporary Protection Directive for those fleeing Ukraine, which successfully delivered rapid residence and labour market access to more than four million people, and which will now run until 4 March 2027 (Council of the EU, 2025). This stands as proof that Europe can offer expansive protection at scale when political alignments and public sentiments are favourable. It also highlights the contrast with more restrictive 'bordering' towards other groups, namely from the Global South, reinforcing the charge that contemporary asylum policy is racially stratified.

'We want our country back'

Beyond the EU, the UK illustrates how nationalist border politics can reshape the asylum regime outside supranational constraints. The 2023 Illegal Migration Act renders claims by people arriving 'illegally' broadly inadmissible and envisages removal to a 'safe' third country, while the 2024 Safety of Rwanda (Asylum and Immigration) Act directed officials and courts to treat Rwanda as safe in domestic law. After the change of government in July 2025, ministers moved to unwind the Rwanda scheme and process thousands of stayed claims at home; repeal of the 2024 Act and elements of the 2023 Act were signalled or under way (Asylum Aid, 2025; AIDA/ECRE, 2025). Clearly, therefore, legislation has often served as a type of performative politics, which is made grimly visible in how refuge can shade into a routinized politics of neglect. The 2024 summer of racist rioting – including the petrol bombing of the

Holiday Inn Express in Rotherham when more than 100 people seeking asylum were inside the building – is an illustration of this (Sinmaz and Vinter, 2024; Vinter, 2024; South Yorkshire Police, 2024). If nothing else, the chanting chorus from rioters of 'We want our country back' is a devastating illustration of how the seemingly extraordinary often turns out to be an amplification of something in the works, a racialized 'crisis ordinariness' (Berlant, 2011: 54), in which asylum governance is loosened from both a legal duty of care and the social solidarities that sustain it.

This sum of narratives and policies' seemingly chronic tendency towards cruelty can be and are challenged, especially at local levels, as was shown spectacularly in the so-called Battle of Kenmure Street in Glasgow a few years earlier, where the neighbours of two men detained by the Home Office for removal – Sumit Sehdev and Lakhvir Singh – successfully mobilized an eight-hour sit-in protest against their deportation (Akhtar, 2021; Brooks, 2021). Such instances might be related to other examples where a recrafting of social imaginaries elevates the capacity of localities to foster new forms of solidarity. The International Cities of Refuge Network, Cities of Sanctuary, the Save Me Campaign and the Eurocities network have all operated within national level racialized opposition to refuge (Meer, 2022a; ICORN, 2025; City of Sanctuary UK, n.d.; Kothen and Blais, 2013; Eurocities, 2025). We will return to these examples, but it is important to signal here a note of caution about a kind of methodological localism that doesn't account for the parallel forms of governance in which asylum increasingly rests, the dehumanization this normalizes, and the moral indifference it produces. The emphasis of the next chapter is on the social production of moral indifference (such that we might alter its reproduction), but it is relevant here to refuse to accept as self-explanatory that failures in the governance of asylum systems are the outcome of people seeking asylum. We can grasp this with the words of the people detained at Napier

Barracks in Folkestone to understand what's been normalized in public policy.

In an open letter published during the COVID 2021 lockdown, people seeking asylum and detained at Napier Barracks wrote: 'It is vital to understand that no one chooses to leave the country they were born in, no one chooses to leave their family and loved ones behind. We came to this country to save our lives, lives which were mostly in danger because of war and persecution. Yet we found ourselves in an army camp and we are surrounded by fences and security guards' (Grierson, 2021). Decommissioned in 2014, Napier Barracks sits on the edge of Folkestone and was hurried into service as contingency asylum accommodation on 21 September 2020 (HMIP, 2021; UK Visas & Immigration, 2021). By mid-January 2021, almost 400 men were on site, housed in multi-occupancy dormitories (up to twenty-eight per room) on beds and mattresses in poor condition; inspectors also recorded multiple incidents of self-harm and suicide attempts within the first months (HMIP, 2021). Napier forms part of the Home Office's initial contingency accommodation estate, which has relied predominantly on hotels and is delivered under the Asylum Accommodation and Support Contracts by three prime providers: Serco, Clearsprings Ready Homes and Mears (House of Commons Library, 2023b; NAO, 2023; 2024a; 2024b; 2025). It is a lucrative market: the NAO reports that in the region of £3.1 billion was spent on hotels in 2023/24, and analysis indicates that Clearsprings alone accounted for more than £1 in every £20 of total Home Office spending in 2022/23 (NAO, 2024a).

That the statutory responsibility of accommodating people seeking asylum is discharged through private firms is an established – if expanded – tendency that has been documented by a variety of research projects (Hill et al., 2021). It involves the distancing of the state from its duties of care, and with it the reciprocal social encounters and moral obligations this should carry, which is inversely correlated with the quality of care that becomes submerged in a costly para-bureaucracy and is detailed in the accounts of people caught up in it; we will return to this issue. Of the 175,500 people awaiting an initial decision on 30 June 2023, 80 per cent had been waiting more than six months (a more than eighteen-fold increase on the number awaiting an initial decision on 30 June 2010). The share of decisions made within six months fell from around 87 per cent in 2014 to around 7 per cent in late 2023 (Refugee Council, 2024; Migration Observatory, 2025b).

For context, the UK has had relatively few asylum applications per capita in recent years, ranking about eighteenth among EU+ countries in 2022 (Chaloner et al., 2022). Since leaving the EU, the UK remains unusual in Europe in having no statutory time limit on immigration detention, and people commonly wait six months to several years for an initial decision (Migration Observatory, 2025a; NAO, 2023). During this time, people are generally not permitted to work (with limited exceptions after twelve months, and a restricted number of occupations) (Home Office, 2024; House of Commons Library, 2024); they are entitled to register with a GP, but wrongful refusals and administrative barriers are widespread in practice (Doctors of the World, 2019; UK Government, 2024); and access to higher education and training is constrained. Asylum seekers are typically ineligible for student finance and often face fee and status barriers, while recognition of existing qualifications is possible but hampered by documentation and cost obstacles (Refugee Education UK, 2025; UCAS, 2025; UK ENIC, 2025; Council of Europe, 2017). Legal advocates working with charities and NGOs describe a situation where:

> There is no way of contacting anybody [at the Home Office] who will take responsibility for any single case so it's just a matter of banging your head against a brick wall … We get phone numbers, we get fax numbers, within a matter of months they become out of service … even if you complain through the

> official complaints system you will get a reply if you are lucky months and months later and eventually, we get an anodyne response … Ultimately, we have to go to court to tell them how to do their job. And we go again, and again, and again … For those months while they are waiting, their mental health had deteriorated massively … I would have to say the majority [of Home Office] decisions show poor reasoning, lack of consideration of the evidence … and a lack of consideration of case law. (Interview)

This is how the 'crisis ordinariness' that surrounds asylum is produced, through system-level behaviour narrated as 'resource strain' – and, with it, moral blame (Berlant, 2011: 18, 109) – such that asylum is presented and understood as a contest between 'undesirable' individuals and the weight of a nation, often filtered through deservingness frames (Chauvin and Garcés-Mascareñas, 2014; Ratzmann, 2021). So capacious is this tendency that we weaponize age attributions to position children and young people as undeserving of access to care, despite sustained evidence that age-assessment practices are error-prone and harmful (Refugee and Migrant Children's Consortium, 2024; 2025; British Dental Association, 2021; Barnardo's, 2025).

Traumatizing the traumatized is out of kilter with the kinds of 'founding myths' that the UK – like most countries – adopts in stories of refuge, in which morality functions almost as a credentializing disclaimer, as illustrated by critical historical work contesting celebratory narratives of the Kindertransport (Craig-Norton, 2019; London, 2000). Working on asylum, however, nearly always illustrates only the very weak 'messianic power' – to quote Walter Benjamin (1968: 254) – which the past might bear upon the present, making glaringly obvious the gap between what we are and what we want to tell ourselves, and the grim realities in between. Remembrance aftercall is a structured and often curated practice to reproduce group membership. Hence, on the very day the Nationality and Borders Act (NBA) came into effect, on 27 April 2002, the Home Office co-sponsored a Yom HaShoah commemoration, a concert to remember the Kitchener Camp in Kent through which 4,000 Jewish refugee men from Germany, Austria, Czechoslovakia and Poland sought refuge in 1939. The NBA and the 2023 Illegal Migration Act, meanwhile, have all but eliminated the fundamental right to seek asylum in the UK, introducing the offence of 'illegal arrival' (with a maximum penalty of four years of imprisonment) and expanding the offence of 'facilitating arrival' to a maximum of life imprisonment.

Such legislation further illustrates the ways in which 'certain human lives are more grievable than others' (Butler, 2004: 30), since, even as asylum in the Global South was becoming increasingly inaccessible, between 2021 and 2023 the UK government created humanitarian routes under which around half a million people, approximately 283,000 from Ukraine and 191,000 from Hong Kong, received a status to live and work in the UK (Home Office, 2023; 2024). According to Butler, this is not an aberration of sentiment but an artefact of framing: administrative and media practices pre-sort those whose injuries register as losses that 'count', reproducing hierarchies of recognizability across 'routes' and categories (2004: 32–5; 2009: 64–6). For example, a meta-analysis of attitudes towards migrants and displaced persons finds a weak preference for those from the Global North over the Global South, a clearer tendency to favour people from the same world region, and (most robustly) 'a strong and systematic preference for Christians as opposed to Muslims', indicating that religion more than geography shapes which displaced migrants are welcomed or rejected (Weber et al., 2024). These results are arrived at by converting outcomes in each study to enable cross-study comparison, though the approach inherits differences in dependent variables (e.g., admission, general approval, citizenship). The pattern aligns with large-scale studies showing consistent European preferences for asylum seekers who are Christian, alongside markers of employability and vulnerability (Bansak et al., 2016; 2023).

The broader point is that we are currently excluding people by region (and, indirectly, religion) as a matter of policy because so-called 'safe and legal' humanitarian pathways have been tightly constrained, with Afghan resettlement routes in particular failing to meet stated ambitions (House of Commons Library, 2024; Home Office, 2023). Hence, of the nearly 1,200 people detained (or formerly detained) at Wethersfield camp since 2023 with whom the refugee charity Care4Calais has been in contact, all were from the Global South (predominantly South Asian, MENA and African nationalities) (Care4Calais, 2024). Operational since July 2023, Wethersfield is an airfield on a remote 800-acre site in rural Essex. Clinicians working with the Helen Bamber Foundation – a human rights charity – have documented, among those held there and at similar mass accommodation sites, survivors of torture and trafficking, people with severe mental health needs and children wrongly treated as adults. Medical NGOs have described a mounting mental health crisis (Dorling and Harris 2023; 2024). Their concerns are warranted: there were around 180 deaths in Home Office housing between April 2016 and December 2023, with 82 of these occurring in such camps since 2020 (Clugston and Walawalkar, 2024).

Asylum and domination contracts

There is, of course, an established literature on how states place some people beyond the moral horizon of equal worth, irrespective of formal membership: A-level sociology still introduces students to Zygmunt Bauman's account of dehumanization in *Modernity and the Holocaust* (1989), which, beyond bureaucratic rationalities, concerns the reframing of sets of people to whom moral obligations no longer apply. In other accounts, such as Giorgio Agamben's discussion of '*homo sacer*' (1998), dehumanization is figured as 'bare life' exposed to sovereign power, stripped of rights and protections. Yet these are oddly de-raced accounts; as argued elsewhere, they underplay the historical and systemic ways in which racial injustice is intrinsic to societies in the Global North, including how nation-states seldom recognize their formation through imperial and colonial systems of racism, or their contemporary legacies in symbols, assets, the built environment and the very criteria of citizenship (Meer, 2022b). For similar reasons, in *Habeas Viscus*, Alexander Weheliye develops a theory of 'racializing assemblages', foregrounding the centrality of race to modern notions of 'the human' as a category for governance (2014: 3–7). Playing on *habeas corpus*, the book joins law and flesh as 'the conjoining of flesh and habeas corpus in the compound habeas viscus', to foreground how legal personhood is built atop racialized corporeality (ibid.: 21). Zakiyyah Iman Jackson (2020) likewise argues that African diasporic cultural production unsettles and refashions 'the human', rather than seeking inclusion within it. Better known is Achille Mbembe's account of 'necropolitics', meaning not only a right to kill, but power over life and death that manufactures 'death worlds' and conditions akin to social unlivability (2003: 39–40). Jasbir Puar extends this by theorizing 'debilitation' as a status in its own right, 'a status unto itself that triangulates the hierarchies of living and dying', and by showing how maiming can be a biopolitical end rather than a mere by product(2017: 37).

Taken together, these accounts furnish a vital horizon in naming how certain lives are rendered less than fully human; but they operate at a level of ontological sweep that illuminates dehumanization and exposure to sovereign power, yet treats racialization as incidental rather than constitutive. Mbembe and Puar clearly address this, but risk flattening the routine instruments through which subordination is manufactured. Weheliye and Jackson, meanwhile, decisively centre race in 'the human', but their interventions offer limited traction on the mid-level levers by which administrative systems can be reset. A domination contract perspective, however, paired with an institutional focus, allows us to appeal to records – such as inspection and audit reports, case law, FOI disclosures – that yield answers to questions such as 'Do routines predictably reproduce racialized and gendered subordination under the cover of neutrality?'. For, if contract theory explains how borders privilege insiders' consent, the domination contract reframes justice at the border as repair and desubordination rather than discretionary charity. In practical terms, that means rolling back devices that manufacture non-protection (broad inadmissibility, mass offshoring), designing credibility processes to challenge predictable bias (interpreters, trauma-informed interviewing, transparent recognition rates, independent oversight), and treating reception conditions, legal aid, appeal rights and timelines as the material means by which the 'right to seek and enjoy asylum' becomes an enforceable relation, and so does not depend on the benevolence of insiders. The UK jurisprudential and policy whiplash around the Rwanda scheme and inadmissibility shows what is at stake: seen through a domination contract lens, the question is not simply whether the border is legally tidy, but whether its design predictably entrenches racialized and gendered subordination under the cover of neutrality. A domination contract lens makes the border's partiality visible, and stabilizes itself through 'an agreement to misinterpret the world' (Mills, 1997: 32), so practices that sort migrants according to credibility, route and country labels appear neutral even as they reproduce hierarchies.

On this view, the contemporary border is 'by definition not neutral', and a state instrument that secures the terms of the contract (Mills, 1997: 97). That frame clarifies why techniques like externalization and offshoring manufacture rightlessness before a claim is heard. The aforementioned UK Supreme Court's judgment on the Rwanda policy cut through neutrality talk in precisely these terms, holding that there were 'substantial grounds for believing that asylum seekers would face a real risk of ill-treatment [and] refoulement', rendering Rwanda not 'safe' (UK Supreme Court, 2023). Parliament then tried to legislate safety via the 2024 Safety of Rwanda Act, even as policy shifted again in 2024–5 towards processing the 'Rwanda cohort' in the UK and revising inadmissibility guidance that structures third country refusal at the threshold (Home Office, 2025).

Pateman's critique reminds us how bordering also reproduces dependency and danger along gendered lines: 'The social contract is a story of freedom; the sexual contract is a story of subjection. The original contract constitutes both freedom and domination' (1988: 10–11). What looks like neutral administration frequently leans on familial dependency and labour subordination regimes (spousal income thresholds, no recourse to public funds), tied to domestic and care work, conditions under which claims to protection from gender-based violence are harder to bring to the surface and sustain. In Pateman's terms, 'political right originates in sex right or conjugal right' (ibid., 11–12); when the border imports private dependence into the public domain, it predictably depresses recognition of persecution, restricts exit options and amplifies coercion in reception and accommodation systems. A domination contract lens identifies the distributional politics concealed by that script. The racial contract operates by coding domination as order and unequal protection as normal politics (Mills, 1997: 14–15); once that background is made explicit, familiar devices (carrier sanctions, maritime interceptions, poor screening of information at first contact) should be read not as neutral management, but as technologies for manufacturing non-protection upstream of adjudication.

The UK Supreme Court's 2023 Rwanda judgment crystallizes the point, where evidence showed a real risk of ill-treatment and refoulement that falsifies the legal fiction of safety. Parliament's subsequent attempt to legislate safety via the 2024 Safety of Rwanda Act and the June 2025 guidance recalibrating inadmissibility both illustrate how discretionary power moves to keep claims outside the circle of enforceable reciprocity (UK Parliament, 2024; Home Office, 2025). Pateman's sexual contract analysis clarifies the gendered mechanics: when residence and status are tethered to spouses, sponsors or employers, 'private' dependence is imported into the public category of the right-holder (1988: 10–12). The result is predictable: barriers to independent claim-formation, chilled disclosure of violence and heightened exposure to coercion in reception and accommodation. Designing for justice therefore requires institutional, not simple attitudinal, reform: guaranteed access to independent legal advice, interpreters and trauma-informed interviewing, recognition audits with disaggregated statistics, shelters and safe housing decoupled from intimate partners and employers, permission to work within clear timelines and independent oversight with powers to compel contractor compliance. On this view, the legitimacy of bordering turns on whether procedures foreseeably reproduce racialized and gendered subordination under the cover of neutrality. Indeed, contemporary UK asylum governance becomes legible as 'organized irresponsibility' (Beck, 2009: 5): a system that normalizes moral indifference by outsourcing care to para-bureaucratic contractors, while keeping protection discretionary in which predictable injuries are recoded as unfortunate 'side effects' instead of acknowledged as the results of how the system is built.

Moral indifference: Omelas or Riace?

'Theory' in the social sciences can have diverse productive purposes beyond postulating testable causality. I've increasingly looked to the narrations of social processes in these accounts, to the banal or performative cruelties these contain, in thinking about how indifference is produced, reproduced and able to flow into and out of public administration. Something is needed that can help us comprehend how unaccompanied children who had crossed the Channel by boat were kept for days without access to beds or showers and how, during the period of curtailed screening, key trafficking indicator questions were not asked until the High Court ordered that they be reinstated (Bulman, 2020; *DA and Ors v. The Secretary of State for the Home Department*, 2020; UNHCR, 2021). This involves not just ideology or the 'crude lying of cynical apologists', as Stan Cohen (2001: xii) once put it, but complex bad faith innocence. It is something that takes us to Ursula K. Le Guin's short story, 'The ones who walk away from Omelas', first published in 1973 and later collected in *The Wind's Twelve Quarters* (1975).

Le Guin was a consummate world-builder brought up by academic social anthropologists; she did graduate work in the humanities and spent the entirety of her professional life as a writer of fiction and essays probing ethics, power and identity in social systems. Published more than fifty years ago, her short story describes a society she names 'Omelas', in which civic harmony is premised upon something atrocious: a carceral contract, the imprisonment and degradation of a child:

> In a basement under one of the beautiful public buildings of Omelas … there is a room. It has one locked door, and no window … The floor is dirt, a little damp to the touch, as cellar dirt usually is. The room is about three paces long and two wide: a mere broom closet or disused tool room. In the room, a child is sitting. It could be a boy or a girl. It looks about six, but actually is nearly ten … The door is always locked; and nobody ever comes, except that sometimes – the child has no understanding of time or interval – sometimes the door rattles terribly and opens, and a person, or several people, are there … The child, who has not always lived in the tool room, can remember sunlight and its mother's voice, sometimes speaks. 'I will be good', it says. 'Please let me out. I will be good!' They

> never answer. The child used to scream for help at night, and cry a good deal, but now it only makes a kind of whining … Some of them have come to see it, others are content merely to know it is there. They all know that it has to be there. Some of them understand why, and some do not.

It is an allegory, of course, but a powerful one that conveys a moral tale of how state violence can carry a broader culpability, including in our knowing or our refusal to know. In Le Guin's story, the world of Omelas is constructed via a narrator who strips away the noise and invites us either to stay and change nothing, or to leave and refuse the choice between statehood and human dignity. The people of Omelas, you see, convince themselves that this cruelty is not only inevitable but the reason they can have what they do have. Misery and suffering are necessary, so long as they are not their own. Perhaps this is to repeat the theory's vice of claiming validity, but I think of Omelas as a composite of material and embodied asylum experiences in our own society. Examples include Home Office asylum reception arrangements for 200 wet and cold arrivals at Tug Haven in Dover, including children and RNLI rescues, being left for hours outside on what the inspectors described as a 'rubble strewn building site', without access to dry clothes (HMIP, 2021; ICIBI, 2022). Some children had been separated from their parents, others physically restrained. David Neal, the former Independent Chief Inspector of Borders and Immigration, previously Commander of Military Police, is recorded as stating that 'conditions in which children were detained at Kent Dover docks were worse than those I'd seen in the detention of adult combatants'. More publicized was the news that some of the unaccompanied children placed in Home Office commissioned hotels go missing (presumed to have been trafficked while under the care of the British state); more than 440 of the approximately 5,400 unaccompanied children (some as young as twelve years old) who were housed in hotels between July 2021 and June/July 2023 went missing

(Ayeb-Karlsson et al., 2024: 6; House of Commons Library, 2023a).

And what of those teenagers who had only just reached the age of 18? Some answers come from testimonies gathered in Glasgow, including that of a young man we're calling Adnan. Adnan arrived in Glasgow via the Asylum Dispersal Scheme in March 2020. He was assigned a hotel room and told the arrangement would be for a maximum of three weeks. It actually lasted nine months. He was not allowed to lock the door, was expected to eat non-halal meals, was subject to curfews and then had his right to leave the hotel removed. Residents were reported to the Home Office and police if they acted outside the system, so that, Adnan recalled, one neighbouring resident was subject to a police investigation for accepting donated clothing from a charity, and another was reported to the Home Office for trying to register with a GP. As time went on, Adnan noted, it became very clear he had been moved into a carceral system. 'Some of the things they were doing', he commented, 'were just not human ... They were very keen on attaching you to the number rather than referring to you by your name.' When he voiced concerns, he was accused of being 'aggressive'.

Documents disclosed by the Home Office in response to a freedom of information request indicate that they don't know who is involved in providing this subcontracted asylum accommodation. They are contractually required to maintain up-to-date lists of subcontractors, but these had not been updated in five years; we know that several of the companies that we know were providing accommodation were found to be missing from the list.

> The moment that you raise your voice, the first initial action that any of the Mears staff would do is pick up the phone, call the police [and] the police would come and then they immediately believe the story of the Mears staff versus the story of the asylum seeker. They will take the asylum seeker to the police station,

> investigate and then an hour or two hours later the [asylum seeker] would come back. (Interview with Adnan)

In another subcontracted accommodation, a young man named Kazim witnessed his neighbour becoming erratic and equipped with a knife. Kazim made a request to a staff member to put a lock on his room so that he might feel safe at night. The provider – which had been subcontracted by Mears – instead called the police, without moving Kazim's neighbour or even providing Kazim with a lock for his door. When the police attempted to arrest the person, they couldn't find him. As a result, Kazim's situation deteriorated and his neighbour became 'really aggressive to me'. So, Kazim explained, with no help from the housing subcontractor or the police, he decided to take matters into his own hands, preferring to sleep on the streets than in his designated housing: 'I went outside of the house. I went to sleep outside. I wasn't safe in this place.'

The Independent Chief Inspector of Borders and Immigration published the results of Home Office property inspections over a twenty-two-month period. Just 23 per cent of Mears properties achieved compliance, while nearly 15 per cent of inspected Clearsprings properties were judged 'uninhabitable' (NAO, 2023).

The ban on the right to work creates destitution-level subsistence provision that is separately managed. Cash transfers were replaced with a voucher system, used intermittently between 2000 and 2009, until the introduction of the Azure card: a pre-paid card run by Sodexo, which was in turn replaced by the Asylum Support Enablement (Aspen) card, provided by Prepaid Financial Services (PFS). The conditions of precarity induced by the card, and how these govern the lives of asylum seekers, are exemplified by Sarah: 'In March, it stopped working. Like, I didn't understand why or when. I couldn't use it in the shop, I couldn't tap it, I couldn't insert it. It won't work.' From one day to the next, she was left without her sole source of income.

> I called them, they said OK, they will sort it out, and then they will send me a new card within ten days. And I asked if I could apply for emergency funding, they said they will let me know. And then ten days passed, and fourteen days passed … It's been now three weeks, and I don't have any food, and I'm really out. I don't have nappies. I don't have anything, I cannot even go out, I don't have bus money to go out.

Isolated from networks of financial support, Sarah was left completely destitute, even though she had a young toddler at home. For five weeks, she received no income and was denied access to emergency support. When her Housing Officer eventually told her that emergency support would be granted, she was given just over an hour to collect it.

It is estimated that the Home Office spent more than £198 million in emergency funding to cover failures in the PFS system, which could have been predicted as, prior to contracting PFS, the Home Office had been doing the same on the previous card system, supplied by Sodexo (Bennani-Taylor and Meer, 2024). What the examples outlined here speak to is the criminalization of a growing population that is subjected not only to indefinite detention or suspended precarity, but to the new and wholly manufactured risks therein that ask profound questions of all of us.

Through the allegory of Omelas, we are reminded that societal complicity in cruelty is not inevitable but chosen; people can refuse arrangements that demand the suffering of some as the price of comfort for the many (Le Guin, 1975). The question, then, is not only about how we diagnose the present, but how we act otherwise, and what practices we might learn from elsewhere to remake the terms of belonging in more just ways.

One answer begins with the story of Domenico Lucano (known affectionately as 'Mimmo'), a former schoolteacher who became mayor of Riace in southern Italy. From the early 2000s, schemes were pioneered in Riace that incorporated displaced migrants and refugees into the life of the town, not as an emergency exception but as a social and economic principle (Foti, 2017; Unsgaard, 2017). Lucano's administration founded City of the Future, explicitly inspired by the Calabrian utopianist Tommaso Campanella. It secured modest funding to support settlement pathways that linked housing, work and welfare (Meer et al., 2021; Progressive International, 2022). Although small in scale (roughly 1,000 people from about twenty countries over time) the cooperative model converted disused and abandoned buildings into homes and workshops, reopened primary schools and language learning spaces, and established health centres (Zolin, 2019; Berardi, 2021; Giuffrida, 2018). This was not regeneration on show but a reanimation of Riace's sociality after decades of depopulation; it treated newcomers as co-dwellers, neighbours and contributors rather than as problems to be managed (Foti, 2017).

In effect, a practical 'right to the city' was staged in Riace that did not peripheralize displaced migrants and refugees. In Henri Lefebvre's terms, it asserted both the abstract claim to urban life and the concrete claim to shared spaces of work, leisure, education, healthcare and accommodation for all urban dwellers (Lefebvre, 1996: 158; see also Purcell, 2003; 2014). Without romanticizing its flaws, the point is that even where formal status was absent, residents enacted a lived right to the city, grounded in everyday cooperation and mutual aid rather than in discretionary charity. Although the model was later undermined (national authorities cut funding and prosecutors pursued Lucano) the 'Riace model' nonetheless travelled to other Calabrian towns. What the Riace model dramatized, then, is not procedure alone, but an ethical-political stance: the cultivation of a sense of 'shared fate', which 'comes by virtue of being entangled with others in such a way that one's future is tied to theirs' (Allen, 2004), together with a recognition of our common 'vulnerability to suffering' that unsettles attempts to hierarchize whose harms count (Butler, 2004). Set against this non-ideal terrain, a range of prominent proposals can be read as complementary routes for institutionalizing what places like Riace experienced. Ayelet Shachar, for example, treats birthright as a form of inherited property and advances the idea of *jus nexi* membership as a way to convert belonging from ascription to relation:

> The *jus nexi* principle is normatively designed to shrink the gap between partaking in actual membership and gaining political voice; it views every long-term resident as a citizen-in-the-making ... *jus nexi* does not force membership upon anyone; it requires long-term residents to display both intent and effort to join the collective if they choose to embark on the path of earned citizenship. The rootedness principle creates a presumption of inclusion on behalf of those whose life-center has already shifted, but it requires individuals to act in order for this eligibility to affect their citizenship status. What is required here is not mere physical presence on the territory, but also the expression of will to become a full member. (2011: 140)

As a kind of right of connection, *jus nexi* can be contrasted with approaches to citizenship that recognize birthplace or ancestry, for, rather than asking where someone happened to be born (*jus soli*) or to whom (*jus sanguinis*), it asks what binds people to a polity in terms of years of residence, schooling, language, work, family life and civic participation. As a result, it places 'rootedness at center stage' and 'counters the absolutist stance that asks us to refer back to the initial act of unauthorized entry or visa overstay' (Shachar, 2011: 140). On this view, membership should follow the fabric of the everyday weave of relationships, intentions and contributions, while supplying a normative criterion that differs from ordinary naturalization, enabling those whose lives are already entwined with a community to hold the status that matches that reality. In Shacher's words, '*jus nexi* allows both democratic accountability and political equality for those whose well-being is directly affected by the legal authority of the polity' (ibid), meaning that in a Riace-like register, those already embedded in a polity's institutional life (working, studying, caring, paying taxes, participating in civic associations) would be recognized as entitled to membership because exclusion becomes a refusal of already existing social ties.

This carries immediate traction at the border, as people consigned to camps, hostels or barges, and subject to spatial and administrative controls, must have a voice in the institutions that govern them. At the same time, and read through the lens of Chapters 2 and 3, membership claims rooted in *jus nexi* would need to name the racial-imperial and gendered histories that structure patterns of who can accumulate recognizable ties, including the criteria used to evidence those ties. Since belonging is itself historically produced inside racialized and gendered social dynamics, where the connection is measured through language credentials, employment histories, criminal records or documentary proof of continuous residence, the result can be a refined deservingness regime that systematically discounts how racialized groups encounter barriers to accumulating legible 'ties'. As such, and where *jus nexi* operationalizes worthiness via market-facing contributions and individualized civic performance, it can undervalue precisely those practices of social reproduction that make collective life possible, but leave thinner documentary traces. If *jus nexi* is applied without naming that history, those whose dispossession is tied to imperial extraction are asked to earn back inclusion through performances of integration in the metropole; an inversion that leaves background conditions intact. Even where *jus nexi* is pitched (as Shachar intends) as an auxiliary route that 'shrinks the gap between partaking in actual membership and gaining political voice', the principle still relies on institutions that decide what counts as connection (2011: 136–7).

A domination contract rejoinder is not that ties should be irrelevant, but that which ties are eligible is itself a product of power. If the ledger recognizes waged work but not mutual aid caregiving, formal volunteering but not community self-help, credentialed language tests but not multilingual family labour, the result is a selective visibility that keeps dominated groups in a state of conditional belonging. Normative repair might expand *jus nexi* by deepening what counts as connection (including care and community labour), cap discretion and anchor relational assessments in an explicit reckoning with racial imperial and gendered starting points. Otherwise, the 'right of connection' risks becoming a refined technology of deservingness, smoothing the edges of exclusion without dislodging the contracts of domination beneath it. Seyla Benhabib's 'democratic iteration' provides a promising route here, namely the approach to renegotiating boundaries and norms, by ensuring 'voice' (2004: 3): 'By democratic iterations I mean complex processes of public argument, deliberation, and exchange through which universalist rights claims are contested and contextualized, invoked and revoked, posited and positioned throughout legal and political institutions as well as in the associations of civil society' (2009: 37).

A Riace-style municipalism is precisely such an iterative practice; it makes room for newcomers' claims to reshape local institutions, from schools and clinics to housing cooperatives and labour markets, and it builds channels through which those changes can develop. Democratic iteration may help name the way municipal practices like the Riace model redraw membership by publicly testing and reinscribing norms through schools, clinics, cooperatives, and councils: 'Through such iterative acts, a democratic people that considers itself bound by certain guiding norms and principles reappropriates and reinterprets these, thus showing itself to be not only the subject but also the author of the laws' (Benhabib, 2009: 38).

Returning to Omelas helps to fix the compass: complicity is a choice, and so is refusal (Le Guin, 1975). The Riace example shows that alternative practices are not only imaginable but practicable, even under conditions of scarcity and political hostility. The task is to move from islands of innovation to an archipelago of institutions in order to reframe the right to seek and enjoy asylum as an enforceable relation rather than a discretionary favour; to convert municipal experiments into national and transnational guarantees; and to ensure that the infrastructures of reception, residence and recognition embody the shared fate and mutual vulnerability that make democratic life possible. Panels, proof requirements and adjudication do not simply test truth; they allocate humiliation, distribute the costs of intelligibility and decide whose account is credible enough to enter the circle of enforceable reciprocity. That is why *procedures* are never merely *procedural*: they are justice machines that can be redesigned either to reproduce bias as neutrality or to treat predictable disadvantage as a design trade-off.

This chapter has argued that the governance of asylum in the UK and Europe is not a system *in* crisis, but a system *of* crisis, deliberately engineered through policies of organized irresponsibility. The 2013 Lampedusa shipwreck serves not as an isolated tragedy, but as a stark prism, refracting the lethal consequences of a contractarian imaginary that rigorously filters membership and protection at the threshold. We have seen how this imaginary is operationalized through a dual movement: the outward projection of borders via externalization deals and offshore processing, and the inward production of indifference through paralysing bureaucracy, outsourced accommodation and a manufactured crisis of ordinariness that normalizes destitution and dehumanization. The theoretical frameworks of the domination and sexual contracts have provided the critical tools to decipher this system. They reveal that bordering is not a neutral administrative function, but a potent technology for naturalizing racialized and gendered hierarchies. It is a process that performs the social contract's exclusionary logic, deciding who may form a reciprocal relationship with the state and who is consigned to rightlessness. The UK's jurisprudential and political whiplash over the Rwanda policy, alongside the grim realities of camps like Napier and Wethersfield, exemplify the high stakes of this design, the predictable entrenchment of subordination under the cover of legal neutrality. Yet, as the allegory of Omelas reminds us, complicity in this system is a choice, not an inevitability. The pervasive moral indifference that allows a child to be sacrificed for collective comfort can be refused. The story of Riace, however imperfect and besieged, offers a glimpse of an alternative ethical-political stance. It models a practice of belonging grounded in 'shared fate' and mutual vulnerability rather than discretionary charity, enacting a Lefebvrian 'right to the city' for all residents. The task is to convert these islands of innovation into an archipelago of enforceable rights, to ensure that reception conditions, legal aid, fair procedures and timely decisions are the material means by which the right to seek asylum becomes a reality.

Ultimately, the question posed in this chapter is not solely how we diagnose the present, but how we act to alter it. Moving beyond organized irresponsibility requires a fundamental reimagining of justice at the border, from an act of sovereign benevolence to an enforceable relation of reciprocity, and from a politics of neglect to a practice of common dwelling. The border, rethought, must cease to be a proving ground for domination and become instead a site where new terms of belonging are iteratively and democratically forged. The techniques that keep protection discretionary at the gate do not dissolve as we progress; they translate. A politics that individualizes catastrophe while externalizing responsibility reappears as institutional innocence in the language of 'global justice' and 'human rights'. The next chapter widens the lens: if law's lexicon misrecognizes structure and contracts instruct hierarchy, what happens when those blind spots travel as universals? And what would a post-innocent vocabulary require of the institutions that speak for humanity?

5

Witnessing, Knowing and Ignoring Injustice

'If I must die, you must live to tell my story', insist the opening lines of a poem from the writer and teacher Refaat Alareer, who was targeted by an Israeli airstrike in December 2023, which killed his siblings and young nieces and nephews alongside him. The poem 'If I must die', written some years earlier, and dedicated to his eldest daughter, carries a number of themes, including the right of Palestinians to narrate their own struggles, something reflected in his own development of teaching spaces to voice and realize this (Aziza, 2024; Just World Books, 2015; We Are Not Numbers, n.d.). The killing, a few months later, of his eldest daughter and her newborn child in a further Israeli airstrike on their Gaza City home was a cruel but characteristic atrocity that could not erase how, in the hours after the killing of Refaat, the poem travelled across languages and platforms, a compact with readers that converted grief into a shared intelligibility of the preposterous status of international justice in the face of continuing and horrific violence, openly perpetrated on a civilian population.[15]

That the grief for Refaat Alareer is voiced in the first person – 'Tell my story' – echoing the line in his poem does more than register hurt; it converts suffering from an administratively managed datum into a political address. It asks us to see his life as a life, bridging the consolations of distance that abstract justice so often permits. Framed this way, first-person mourning is not merely expressive; it is constitutive of a claim to justice. It disrupts the prior sorting of whose voices are audible and whose injuries are rendered statistical, insisting on recognition before adjudication, on being taken as a speaker of injustice rather than a distant object of policy. As Butler (2009: 14) insists, 'the apprehension of grievability precedes and makes possible the apprehension of life'. Thus, where public frames never attach grief, lives are unworthy of attention, such that losses barely appear relevant; this is something that teaches us whose deaths merit narration and whose pass unmarked (cf. Butler, 2004: 32–3). In that shift from third-person classification to first-person address lies the conceptual work that abstract schemas evade – the reallocation of recognizability, the remaking of the 'we' that counts losses and the exposure of the normative frames that withhold public grief from some, while lavishly extending it to others.

Read this way, Alareer's poem is neither an ornament to moral argument nor a lament to be filed under 'poetry'. It is a method that compels us to hear the human not as a category already decided elsewhere, but as a claim upon us everywhere, made from within structures of domination that the language of global justice too often brackets as context (Ba, 2021). For example, although the language of human rights promises universality, it all too often sorts lives by their legibility and grievability; who is heard as a rights-bearing subject and who remains a case, a threat or a statistic. The international machinery that claims to vindicate 'humanity' frequently individualizes catastrophe, abstracts it from the structures that produced it, and then returns us to the old hierarchies of who may speak and on what terms, and the question of to whom repair is owed. Set against that horizon, Alareer's poem is not only elegy but method, a refusal of the frames that render some deaths unspeakable and some claims unintelligible; a pedagogy that begins from situated narration rather than from the administrative thresholds of admissibility; a reminder that justice, to be more than a label that the strong attach to order, must be authored by those who live its absence (Aziza, 2024; Serhan, 2023). When Euro-Atlantic discourses of global justice and human rights ask us to move immediately to principles and procedures, Alareer's life's work drags us back to the prior question (who gets to be the 'we' of the human, and on what narrative terms) and demands that the answer be built from voices that were meant to be marginal, translated and filed away (*We Are Not Numbers*, n.d.; Edwards, 2023).

Against that backdrop, the migration from national to global scales should not mislead us into thinking the problem is new. What Chapter 1 named as law's 'operative lexicon', its conversion of structural harm into micro-disputes, returns globally as the etiquette of impartiality. What Chapter 2 reconceived as 'domination contracts', the social technologies that fabricate hierarchy while calling it order, reappears in the international sphere as institutionalized innocence: a universalism that speaks for humanity by ventriloquizing those it marginalizes. And what Chapter 3 showed at the border, the manufacture of non-protection upstream and the normalization of crisis as administrative common sense, opens outward as a politics that individualizes catastrophe while insulating the historical production of vulnerability from remedy. In short, the blind spots travel; they do not dissolve.

The argument so far has moved from the 'double hermeneutic' of justice, how concepts travel into institutions and back again, to the limits of a canon that secures elegance by bracketing the social world it orders. In Chapter 1 we returned to the archive not to venerate it, but to see how its argumentative moves still organize today's vocabularies. Thrasymachus' provocation, that 'the just' serves the stronger, was not finally answered so much as domesticated; Socrates' win exposed logical slippage but left intact the sociological insight that power scripts moral language.

That is why the chapter pressed beyond jurisprudence to law's 'operative lexicon', recognizing how this atomizes structural harms into micro-disputes and defaults to 'reasonableness' as status quo, making a system pervasively lawful and yet systematically unjust.

Chapter 2 then named the concealed architecture: domination contracts. Building on Pateman's sexual contract and Mills's racial contract, we took domination rather than aberration as the baseline, and recast the social contract as a technology that generates norms and teaches administrators how to apply them in ways that stabilize hierarchy. Mills's revisionist wager, that contract theory can be re-tooled for rectification, only sharpened the methodological pivot: begin from group domination, historical realism and non-ideal theory, not from a population of interchangeable individuals behind a veil of forgetfulness. Chapter 3 then showed how this plays out at the border, where the 'contract' is kept from forming at all: inadmissibility rules, offshoring and externalization manufacture non-protection upstream, while a politics of 'crisis ordinariness' naturalizes moral indifference as administrative common sense. The Lampedusa prism and the UK's accommodation regime (Napier Barracks) made concrete how para-bureaucratic outsourcing and slow violence routines turn rights into discretionary benevolence. This chapter widens the lens: if the contract's blind spots travel, what happens when they reach 'global justice' and 'human rights'?

A rolling constitution?

One way to approach the idea of human rights is to view something like a rolling constitution that reflects accumulated contestations, sometimes widening to address cross-border harms and fair social and material outcomes (Fraser, 2008; Sen, 2009; Madhok, 2024). The story of human rights is neither linear nor purely European; it emerges from entangled struggles over authority, dignity and political membership that stretch across empires, revolutions and social movements. As a cumulative activity, human rights might even comprise medieval charters such as the Magna Carta, which circumscribed sovereign power in the language of liberties for specific estates, planting early seeds for claims against arbitrary rule (Carpenter, 2015). We have already seen how social contract thought translates such sentiments into more general principles of individual freedom and consent, even as they narrow its subjects in practice, excluding enslaved people, women and colonized populations. Nineteenth-century campaigns against slavery, and the growth of labour, women's and minority rights movements, arguably widened the circle of rights-bearing subjects and expanded the repertoire from civil and political liberties to social claims concerning work, welfare and education (Hochschild, 2005; Rappaport, 2000; Marshall, 1950). Less often stated is how these pressures travelled through imperial circuits as anticolonial activists stressed the limitations of prevailing idioms of rights, and pressed for self-determination, racial equality and democratic inclusion, culminating in debates about mandates in the interwar period and, later, in the politics of decolonization (Pedersen, 2015; Burke, 2006; Getachew, 2019).

The catastrophe of the Second World War arguably catalysed a normative consolidation in the UN Charter (1945) and the Universal Declaration of Human Rights (1948), which established binding covenants and regional systems, including the European, Inter-American and African regimes (Morsink, 1999; Shelton, 2013). From the 1970s, human rights acquired a distinctive transnational infrastructure (treaty bodies, courts, NGOs and advocacy networks) that professionalized monitoring and reframed dissident claims in legal-moral terms (Keck and Sikkink, 1998; Hopgood, 2013). This 'breakthrough' era, as some describe it, popularized the language of universal rights and the supposed protection of individuals against state terror, even while social and economic rights, and collective claims to development and culture, advanced more unevenly (Moyn, 2010; Alston and Goodman, 2013).

At the same time, narrations on the emergence of human rights typically avoid confronting its exclusions and imperial entanglements. Feminist, postcolonial and third world approaches to international law (TWAIL) scholarship have shown how hierarchies of race, gender and civilization were baked into the international order, and how contemporary regimes can reproduce paternalism unless they are repoliticized and regrounded in democratic struggle (Anghie, 2004; Mutua, 2001; Bhambra, 2014). These critiques do not reject human rights so much as demand their reconstruction, expanding the subjects, sites and scales of protection to include borders, carceral systems, digital infrastructures and planetary ecologies (Benjamin, 2019; Couldry and Mejias, 2019; Knox, 2020). The point is that human rights did not spring fully formed from a single European moment. Their emergence is better understood as a braided history of claims, institutions and imaginaries that were repeatedly assembled, tested and reworked across different worlds; canonical accounts often begin with natural law philosophizing, move through the age of revolutions and culminate in postwar internationalism. According to Sumi Madhok, such accounts typically fix the epistemic centre in the Euro-Atlantic and treat the rest as belated recipients, a stance she calls 'time–space provincialism' (2024: 3). This provincialism underwrites a 'politics of origins' that racializes authorship (rights are said to originate in, belong to and travel from 'the West') and it organizes debate into stock binaries such as West/non-West and universalism/particularism (ibid.). Reconstructing emergence from 'most of the world' shifts the timeline and the map. Here, rights crystallize in what Madhok terms 'vernacular rights cultures', that claim entitlements (*haq*) and re-specify whose injuries count, which institutions must change and what it is that justice demands across borders (ibid.: 10, 18).

Such mobilizations do not treat rights as thin, humanitarian moralism; they tie rights to anti-imperial and anti-exploitation agendas and contest legal and political architectures that have historically excluded racialized, Indigenous and caste-oppressed peoples (ibid.: 2, 10). On this view, the emergence of human rights is inseparable from social movements as epistemic sites where new concepts are coined, translated and fought for, while remaining alert to the risks of romanticizing movements or shrinking them into the 'local'.

There is a deeper argument about the contingency legal foundations (Pahuja, 2011), but a more modest point lies in what justice literature terms a 'third-generation norm of legitimacy' – i.e., respect for reasonable cultural diversity. This norm must be considered on a par with first-generation rights (civil and political) and second-generation rights (economic, social and cultural), thereby modifying and enriching them all (Buchanan, 2004). The meaning for human dignity is that for the UDHR to be meaningfully adopted outside its Western context, it must connect with the cultural and circumstantial realities of diverse societies. While the UDHR is rightly considered a moral minimum, people do not experience their lives solely as individual rights-bearers. In many societies, respect for dignity includes the recognition that life is lived in groups, families, communities and peoples, and that justice requires the distribution of power and recognition to both individuals and collectives, not just in law but also in the offices of state. This pluralistic vision is enshrined in other foundational documents. The Bangkok Declaration asserts that human rights, 'while universal in nature, must be considered in the context of a dynamic and evolving process of international norm-setting, bearing in mind the significance of national and regional particularities and various historical, cultural and religious backgrounds' (World Conference on Human Rights, 1993: para. 8). In contrast to the UDHR's exclusive focus on rights, the African Charter on Human and Peoples' Rights (1981) incorporates duties, stating that every individual has a duty 'towards his family and society, the State and other legally recognized communities'. Similarly, the Cairo Declaration on Human Rights in Islam presents an alternative instrument, enshrining different values and understandings, including that 'All men are equal in terms of basic human dignity and basic obligations and responsibilities' (Organization of the Islamic Conference, 1990: art. 1(a)). The existence of these documents testifies to a global desire for human rights, but they also serve as a critique of the parochialism embedded within the UDHR.

Saving us from hell?

On the fifth anniversary of the UDHR, Dag Hammarskjöld (1953), the second Secretary-General of the United Nations, offered a sobering assessment: 'The United Nations was not created in order to bring us to heaven, but in order to save us from hell.' The stark realism of this statement resonates profoundly in the light of contemporary ordeals, where populations nonetheless endure a kind of hell on earth. To bear witness to this suffering from a position of relative comfort and safety is sometimes termed 'vicarious suffering', a concept that feels perverse when juxtaposed against the first-hand, visceral agony of civilians in conflict zones. This is starkly evident today in Gaza, where children trapped under debris have been heard pleading with rescuers to save their parents or siblings instead of themselves, and among the survivors of horrific violence carried out in Israeli kibbutzim (Alsaafin and Humaid, 2023). Such images of raw human desperation are difficult to un-see, and force upon us two urgent lines of inquiry.

First, how can such profound suffering persist despite the elaborate patchwork of international human rights law (IHRL) and international humanitarian law (IHL) cumulatively developed over the past seventy-five years? As distinct but complementary legal bodies, they are formally dedicated to protecting life, health, and human dignity. Their repeated and catastrophic failure demands critical reflection. The approach to this question is framed not by legal doctrine, but by a sociology of justice, particularly racial justice, which highlights the chasm between the aspirational optimism of legal frameworks and the grim realities of political expediency that routinely undermine them.

This perspective is qualified because these documents were largely forged in the fires of atrocities within Europe, representing a hard-won ambition of formerly imperial states not to repeat such horrors, at least on one another (Freedman, 2022). However, this very process creates what the late Lauren Berlant (2011) termed 'cruel optimism', the condition of being attached to a compromised and ultimately obstructive fantasy of a good life that is itself an impediment to being able to flourish. We encounter an impasse, unable to detach ourselves from systems that are clearly failing, while clinging to the hope that they might one day function as intended. A paramount example is the role of state practice (particularly by powerful, 'law-conscious' states) in actively shaping what is deemed lawful in war. Through the invention of new weapons and new legal justifications for conflict, these states perform immense intellectual and political labour to frame violence as legal, thereby normalizing the very acts that the spirit of IHRL and IHL was designed to prevent (Weizman, 2011). This process illustrates the social production of moral indifference, where legal interpretation becomes a tool for legitimizing brutality.

The normalization of extreme violence is starkly visible in contemporary conflicts. The scale of force that has been visited on Gaza, where fully half the population are children, and against the backdrop of core principles of international humanitarian law, makes absurd the duty of legal distinction that forbids the deliberate targeting of civilians (Henckaerts and Doswald-Beck, 2005: Rule 1); the proportionality that bars attacks whose expected harm to civilians would be excessive relative to the concrete and direct military advantage anticipated (ibid., Rule 14); the limits on force to what is strictly required to achieve a legitimate military objective (Melzer, 2008); and the humane treatment safeguards for civilians under occupation alongside captured or injured combatants (OHCHR, 1949).

Read through the lens developed in Chapter 1, this is not only a ledger of alleged violations, but a stress test of the moral vocabulary that makes some losses apprehensible and others disappear. As Butler (2009) argues, grievability is rationed, the public apprehension of a life as a life is unevenly distributed and, where grievability does not attach, devastation scarcely registers. In colonial and racial orders, that rationing has long histories, the 'thingification' named by Césaire (2000) as the ordinary work of empire, so that whole populations can be rendered statistically visible yet morally quiet. What we call the social life of justice is precisely this loop between concepts, institutions and perception: categories train what can be seen; institutions operationalize those categories; perception then returns, certified as common sense. Breaking that loop demands an ethic of witnessing that refuses the hierarchy of the grievable and binds remembrance to redesign, rather than consolation.

This is why a typical legal question ('Were the rules broken?') cannot be the only question. Earlier chapters have insisted on duties of design before harm, the forward-looking obligation to build institutions that prevent predictable injury and to discipline discretionary power so that words become worlds differently. In the context of armed conflict, that implies not just after-the-fact attribution of liability, but upstream guarantees (on targeting review, civilian evacuation and aid corridors, independent monitoring, and material reparations) that make compliance structurally likely rather than aspirational. War may be a legal undertaking, but wilful violations of these obligations constitute war crimes; the deeper concern is whether IHL and IHRL can sustain their normative integrity without a politics capable of reauthorizing the very institutions that decide what – and who – counts. On the account advanced here, integrity will not come from invoking neutrality, but from redesigning the grammars and guardrails through which grievability, protection and accountability are administered in practice.

The collapse of dominant legal and normative frameworks is documented in the harrowing testimonies from the ground in Gaza. As bombardments escalated, parents resorted to writing their children's names in permanent marker pens directly onto their skin, a desperate measure to ensure they could be identified if killed, as traditional identity bracelets had become unavailable (Alsaafin and Amer, 2023). Speaking through tears, Sara al-Khalidi, a mother of four, emphasized: 'The world should know about these children … they are not numbers, but names, stories and dreams.' Similarly, 13-year-old Mayar Abu Daqqa described marking her own name on her body, noting that surviving children were frequently left 'in a state of shock and fear and are unable to speak' (ibid.). These acts reflect what Butler describes as the precarity and 'differential distribution of grievability' that marks certain lives as more disposable in conditions of violent conflict (2009: 31).

The sense of safety in Gaza has been obliterated. Ambulances, protected under IHL, have been targeted, and families complying with evacuation orders have themselves become victims of attacks (Shurafa and Kullab, 2023; Federman et al., 2023; Beaumont, 2023), acts that violate the Geneva Conventions and erode the minimal protections intended for civilians and medical personnel (Henckaerts and Doswald-Beck, 2005). Medical triumphs have tragically unravelled; in one documented case, a newborn rescued from her deceased mother's womb later died in an incubator deprived of electricity and essential medical supplies (Reuters, 2024a). Such scenarios illustrate how armed conflict systematically dismantles healthcare infrastructure, exacerbating health disparities and causing preventable deaths (Rubenstein and Bittle, 2010). The long-term suffering is profound. Thousands of children now face lifelong disability, multiple surgeries and chronic pain, compounded by the near total absence of adequate rehabilitation facilities (Al Jazeera English, 2023; 2024). This prolonged trauma echoes Derek Summerfield's (2000) analysis of war's enduring psychological and physical scars, which severely compromise the future recovery and wellbeing of young populations. Beyond immediate physical injuries, many civilians endure slow, invisible deaths within overcrowded shelters, succumbing to malnutrition, dehydration, and rampant infection under dire sanitary conditions (Debre, 2023). These indirect deaths, frequently overlooked in casualty figures, are profoundly impactful indicators of the comprehensive collapse of health and social infrastructure during conflict (Wise and Darmstadt, 2015).

These accounts underscore the truth that behind every statistic lies a deeply personal narrative of memory, relationship and unrealized dreams. These are stories that survivors urgently wish the world not only to hear, but to genuinely comprehend and remember. Understanding these individual narratives within the broader patterns of conflict remains critical to appreciating the full human cost of war (Nordstrom, 1998). Gerry Simpson recognizes the need to prise the field away from technocratic utility and open it to other registers by 'speaking different sorts of international law or … speaking international law in different sorts of ways' (2021: 6, 2). A central diagnosis concerns international law's prevailing authorial persona and prose. Simpson argues that much doctrinal writing disavows the lived texture of practice, producing an 'absence of "life" in the writing of international law', policed by the figure of the international lawyer as a 'person from nowhere … a person with little or no inner life to speak of' (ibid.: 31). The point is neither confession nor mawkishness; it is that a disciplined attentiveness to feeling can widen what law is able to notice and name without collapsing judgment into sentiment (ibid.: 29–31). If so, it is not only what the law can adjudicate, but also who will stand and say what has been done.

Witnessing and the 'grim and often smiling knowing'

Witnessing in this sense is not a supplement to justice but part of its very specification, for it names the labour of making violence visible when prevailing categories would prefer not to see, and it positions the speaker, and the listener, inside the scene. This is why this chapter moves next to the ethic of bearing witness to prise open the distance at which global idioms ask us to stay, and to insist, with Alison Phipps (2019: 13) that proximity is not only geographic, but moral and institutional. Phipps draws upon the symbolic power of the post-Second World War promise of 'never again'. While the material circumstances are different, the ethic of witnessing and solidarity born from that historical moment continues to determine action and shape new ethical responsibilities within the polity, particularly among groups of individuals (ibid.: 12).

This action is guided by a moral code that Phipps identifies within the Refugees Welcome movement and among refugees themselves: 'When human beings are caught up in systems which inflict great suffering upon them, people of conscience have a responsibility to bear witness' (2010: 12). This code dictates that those with privilege must offer solidarity and practical action, learning from direct experience rather than second-hand assumptions. Phipps characterizes the vast array of solidarity work since 2015, from media and arts to legal action and humanitarian endeavours, as 'the international, multilingual, and cultural work of bearing witness' (ibid.: 12–13). While acknowledging the deep body of academic work on testimony in legal theory (Scarry 2010; Choo 2015; Dennis 2017), Phipps focuses on the metaphorical power of witness-bearing as an act that extends beyond a physical visit. She draws on Butler's (2011) distinction between responding to suffering at a distance and responding when one is proximate to it. This distinction is key to understanding the significance of witness-bearing. In law, a witness is usually proximate and provides testimony as a civic duty, a role central to justice. However, Phipps argues this ethical obligation now permeates the public sphere, where witnessing through media and art poses a direct question to the conscience: 'Will you bear witness? Will you use your body, time, intellect, memory, speech, writing, and actions to serve the rule of justice, the common good, the rights of humanity?' She notes that this sense of ethical responsibility, while underpinning acts of solidarity, can also be found in groups who bear witness to a perceived injustice against their own codes of ethnic purity (2019: 13).

For Phipps, bearing witness is a transformative act of the present and of memory that imposes a heavy burden. The weight of confronting the erosion of refugees' rights leads individuals to extraordinary actions, from providing humanitarian aid to performing acts seen as upholding natural justice. This requires a form of stoicism, a refusal to flinch from the discomfort and helplessness of confronting the consequences of one's own society's policies. Individuals bear this judgment alone and take on costly tasks, with the most powerful testimonies often coming from refugees who are 'experts by experience' (Phipps, 2019: 15). A profound consequence of this long-term engagement, Phipps concludes, is that one can lose one's bearings. The foundational European laws and conventions protecting freedom of movement and asylum have been so undermined by political mechanisms that it becomes difficult to maintain. Those who endure this work, allies and refugee actors alike, share a 'grim and often smiling knowing' that becomes essential for shouldering the disorienting and heavy load (ibid.: 22). Yet the ethic of witness fails if it does not translate into design. The point is to disable the devices through which slow death is rendered technically invisible and thus politically deniable. Hence the turn to famine, to the way thresholds, classifications and channels of aid become tools in a repertoire of 'lawfare', where legality is engineered to launder intent (Weizman, 2011; Dannenbaum, 2018). Watching, and naming, how intent is built into supply chains, access regimes and the destruction of civil infrastructure move us from the consolations of procedure to the hard question of result, of who is kept alive, on what terms and by whose decision.

Manufacturing famine

As we see drone footage of the dust, thick with the pulverized concrete of homes, universities and hospitals, that settles over a shattered Gaza, the material reality is one of almost incomprehensible devastation. More than 62,000 dead (see note 15), a population starved by siege, and a landscape rendered uninhabitable by the equivalent of two nuclear bombs worth of explosives (UN Special Committee, 2024). This is the visible catastrophe, live-streamed and documented. The crisis in Gaza exposes a profound and often deliberate chasm between the formal architecture of international law and the political mechanisms required to enact justice. Alex de Waal's analysis (2025) reveals that the systems designed to objectively measure suffering – such as the Integrated Food Security Phase Classification (IPC) – was strategically manipulated to evade legal and moral accountability. The high technical threshold for a formal 'famine' declaration, requiring specific, verifiable data on food access, malnutrition and mortality, creates a loophole. As de Waal argues, a state can engineer a situation where catastrophic hunger (IPC Phase 5) is undeniable for the population, yet the precise, concentrated data points needed to cross the technical 'famine' line are systematically obscured through restrictions on access, aid and information. This creates a perverse reality where the absence of data, actively enforced, becomes a defence against the 'famine' label, a phenomenon previously observed in Ethiopia's Tigray region (Maxmen, 2021).

This technical circumvention is compounded by the specific nature of the crime of starvation under international law. The

Rome Statute of the International Criminal Court criminalizes 'intentionally using starvation of civilians as a method of warfare by depriving them of objects indispensable to their survival, including wilfully impeding relief supplies' (ICC, 1998: Art. 8(2)(b)(xxv)). As de Waal notes, the critical element is *intent*, not the body count required for an IPC famine classification. This legal standard shifts the focus from the technical outcome to the policy actions. A report by UN special rapporteurs on the situation in Gaza concluded that 'Israel's extensive restrictions on the entry of aid and essential goods, and its failure to provide basic necessities, have led to man-made starvation' (UN Human Rights Council, 2024: 12). This aligns with the legal opinion of scholars like Tom Dannenbaum, who argues that siege warfare that uses hunger as a weapon constitutes 'societal torture', a deliberate process of breaking social bonds and human dignity that is 'normatively reminiscent of torture' (2018: 29).

However, the enforcement of these laws is neutralized by geopolitical power and the politicization of humanitarian mechanisms. The US role, as detailed by de Waal, provides a textbook case of this dynamic. The suppression of the Famine Early Warning Systems Network report by USAID officials and the invocation of a never-before used clause to override its findings demonstrate that technical early warning systems are vulnerable to political override (de Waal, 2025). Furthermore, the US creation of National Security Memorandum-20 acted as a political workaround to more stringent legal obligations under the 1961 Foreign Assistance Act. NSM-20 required assurances from allies on compliance with international humanitarian law, but vested ultimate assessment authority in the secretary of state, a political appointee, rather than in an independent legal body. This process, which resulted in a positive certification for Israel immediately before a major offensive that strangled aid flows, illustrates how policy can be designed to create a façade of compliance while shielding perpetrators from consequences (Chomsky and Pappé, 2013).

The weaponization of lawfare is another critical dimension. Israel's campaign to dismantle UNRWA (the primary humanitarian agency with the operational capacity to distribute aid at scale), based on allegations against a small number of staff, directly impaired the humanitarian response. This action, coupled with the systematic targeting of Palestinian police forces who were attempting to secure aid convoys, engineered a collapse of public order. This created conditions where looting became inevitable, which Israel then cited as evidence that Hamas was stealing aid, thereby justifying further restrictions. This creates a circular logic whereby the perpetrator of the siege generates the chaos that validates its continuation, a strategy that Weizman (2011) might describe as the 'logic of humanitarianism' turned inside out.

Ultimately, existing legal and policy frameworks can be actively inverted. The tools meant to ensure accountability (the IPC, the Geneva Conventions, the Rome Statute) are exploited as instruments of a bureaucratic and legal battle. The perpetrator state engages in a form of 'lawfare', using the language of law and procedure to provide a veneer of legitimacy for actions that violate its spirit (Dunlap, 2001). The result is a situation in which, as one Gaza resident quoted by de Waal (2025) stated, 'they have reduced us to what they want us to be … subhumans living in filth'. Justice, in this context, requires moving beyond the technical debate over famine thresholds to an unequivocal focus on the intentional acts of deprivation, the political mechanisms of impunity and the societal destruction that constitutes the core of the crime of starvation. To hold together elegy and institution is therefore to abandon innocence as a scholarly posture. It is to accept that any universal worth having must be authored from below and across, pluralizing the 'we' of the human by building remedies that reckon with domination rather than taking it for granted (Ba, 2021; Butler, 2009). Only then can witness get to be more than testimony, becoming the principle by which we redesign the floor of protection so that grievability is not rationed by history's hierarchies, but guaranteed in spite of them. As Jacqueline Rose (2019) has argued: 'There will be no political emancipation for anyone until we all recognise the corpse still lying on the road, the continuing injustice, the work that remains to be done.'

The discussion so far confirms the argument that racialized conceptions of the human still organize the very institutions through which justice is imagined and pursued. The earlier discussion treated human rights as a contested, pluriversal formation – forged in revolt, reshaped through decolonization and social movements, and continually reinterpreted against structures of domination. This is something that, according to Oumar Ba, mainstream global justice theory so often misses, even while it 'grapple[s] with questions such as what is owed to the global poor ... [from] people living in wealthy countries toward "distant others"' (2021: 375–7). He is blunt that 'global justice is inherently a racialized discourse, and the architecture of international law and justice is entrenched in and perpetuates racialized hierarchies of humanity', and that current critique often still rests on 'liberal cosmopolitanism ... operat[ing] in a racialized superstructure' (ibid.). This dovetails with Madhok's earlier critique of Euro-Atlantic 'time–space provincialism' and the call to engage vernacular rights cultures.

The ICC crystallizes Ba's institutional point. As he puts it, the court is 'a political agent and actor (an identity that it refuses to embrace)', which helps reproduce a geography of culpability that tracks imperial legacies rather than structural repair (2020: 160). Read alongside our earlier chapters, this is the same mechanism on a different scale: norms produced within domination contracts applied as if they stood above history, converting collective, historically produced harms into case-by-case thresholds and individualized responsibility. Where orthodox global justice theory asks how to distribute across borders, the domination contract lens asks how those borders (and the law of peoples behind them) were made, and who is kept beyond enforceable reciprocity. If justice is to be more than a legitimating label, then (a) human rights must be a floor specified by those most exposed to domination, not a ceiling policed by implicated institutions; and (b) global design must shift from discretionary, case-led juridification to duties of result, from individualized desert to collective repair, and from Eurocentric guardianship to plural, transnational authorship of norms (Ba, 2020: 160; 2021: 375–7).

'If I should die …'

The story of Refaat Alareer – his life, his work and his death – becomes a profound synecdoche for the broader Palestinian narrative of resistance and erasure, and the relentless pursuit of voice (Just World Books, n.d.). Alareer embodied the act of witnessing not as a passive observer, but as an active participant in the forging of a collective identity. His directive, 'If I must die, you must live to tell my story …', transcends the personal, evolving into a collective imperative for a people whose very existence is contested (Alareer, cited in Serhan, 2023). His legacy, carried forward through the writers of *We Are Not Numbers* (n.d.) and his posthumously published works, represents a defiant form of knowing, a refusal to be silenced or rendered abstract (Just World Books, 2024]). Yet, as this chapter has argued, this knowing exists in stark tension with a pervasive and often deliberate global ignorance, facilitated by the very systems purportedly designed to prevent such injustices.

The catastrophic suffering in Gaza, documented in the harrowing testimonies of parents writing their children's names on their skin and the slow, invisible deaths from starvation and disease, exposes the cruel optimism at the heart of the international legal order (Alsaafin and Amer, 2023; Alsaafin, 2025). The elaborate frameworks of IHRL and IHL, born from the promise of 'never again', never forced a reckoning with the identity of human rights themselves, nor the social production of moral indifference that it enables. The universalism of the UDHR, drafted without the voice of colonized peoples, is rightly challenged by pluralistic visions from the Global South, such as the Bangkok (1993) and Cairo (1990) Declarations, which centre duties and communal identities alongside individual rights. For human rights to be more than a parochial fantasy, they must be redefined through this pluralistic lens, robust enough to acknowledge that lives are lived not just as individuals, but within families, communities and peoples, collectives whose destruction constitutes a unique form of 'societal torture' (Dannenbaum, 2018: 29). Ultimately, this chapter argues that justice in the face of such manufactured ignorance requires a particular kind of witness. It requires moving beyond what Phipps (2019: 13), drawing on Butler (2011), identifies as responding to suffering from a distance. It demands a proximate, ethical response to the question, '*Will you bear witness?*'. This is the heavy burden of confronting the erosion of fundamental rights and refusing to flinch from the consequences of one's own society's policies. To speak the name of Refaat Alareer, to recount the stories of Sara al-Khalidi's children and to detail the intentional manufacturing of starvation is to engage in this transformative act. It is to use one's body, intellect and voice to serve the rule of justice and the common good, recognizing that, in the silence of institutions, the responsibility falls to people of conscience. Bearing witness will not, in itself, save us from hell. But it is the necessary first step in rebuilding the promise of heaven from the ashes of its betrayal. Bearing witness is the beginning, however, not the end, of institutional responsibility. If a post-innocent grammar binds obligation to the sites where vulnerability is produced, then climate adaptation is a further test, a field that often speaks technics, while reproducing historical stratification. The next chapter brings the argument home to infrastructures, housing, health and planning, asking how adaptation can be rebuilt as desubordination by design, so that race and coloniality are treated not as afterthoughts, but as determinants of who gets to survive, and on what terms.

6

Out of Sight, Out of Climate Justice

In the summer of 2022, the Indus basin burst its banks rendering villages in Sindh and south Punjab indistinguishable from the river itself. Families climbed onto rooftops with whatever they could carry; when they returned months later, the mud houses had cured and cracked like overfired pottery. Parveen Bibi, one of many who would later be quoted describing a splintered home and ruined fields, found the cotton and wheat that should have supported her family had been reduced to rot. The statistics bear out her story at scale: around 33 million people were affected and nearly 8 million were displaced, with losses and damages topping US$30 billion (World Bank, 2022; Government of Pakistan et al., 2022; OCHA, 2023). Researchers and humanitarians now treat the 2022 Pakistan floods as one of the largest disaster displacement events of the past decade, a benchmark of what climate disruption looks like when it collides with poverty, land precarity and debt (IDMC, 2023; 2025). The aftershocks have been long-lasting. Post-disaster assessments recorded damaged irrigation channels, silted wells and persistent standing water that delayed sowing, compounding food price spikes and household indebtedness (Government of Pakistan et al., 2022). The poorest effectively 'lost a season', not only in agricultural time, but in social time: marriages postponed, school fees unpaid, migration decisions forced. And while the cameras moved on, the water returned. In 2024 and again in 2025, heavy monsoon and riverine flooding struck many of the same districts, with Punjab and Sindh once more declared disaster zones; millions were affected or displaced, and survivors like Parveen Bibi described coming back to fields stripped bare (OCHA, 2024; 2025c). Each recurrence hampers recovery, because households that lack insurance, savings or secure land title must rebuild from a lower base every time, often by taking new high-interest loans that mortgage the next harvest (Humanitarian Outcomes, 2022; UNHCR, 2024).

Placed against the arc of this book, these scenes are not exceptions but exemplars: the river and the heat trace the seams cut by tenancy, debt, gendered assets and brittle care, turning hazard into harm by design. The argument of this chapter is that these experiences demand that 'adaptation' to climate change must be recast from coping after the fact to redesign before harm: an institutional project that makes recurrent losses impossible by design rather than tolerable for those who can pay. This chapter has earned the normative space to argue in favour of recasting adaptation in this way, having established, in Chapter 1, historicity over abstraction and concepts answerable to movements and evidence; adaptation here takes up that method as practice, shifting inquiry from 'Who failed to cope?' to 'Which arrangements predictably manufacture harm, and who must redesign them?'. The task is to make language answerable, to convert resilience from etiquette into enforceable thresholds, and to treat care, land and housing as the levers by which social life is protected in climate time. This book has shown, moreover, that justice begins not with hazard but with design. We do not inherit a neutral social field upon which storms later play; rather, we inherit institutions already arranged to make some losses ordinary and other losses exceptional.

If Chapter 1 insisted that justice is a practice for building arrangements that hold when reassurance is scarce, Chapter 2 revealed how justificatory habits domesticate history to preserve those arrangements. In this chapter, we treat adaptation less as coping and more as redesign, naming the routines that make harm predictable and refusing their quiet renewal. Chapter 2 treated the canon not as an object of veneration, but as a living archive of argumentative moves that still train our institutions what to see and what to miss. Law's 'operative lexicon' shrinks responsibility to what can be litigated, dissolving structure into micro cases; the result in climate policy is a repertoire of post hoc adjustments whose neutrality conceals patterned exposure. Reading from Plato to Rawls as an infrastructure of inference permits the pivot we make here, from ideals to arrangements, from liability after the fact to duties of design before the harm. What travels as adaptation is not empty; it often smuggles in the contracts that organize dependency. Chapter 3 named these as domination contracts, sexual, racial and settler, through which civic membership was masculinized, personhood racialized and extraction normalized. When the same architecture is left intact, 'green' improvements become engines of displacement, externalizing risk onto tenants, casualized workers and precarious status-holders, while describing the outcome as 'resilience'. To begin from domination is not to abandon normativity; it is to earn it by making design the site of repair. Chapter 4 showed how 'crisis ordinariness' is manufactured upstream, through inadmissibility, offshoring and para-bureaucratic outsourcing, so that protection becomes discretionary benevolence. Climate mobility will inherit that script unless reception, status and services are specified as rights with credible procedures and independent oversight. In other words, climate adaptation that leaves bordering untouched will reissue rightlessness at scale. In each case, the test is unapologetically institutional: do rules reduce the discretion through which domination is reproduced, or do they relocate risk while naming the result 'resilience'?

Chapter 5 argued that first-person address is not decorative to justice but part of its specification: grievability must precede adjudication, and remembrance must bind itself to redesign. Read here, testimony about flood, heat and slow attrition cannot be abandoned at the register of lament; it must be converted into influence, into authority over budgets, thresholds and timelines, so that the same bodies and postcodes do not secure the next 'exceptional' event. Bearing witness becomes a constitutional act when it compels institutions to count what they once rendered unspeakable. Witnessing here is not as a sombre register, but as a constitutional one. If those who bear the brunt of hazard are permitted only to narrate their losses, the cycle resets with fresh devastation. Chapter 5 argued that grievability must travel with enforceable obligation: voice must convert into authority over budgets, standards and timelines (Fraser, 2008: 16–24).

In this chapter we move from concept to site. We trace how racial and colonial domination contracts render losses ordinary; we show how absence in datasets becomes absence in protection; and we return to the Pakistan floods and England's heat to specify what reparative design would look like in practice – namely, land regularization and fair credit; enforceable housing heat standards, community authority over adaptation spend and reception infrastructures sized for predictable mobility. Where these are present, adaptation interrupts the schedule of loss. Where they are absent, the water and the heat simply find their way back. Changes represent both evidence and remedy. Evidence must include distributional assessment as a duty, not an annex, co-produced with communities that have influence over budgets, thresholds and timelines. Remedy must embed anti-displacement practices in financial terms so that green investment does not relocate risk from floodplains to eviction courts; it must treat care as critical infrastructure rather than a discretionary add-on; and it must legislate for climate mobility as a reciprocal right rather than leaving protection to para-bureaucratic drift.

The injustice of climate change

Climate change is driven primarily by human-generated greenhouse gases, above all carbon dioxide from fossil fuels and industry, alongside methane and nitrous oxide from agriculture and other sectors. Historically, cumulative CO_2 emissions since 1850 are so large that they have already consumed most of the carbon budget compatible with the 1.5–2°C target (IPCC, 2022a; IPCC: 2022b). These emissions are highly unequal within and between countries, since a small, affluent share of the population produces a disproportionate fraction of global emissions. The World Inequality Lab estimates that the top 10 per cent of global emitters generate almost half of all greenhouse gases, and the top 1 per cent more than the entire bottom 50 per cent (Chancel et al., 2023: 3–4, 8). Earlier analysis similarly showed that the richest 1 per cent were responsible for a large share of emissions growth since 1990 (Oxfam, 2020: 1; 2023: 3–6).

The unequal impacts of climate change follow from how risk is produced. The IPCC frames climate risk as a function of hazards, exposure and vulnerability, with equity and justice central to understanding outcomes (IPCC, 2022a). This means that identical hazards (e.g., heatwaves) do not translate into identical harms: who is exposed (e.g., those living on floodplains or in informal settlements) and who is vulnerable (e.g., in terms of poverty, discrimination, health status, age, disability or precarious livelihoods) determine the scale of loss. Opportunities for climate-resilient development are not equitably distributed, with risks and development challenges concentrated in developing regions and particularly exposed sites such as coasts, small islands, deserts, mountains and polar regions. The IPCC also finds that losses and damages are already occurring, some of which are irreversible, and that, as warming increases, losses grow and are strongly concentrated among the poorest and most vulnerable, even where adaptation occurs (ibid.: 24–5).

If the climate crisis exposes anything with unusual clarity, it is the social life of justice. The water does not just rise; it seeks out the seams already cut into the social fabric, finding tenancy that is informal, labour that is precarious, care systems that are stretched to breaking, and administrative routines that decide, quietly and on a daily basis, whose losses count more than others. That is why the same flood levels turn, in some places, into a season lost and, in others, into an insurance claim processed and paid. The hazard is meteorological; the harm is institutional. We cannot, then, leave adaptation as an inventory of technical adjustments while the architecture that distributes exposure and recovery remains unchanged. To do so would be to accept, in a new register, the old habit of translating structural injury into a problem of post hoc allocation. This chapter seeks to show how that translation works: a chameleonic policy lexicon in which adaptation travels easily precisely because it does not name the racialized and colonial histories that structure vulnerability, allowing green improvements to double as engines of displacement and resilience to become the etiquette of unequal survival. This is the social life of justice in climate time: the point at which meteorology is converted into administration, where resilience becomes the etiquette of unequal survival and adaptation the policy language that travels precisely because it refuses to name what it is that structures vulnerability.

These structural inequalities surface across domains. Food and water security are undermined most in vulnerable regions – Sub-Saharan Africa, South Asia, Central and South America, and Small Island Developing States – as droughts, floods and heatwaves intensify, with knock-on effects on nutrition and health (IPCC, 2022a: 9–10). Cities face rising risks from heat, flooding and infrastructure disruption, with impacts sharpened by the urban heat island (UHI) effect and by social and spatial inequalities that determine who can cool, insure, rebuild or relocate (Dodman et al., 2022; IPCC, 2022a: 14). Displacement is already occurring and is projected to expand; modelling for six world regions suggests that there will be up to 216 million internal climate migrants by 2050 unless strong action takes place (World Bank, 2021: 3–5, 9). Health burdens are also unequal: the Lancet Countdown documents that global health remains at the mercy of fossil fuels, with risks rising fastest where capacities and finance are most constrained (Romanello et al., 2023). Air pollution is closely linked to fossil fuel combustion and is another illustration of stark environmental inequality. In 2021, air pollution contributed to 8.1 million deaths worldwide, with populations in low- and middle-income countries exposed up to four times pollution levels than those in high income countries (HEI/IHME, 2024: 3, 13, 2, 7, 28).

In short, climate change is caused predominantly by unequal, historically accumulated and highly skewed emissions from fossil-fuelled production and consumption. Its harms are patterned by social structures – poverty, governance capacity, infrastructure, discrimination, colonial legacies – and by place, such that those who contributed least generally face the greatest risks and tightest adaptation constraints. The upshot, in the IPCC's terms, is that equity and justice are not add-ons, but preconditions for effective risk reduction and climate resilient development (IPCC, 2022a: 28–9).

'Adaptation' and chameleonic concepts

Motivated by a need to think in terms of consequences, namely by anticipating the negative impacts of global warming and accordingly adopting proactive measures, the language of 'adaptation' has become key in policy approaches tackling climate change (Berrang-Ford et al., 2019). Sometimes discussed alongside the very different objective of 'mitigation' (concerned with reducing overall greenhouse gas emissions either by cutting sources or enhancing 'carbon sinks'),[16] it is important to be clear about their fundamentally different orientations, even while recognizing their shared provenance (IPCC, 2023: 126; Denevan, 1983; Kellogg, 1987) and trajectory into the global policy lexicon. For example, in their study of the developing emphasis of the UN Framework Convention on Climate Change (UNFCCC), Venturini et al. note that, while 'adaptation and mitigation issues are both visible in the UNFCCC negotiations', mitigation has 'from the very beginning been a top priority', and adaptation activities only came to prominence 'when countries began to fail to achieve their mitigation objectives' (2019: 1). Thereafter, adaptation has been a staple of each landmark global climate change agreement (UNDP, 2007; Mor et al., 2023). Furthermore, the 'Adaptation Fund' established in the 1997 Kyoto Protocol was reaffirmed in the Copenhagen Accord in 2009 and the Paris Agreement in 2016, even though the 1997 treaty was widely deemed unsuccessful given that it was not ratified by the US or, therefore, China (Victor, 2004; Owen, 2020).[17]

It is through this route that adoption of the Adaptation Fund by bodies such as the IPCC has been received with a justified urgency, and in ways that have seen adaptation enlisted by a diverse constituency of actors (including supranational organizations as well as national governments) and across a variety of approaches, much as if it were a 'chameleonic' concept. That is to say, and borrowing from Katherine Smith's study of policy ideas, stated goals and the means to pursue them, adaptation approaches appear 'able to move further into policy either because they overtly complement institutionalized ideas' or have 'chameleon-like qualities which facilitate their translation into policy' (2010: 181). This understanding helps explain the seeming appeal of the concept, but, and as shown below, it also contains clues as to why prevailing adaptation approaches have been inattentive to the racial determinants of vulnerability to climate change. For example, the IPCC defines adaptation as a 'process of adjustment to actual or expected climate change and its effects, which seeks to moderate harm or exploit beneficial opportunities' (2022a: 2898). It is 'chameleonic' in that we can include short-term behavioural change, such as closing shades on windows and drinking plenty of water during heatwaves; keeping warm and using home energy efficiently in cold weather; supporting public education that promotes broader community awareness and knowledge of weather-related risk at a population level; and encouraging large-scale infrastructure agendas, emergency management, hazard planning and associated risk assessments (Berrang-Ford et al., 2019).

In their systematic review, Porter et al. (2014) usefully distinguished between four types of action deemed as adaptation: (1) the aforementioned behavioural actions, (2) technical and infrastructural actions seen in planning and construction, (3) institutional responses such as creating policies, programmes, regulations and procedures, and (4) ecosystem or nature based responses such as the regeneration of flora and the use of green and blue spaces (especially in cities). Notably, The UK 2008 Climate Change Act (CCA) appeals to a mixture of these adaptation actions in providing a legally binding framework. It foregrounds as a priority better inland flood defences and preparedness for coastal erosion, energy security and the possible impact on agriculture. The CCA, moreover, places a legal burden on the UK government to undertake a climate change risk assessment (CCRA) every five years, before rolling out a National Adaptation Programme (NAP). The governance of these commitments is partially devolved to the four administrations of the United Kingdom. In this respect, and as a policy variable that might alternate and operate at multiple levels, and in the case of Scotland, there is a devolved statutory framework on adaptation set out in the 2009 Climate Change (Scotland) Act. The Scottish government has on occasion hinted at a distinctive approach. For example, it has stated that 'climate change poses risks to Scotland beyond those identified in the UK Climate Change Risk Assessment (UKCCRA), including the unequal impacts of climate change on the most vulnerable in our society', and implied that 'an outcomes-based approach' pursued in Scotland 'allows us to address this' (Scottish Government, 2019: 21).

As Scotland's 2019–24 adaptation programme came to a close, however, the Scottish government signalled alignment with Westminster through the adoption of 'carbon budgets' used by both the UK and Welsh governments; it also renounced its ambitious flagship target of reducing greenhouse gas emissions by 75 per cent by 2030. The 2019–24 adaptation programme did not contain a single mention of either race or ethnicity in its 229 pages, even as it stated: 'The Scottish government champions climate justice, and promotes a people-centred, human rights approach that shares the benefits of equitable low carbon development, and the burdens of climate change fairly' (Scottish Government 2019: 10). In this respect it was consistent with similar absences in the UK government's National Adaptation Programme (NAP3) and the fourth strategy for climate adaptation reporting, discussed further below (UK Government, 2023). The importance of these oversights can be shown through an understanding of multifinality and vulnerability, in that what appears as a singular meteorological event is, in practice, a social multiplier. The same heatwave threads itself through tenancy status, building stock, wage security and care infrastructures; the same flood seeks out unregularized land, borrowed money and seasonal assets. Previous chapters have looked askance at tidy principles that abstract from these histories (Rawls, 1999 [1971]: 53, 76–7). Here, that scepticism does its most urgent work: adaptation is not a distribution of sandbags after the fact, but a reauthoring of the institutions that decide where the water will finally settle. That the UK and devolved adaptation programmes can span hundreds of pages without naming race or ethnicity is not an administrative oversight, but the predictable effect of the operative lexicon we critiqued in Chapter 2 and the domination contracts that surfaced in Chapter 3. A neutral grammar converts racialized geographies into 'context' and treats differential harm as an implementation wrinkle. A 'justice-first' adaptation reverses the sequence: it specifies data that renders disparities visible; it allocates decision rights to those most exposed; and it builds enforceable standards so discretion cannot launder subordination through guidance.

Multifinality and vulnerability

Despite the variety of ways in which adaptation approaches have been understood, and how adaptation has been interpolated in the policy process, the key issue of multifinality in the impacts of climate change continues to be peripheral. With a provenance in systems theory, (Von Bertalanffy, 1968) multifinality describes the different outcomes of a common cause. In this usage, multifinality recognizes how, in social systems, 'the effect on functioning of any one component's value may vary', and that these 'effects will depend on the conditions set by the values of additional components with which it is structurally linked' (Cicchetti and Rogosch, 1996: 598). Its adoption in policy studies retains the core analytical concern, namely how 'the same mechanism can generate differential policy outcomes dependent on the context in which it operates' (Kay and Baker, 2015: 7). For the purposes of this chapter, it helps to grasp how certain social dynamics render some populations more vulnerable to its effects. What, however, is meant by vulnerability?

Borrowing from Kelly and Adger (2000: 328), vulnerability refers to 'the ability or inability of individuals and social groupings to respond to, in the sense of cope with, recover from or adapt to, any external stress'. The key point to emphasize here concerns the way vulnerability is describing a structured capacity to respond to climate change and not the anticipation of likely adaptive behaviour. This is what is meant by the social determinants of vulnerability, in which direct and indirect racial inequality operates at a systemic level. It is very rare, for example, to hear concepts such as 'weathering' the 'life-course' within adaptation approaches, even though a large body of inquiry has established that the accumulated social stresses these terms denote come with being a racial minority (Phelan and Link, 2015; Geronimus et al., 2020; Razai et al., 2021). The need to connect a multifinality in exposures to differential vulnerabilities is also found in Schlosberg et al.'s work on climate justice research with Aboriginal communities in Australia. These authors insist on the need to include more than a 'focus on the biophysical risks of climate change' and expand to consider 'the more organic concern with vulnerability in everyday life illustrated by community groups' (2017: 420).

These are especially helpful emphases because the challenge in addressing racially structured differences requires us to think of vulnerability in adaptation approaches as something akin to a multidimensional concept that harnesses our existing knowledge on inequalities as well as established approaches to addressing these. This would allow us to better register differentiated levels of adaptive capacity for racialized communities as well as the structural impediments to this; and also how these may be incorporated (or overlooked) within prevailing climate adaptation planning and action strategies and whether corresponding strategies meet the issue of climate change without accounting for existing social inequalities across domains. There has hitherto been no consideration of this in the UK by either the Westminster or devolved administrations.

The UK government has stated 'a need to address the interdependency and inequality of risks' but makes no further mention of what these are and how they may be understood (UK Government, 2022: 10). Signalling a misalignment between policy aspirations and community experience, the technical report for the third UK climate change risk assessment (CCRA) identifies sixty-one climate risks cutting across multiple sectors of society, but it contains not a single mention of race (or possibly cognate means of discussing this in terms of ethnicity or structural discrimination) (BEIS/Defra, 2022). This is despite the UK Environment Agency's warning that recent analysis of social vulnerability to flooding highlights the disproportionate disadvantage experienced by ethnic minorities, particularly Black ethnic groups (Environment Agency, 2021; Sayers et al., 2020). Such oversights are unlikely to be addressed as long as progress and implementation instruments reproduce the gaps. For example, in the Climate Change Committee's most recent and otherwise comprehensive 364-page report to Parliament (CCC, 2023), the UK's leading climate scientists made not a single mention of race in the context of adaptation progress and only one reference to ethnicity, which itself was accompanied by a recognition that 'there is limited data available to assess progress in achieving enablers for this outcome' (ibid.: 264). This absence in the dataset is not a technical oversight but a distributive decision. When administrations omit race, tenure or immigration status from risk-planning, they have decided in advance who will be seen and therefore who can claim. The remedy is not annexed statistics but an epistemic duty: no adaptation spend without distributional assessment, and no assessment that is not co-produced with binding community authority (ibid.: 264; ONS, 2020: 2; Groundwork UK, 2022). Once we name racial and colonial domination as a constitutive contract of the modern order, vulnerability stops looking like bad luck. Heat islands map onto redlining and overcrowding; flood exposure onto dispossession and infrastructural neglect; triage onto budget lines recited as common sense. If legitimacy and protection are to mean anything, the state cannot license arrangements that manufacture 'ordinary' loss for entire populations (Pateman, 1988: 2–4, 10; Mills, 1997: 3, 14–15), such that 'adaptation' approaches worthy of the name should begin by voiding domination clauses in housing, work, welfare and planning.

Racial determinants of vulnerability in the UK

The prevailing omission of race in UK adaptation approaches is not unconnected to the dearth of research on the differential impact of climate change in the country. This situation makes for a striking contrast with the US, where it is long established that the health risks of climate change are significantly higher for racial minority groups (Brodine, 1972; Higgins, 1993; Tuana, 2019). This has given rise to a broader analysis of political economy, racial disparities and climate justice, especially in the 'critical environmental justice studies' scholarship (Pellow and Brulle, 2005: 18). It is also illustrated in Laura Pulido's connections between climate vulnerabilities and what she has termed the 'environmental racism gap', which she uses to describe persistent inequalities in environmental outcomes for minoritized groups as being 'manifest in practices, regulations, and outcomes' (2017: 524–5).

Despite fewer such studies in the UK, what social science approaches allow us to grasp is how prevailing inequalities establish likely differential racial vulnerabilities to climate change, not least by connecting these inequalities across multiple social domains. Social policy as a disciplinary tradition is able to span the study of public policies, market operations and personal and social relationships, as these mediate, and are mediated by, state institutions and welfare services. If we are to take seriously the earlier argument that vulnerability to climate change must include a description of a structured capacity, then this requires us to focus on residential settlement and housing, typically viewed as a key means of gauging the distribution of social goods and life chances (Somerville and Sprigings, 2005). This reveals, for example, that Black and ethnic minority residents in cities have significantly less access to green spaces than white residents (in one study this was eleven times less) (Dobson et al., 2019). This is especially relevant in the context of consistently warmer surface and/or air temperatures in UK cities compared with suburban and rural surroundings and the rise of UHIs.

UHIs are a progressively common feature of urban life and result from a concentration of dark surfaces and lack of vegetation, encouraging greater heat absorption during the day and increased re-emission during the night (Sandink, 2013). Black and ethnic minorities are disproportionately resident in the locations of prominent UHIs in London, Birmingham, Manchester, Leeds and Liverpool (Chowienczyk et al., 2020: 527; cf. Burbidge et al., 2022), all of which have long been connected with heat-related health impacts and elevated rates of mortality and co-morbidities, and are part of a wider pattern in which heat-related deaths increased by 68 per cent between 2000/4 and 2017/21 (Romanello et al., 2022).

Access to green spaces is therefore vital, and yet the ONS (2020) reports that ethnic and racial minorities are nearly four times as likely as white people to lack access to outdoor space at home, such as a garden (private or shared), patio or balcony, and two and a half times less likely than those of white ethnicities to have a private garden, even when comparing people of similar age, social grade and living situation (such as location and living with or without children) (cf. Curran and Hamilton, 2017; Haycox et al., 2025). At the same time, we know that these same groups also have significantly less access to public green spaces more broadly (Groundwork UK, 2022). This is partly about proximity, as they 'are less likely to live within short walking distance of a green space than people that identify as White (39 per cent compared to 58 per cent)' (ibid.: 3). It is also related to documented local and national housing strategies that have resulted in 'territorial stigmatisation' (Hill et al., 2021), and includes Black and ethnic minority respondents feeling 'out of place' in rural and country settings (Collier, 2019; Foster, 2021; Haycox et al., 2025).

Notably, Barnes et al. (2008: 28) show that Black families are much more likely to experience persistent bad housing conditions with poor insulation: one in ten such households compared to one in twenty for their white counterparts. This is not a direct measure of the impact of climate change on households, but a means of gauging unsatisfactory housing conditions that make these groups more susceptible to its impact. It is precisely in the connections between different social policy domains that racial inequalities become entrenched and reproduced, and the racialized patterns of exposure and sensitivity to climate harms also become apparent and remain prevalent despite compounding factors and variations (Meer, 2022a). Currently, nearly 97 per cent of Britain's Black and ethnic minorities live in urban and peri-urban settings (ONS, 2020; 2022a; 2022b) and, as Morris and Naz have argued, this locks in 'certain forms and activities, and impedes or prevents others', and reflects 'both structural conditions as well as constraints' (2021: 42). That there is a societal pattern in which ethnic and racial communities bear heavier burdens of urban exposure, however, has typically been understood in terms of socioeconomic status and health inequalities (Jerrett et al., 2001; 2004; Marshall, 2008; Richardson et al., 2013).

To think about social determinants otherwise requires us to use concepts and categories that hold an explanatory function in detailing how racial injustice is almost in 'the design of things' (Murakawa and Gilmore, 2020). This is not straightforwardly easy to quantify, but the argument in this chapter is that we should seek to make connections across histories and across social domains in order to recognize the accumulated disparities that help explain vulnerabilities. For example, the experience of residing in UHIs is moderated not only by good access to green spaces, but also by the quality of housing and degree of insulation to keep homes cooler (in addition to greater energy efficiency in colder climates). The argument so far has moved from basins and budgets to contracts and categories; but the same language only becomes incontestable when it is read back through the body, the building and the block. What follows are two case narratives showing how a supposedly neutral hazard is braided to tenancy, insulation, income, care and the administrative habits that decide what must be proved and by whom. They also correct the policy temptation to smooth away difference: the mean temperature that hides the lack of ventilation in attic flats, the citywide air index that forgets the school run along the arterial road. If adaptation is about redesign rather than etiquette, it must be specified where harm is actually apparent in leases and standards, in retrofit details and service thresholds, in data that count what has been treated as background. From grievability to governance, these two indicators of climate injustice (indoor heat and traffic-borne pollution) are not only institutional artefacts or weather events, but administrative choices made visible in a single bedroom or on a single street.

Too hot to live

When the UK first recorded a temperature of 40°C in July 2022, a shift occurred from episodic 'continental' heat to domestic exposure: what was once a meteorological headline materialized as prolonged indoor heat in ordinary rooms (Met Office, 2022; WWA, 2022). Subsequent mortality estimates underscore the scale: in the summer of 2022, England experienced approximately 2,985 excess deaths across five heat episodes, disproportionately among those aged over 65 and concentrated in the most intense periods (UKHSA, 2025; ONS, 2022b). These outcomes are not 'acts of God' but the arithmetic of vulnerability: the physiology of ageing, medicines that dehydrate or blunt thirst and homes that trap heat. In many inner-urban neighbourhoods, where Black and ethnic minority residents are overrepresented, high-risk housing typologies, top-floor or single-aspect flats with little cross-ventilation and limited resources for cooling turn background exposure into predictable harm (Cole et al., 2024; CaCHE, 2024).

Urban form – that is, the city's density, surfaces and limited vegetation – amplified the scale of these conditions as London's UHI effect raised nocturnal temperatures relative to surrounding areas, impeding overnight recovery essential for health. Recent analysis attributes more than one-third of heat-related deaths in Greater London during the July 2022 heatwave to the UHI effect, highlighting how built-environment factors (surface materials, density and limited vegetative cover) convert ambient heat into elevated temperatures overnight (Simpson et al., 2024). For older residents, and for communities already carrying racialized social and health inequalities, a marginal difference of a degree or two is clinically consequential (Simpson et al., 2024; UKHSA, 2025). Within the housing stock, thermal inequalities track architectural features. Empirical studies of indoor temperatures show mid- and top-floor flats running hotter than ground-floor and non-flat dwellings, with higher night-time temperatures that limit physiological reset (Cole et al., 2024). Policy analyses label this 'overheating', but reports from residents themselves emphasize breathlessness and sleep disruption. English housing briefs identify familiar design legacies, insufficient external shading, extensive south-facing glazing without blinds, dark roofing and sealed windows installed for energy efficiency, which elevate living-room discomfort and preclude safe bedroom temperatures (CaCHE, 2024). These features are disproportionately present in lower-cost, higher-density housing, intersecting with racialized disadvantage. High temperatures in the UK are now vastly more probable given anthropogenic climate change; what would previously have been 'extremely unlikely' now falls within expectation (WWA, 2022; Carbon Brief, 2022). The policy implication concerns recurrence, not singularity: with repeat heat episodes close to certain, background vulnerabilities (ageing, low income, poor-quality housing) operate as a conveyor turning heat into harm. In England's 2022 season, for example, 8–17 August alone saw an estimated 1,458 excess deaths among over-65s (excluding COVID-19), underscoring that cumulative duration and sequencing matter alongside peak days (UKHSA, 2022; ONS, 2022b). Where racialized communities are more exposed to overheated flats and hotter night-time streets, recurrence converts inequality into mortality (Simpson et al., 2024; Cole et al., 2024).

Micro-scale interventions nonetheless demonstrate tractable levers: the provision of a basic fan, welfare calls before the heatwave starts, targeted household advice, shading retrofits undertaken by social landlords, street tree-planting in high-exposure corridors and proactive clinical outreach are all associated with reductions in heat stress (POST, 2024; Simpson et al., 2024). Framed this way, the episode is not primarily a narrative of individual fortitude, but a ledger of institutional choice. Persistent exposure to heat without ventilation in attic flats, deferred retrofit cycles, and enduring care infrastructures that default to low-level advice ('keep curtains closed') illustrate how administrative arrangements mediate survival. Thermometers register temperature, not injustice, yet distributive and procedural choices determine who can survive equivalent heat loads. To classify 2022 as a 'natural disaster' misreads the causal structure: the hazard is meteorological, but the harm is administrative, deriving from planning standards, enforcement capacity and whether guidance possesses legal force (UKHSA, 2025; ONS, 2022b; Simpson et al., 2024). Where policy relies on non-binding guidance, discretion proliferates and predictability declines; where enforceable standards permit tenants to compel landlords, residents to compel councils and councils to compel contractors, minimum thresholds become achievable rather than aspirational. A just adaptation stance therefore reclassifies care as critical infrastructure rather than an emergency add-on: home-care hours, community pharmacies, cooling centres, and neighbour-to-neighbour schemes constitute the actual grids of survivability and should be budgeted for and governed accordingly – especially for Black and ethnic minority communities facing compounded risks (Romanello et al., 2023: 5, 115; IPCC, 2022a: 14). In practice, this means enforceable indoor temperature safeguards, mandated shading and ventilation retrofits in high-risk stock, funded green street networks in UHI hotspots, proactive and culturally appropriate health communications and pre-emptive check-ins with clinically vulnerable residents before and during heat events (POST, 2024; CaCHE, 2024; Simpson et al., 2024).

Ella's story

These concerns are wide-ranging but no less prominent in the vulnerability of exposures to air pollutants; 'air pollution and climate change are deeply interconnected because the chemical species that lead to a degradation in air quality are frequently co-emitted with greenhouse gases' (Pinho-Gomes et al., 2023: e727). Road traffic, for example, is the single largest generator of nitrogen dioxide and particulate matter in British cities (Lee, 2022), and illustrates that, while 'substantial risks to the population are associated with air pollution and climate change separately, each can exacerbate the effects of the other' (Pinho-Gomes et al., 2023: e727). The story of Ella Kissi-Debrah, a young girl from Lewisham in South London, is therefore salutary. In keeping with something of a narrative turn in policy studies, and a range of scholars emphasizing the importance of episodic storytelling for grasping policy problems (see, for example, Polletta, 2006; McBeth et al., 2014; Kubin et al., 2021; Fraser and Gillon, 2023), Ella's story is presented as an account that elucidates a specific issue, since she is the first person in Britain to have air pollution listed as a cause of death.

Ella's story is not cited as a representative sample but, rather, as a landmark case that is 'characterized by very low levels of disagreement' on the facts involved (Jones et al., 2014: 6).

It is also a policy-relevant story, as her family's campaign to reopen the coroner's inquiry into her death, initially attributed to acute respiratory failure, has become a reference point to a variety of stakeholders (Carrington, 2023). In this regard, and as Donna Houston and Pavithra Vasudevan have argued, 'storytelling is not just about narratives, it is about recognising emergent cultural, temporal and environmental realities shaped by the material presence of toxics and toxic environments' (2018: 248). Three weeks after turning nine, Ella suffered a fatal asthma attack in her home. She had been a healthy child, playing football and practising gymnastics, and with no underlying issues prior to exhibiting breathing difficulties at the age of seven when she was diagnosed with asthma. In the two years that followed, her mother Adoo describes how Ella would cough 'so much she blacked out', experiencing what she came to know as a '"coughing syncope" caused by lack of oxygen to the brain' (Ella Roberta Family Foundation, 2023). All of Ella's short life had been spent in Lewisham, a historically multiracial borough that also has one of the highest densities of traffic in any urban setting in Britain today. Growing up near the South Circular, 'one of London's most notoriously congested roads' (Marshall, 2020), and travelling to her school a 'half hour walk away, mostly on the pavement beside nose to tail traffic' (ibid.), meant that Ella's exposure to both outdoor and indoor traffic-related air pollution was total, with no respite from the associated mixture of gasses and fine particulate matter (National Toxicology Program, 2019). Indeed, on revisiting the circumstances of her death, the coroner, Philip Barlow, concluded: 'Air pollution was a significant contributory factor to both the induction and exacerbations of her asthma. During the course of her illness between 2010 and 2013 she was exposed to levels of nitrogen dioxide and particulate matter in excess of WHO guidelines. The principal source of her exposure was traffic emissions. During this period there was a recognized failure to reduce the level of nitrogen dioxide to within the limits set by EU and domestic law which possibly contributed to her death' (Courts and Tribunals Judiciary, 2021: 1–2). The coroner's findings were consistent with research from the US, for example, which has long established clear links between minorities, high-traffic neighbourhoods and respiratory issues in children (Gilliland et al., 2001).

Most obviously, this work has established that children living near busy roads are at an increased risk of developing asthma, and specifically that respiratory health in children is adversely affected by outdoor nitrogen dioxide (Gauderman et al., 2005), including when children play outdoor sports (McConnell et al., 2002). In the UK, there is limited literature typically focused on London, but what there is is unambiguous in reporting that the highest levels of air pollution can be found in ethnically diverse neighbourhoods, defined as those where more than 20 per cent of the population is non-white (Fecht et al., 2015; Brook and King, 2017).

One of the consequences of overlooking racialized geographies is that the racialized inequalities they contain are reproduced in adaptation strategies expressed in approaches to urban greening, which have been especially prominent in some economic attempts to address the twin objectives of economic renewal and net zero commitments (Haycox et al., 2025). Sometimes pitched as a 'green industrial revolution', the possibility that the economic, ecological and social benefits of greening initiatives are unequally distributed, especially with respect to the accessibility and utility discussed earlier, risks exacerbating existing disparities and vulnerabilities (Anguelovski and Connolly, 2021). Resilience that raises land values without protections simply relocates risk from floodplains to eviction courts. If adaptation projects translate into rent spikes and property speculation, they become a domination contract by greener means. The design correction is straightforward: embed anti-displacement mechanisms – such as community land trusts, right to remain covenants, rent caps triggered by public works – into the finance itself (cf. Fraser, 2008: 16–24; see also Groundwork UK, 2022).

The UN special rapporteur E. Tendayi Achiume has argued that 'environmental, climate and racial injustice are the institutionalized status quo' (2022: 3). This chapter responds by making the case for social policy to be at the forefront of rethinking climate adaptation approaches, namely by foregrounding the social determinants of vulnerability. Focusing on Black and ethnic minorities in Britain, it has insisted on the need to pursue this argument by connecting up differential exposures with differential vulnerabilities and differential access to space and services. What adaptation approaches urgently require, therefore, is consistent recognition of the ways in which existing racial disparities contribute to climate change vulnerabilities, and in ways that do not uncouple their constituent parts from one another. At the same time, this is also a challenge to climate change researchers and funders to prioritize primary research that examines how adaptive measures can attend to these inequalities across hazard, planning, social vulnerability and long-term risk assessments.

Multidisciplinary work spanning environmental and social science, the physical environments of cities and their biophysical attributes is still a relatively small component of research funding allocations, even while the incorporation of perspectives on social drivers such as the economy, policy and culture is deemed inseparable to how climate change is experienced. This is no less a priority than grasping how an increasing awareness and knowledge of weather-related risk and emergency management is also attentive to existing ethnic and racial disparities. It includes prevailing impediments in the urban environment and where adaptation policies can exacerbate existing inequalities. As Manon Burbidge et al. have argued, current approaches are inadequately 'weighted in the actual political, social and economic decisions that are made about how to manage, reduce, and adapt to risk on a community level' (2022: 163).

The status quo is further illustration of how approaches to public policy that originate only from institutionally privileged locations ignore those who are hurt by public policy that is designed and implemented without the inclusion of their experiences. A sustained space for understanding the relationships between environmental science, urbanization and stratification is therefore critical to addressing policy approaches to adaptation. Social policy is equipped to pursue this by foregrounding the social conditions that heighten vulnerabilities to climate change. It is especially well placed to consider how prevailing approaches to climate change might better address existing inequalities that are further compounded by environmental challenges, but also be alert to the possible unintended consequences of interventions that exacerbate these even more. Much as we accept that the impact of poverty can be evident across different domains over the life course, and indeed might be transmitted from one generation to the next, and therefore require context specific interventions, so we must be open to the ways in which racialization plays a cumulative role.

Specifically, this involves the long-term impact of the compounding effect of discrimination and social stress, differences in residential exposures, income and housing conditions, and differential vulnerabilities in underlying health conditions and comorbidities, as well as differential access to treatment and other forms of support. This last point is important because we should ask why we would expect disparities in labour markets, health and housing not to feature in vulnerabilities to climate change. The challenge this chapter identifies is to maintain a broad focus on the underlying determinants, and not allow climate risks to be separated from their social exposures. Vulnerability cannot be explained in isolation. At an elementary level, this requires the inclusion of race and ethnicity in data collection on adaptation progress, and its integration into governmental analysis and reporting of such data. Going forwards, adaptation can only be credible if it is built to confront race-structured climate risk by measuring it, reporting it and designing interventions that change the underlying conditions that produce it. After the storm, the choice is deceptively simple. Either adaptation becomes a new etiquette for unequal survival – green efficiencies draped over familiar hierarchies – or it becomes the arena in which we revoke the permissions that made yesterday's losses normal. This book has named those permissions as contracts (Pateman, 1988: 2–4, 10; Mills, 1997: 3, 14–15), traced their borders (Benhabib, 2004: 3; 2009: 37–8), enrolled witnessing as standing (Fraser, 2008: 16–24) and returned to adaptation as design. The measure of success is plain: do our institutions make predictable harm impossible by design, or merely tolerable for those who can pay? If the answer is the latter, we have not adapted; we have relocated risk. The work of justice is to refuse that relocation. If earlier chapters moved from canon to contracts, borders and witness, this one names climate adaptation as the field on which those arguments must now be built into thresholds, budgets and rights. My concluding chapter calls this a method and a brief: treat domination as baseline; widen the legal lexicon from fault to design; re-tool contract language for non-ideal worlds so obligation tracks benefit and injury through time; and build borders and memory that binds acknowledgement to duty, instead of apology to closure. Justice, here, is desubordination by design, answerable tomorrow morning in the institutions we are prepared to build.

7

Justice after the Trouble: Institutions, Memory, Borders

We began this book with an apparently simple question: 'What does justice mean in an unjust world?' The simplicity was always misleading. The world we must answer from is not an empty stage where impartial principles are auditioned; it is already populated by institutions that distribute risk, attention and repair unevenly, by histories that weight the dice before anyone throws them and by vocabularies that make some harms visible and others routine. Injustice therefore is more than an absence; it is an outcome engineered through specific technologies and lexical capture, whereby the powerful script the moral vocabulary (from law's operative lexicon that narrows responsibility to the litigable, to Rawlsian abstraction that brackets history, to technical definitions of 'famine' that evade starvation as a crime); bracketing and erasure, where patriarchy is styled as 'private', race as 'irrelevant', colonial history as 'past', and climate vulnerability as 'natural'; the manufacture of non-protection, in which systems are designed to prevent claims from being heard at all; and the social production of moral indifference through bureaucratic routinization, outsourcing and the narrative of crisis ordinariness, with Omelas as the starkest image.

Confronting this requires a critical method in a specific sense: not anti-empirical or anti-theoretical, but a style of inquiry that binds explanation to anti-domination. To this end, three commitments guided our analysis. First, historicity over abstraction, since moral language is a battleground and concepts are historical artefacts with users and effects (making it impossible to understand the UK's asylum system without the history of empire, or climate vulnerability without racial capitalism). Second, reflexivity about our tools, since social-scientific categories can loop back to entrench the very blind spots they aim to cure, and our task is to build concepts that 'carve at the joints' of social life rather than at the joints of our disciplines. Third, normativity without paternalism, since a refusal of value-free description must remain accountable to those most exposed to harm. The organizing questions for the book remain: where is justice located, who gets to name it, and which institutions turn claims into guarantees?

The argument that has unfolded insists that distribution matters, but on its own it can obscure how goods and burdens came to be maldistributed and how the very metrics are set by power. The domination contract shifts emphasis from allocation to relation and structure, showing how injustice is a relation of domination, and a structured incapacity to participate as an equal in social and political life. Carol Pateman's sexual contract is pivotal because it shows subordination not as receiving less of a pre-existing good, but as being constituted as a different kind of person within the legal and social order, whose consent is framed by dependence. A reparative agenda follows in seeking to dismantle technologies of domination (rolling back devices that manufacture non-protection, redesigning credibility processes against predictable bias, and treating reception conditions, legal aid and timely decisions as the means by which rights become enforceable); institutional redesign (changing the rules of the game, not just the allocation of prizes, with proposals like *jus nexi* and democratic iteration tying membership to social connection rather than ascribed identity) (Shachar, 2011; Benhabib, 2004); and epistemic repair (confronting the 'epistemological contract' [Mills, 1997], filling in memory holes, centring marginalized knowledges, challenging 'white innocence' [Wekker, 2016]). This is what connects climate justice to migrant justice and the struggle against racial patriarchy: facets of a single imperative to repair a world organized by domination through institutions grounded in reciprocity, recognition and a relentless honesty about history.

To 'stay with the trouble' (Haraway, 2016) then is not to dwell in melancholy, but to make the impasse analytically visible and practically revisable. Optimism here is a practice of design, a commitment to build institutions, relationships and languages that can sustain a more just common life. If this book has tracked a single insistence, it is that justice has a social life in which our concepts become worlds when they are taken up by law, policy and administration; concepts travel into budgets, contracts, eligibility criteria, procurement rules, guidance and oversight, and then travel back again as common sense. The argumentative spine has been that we treat domination as the baseline rather than a deviation: the 'original contract' of modern polities is hardly a pact among equals, but a layered architecture of sexual, racial and settler compacts that normalize hierarchy while narrating equality (Pateman, 1988; Mills, 1997). A politics that begins from that position will not mistake systemic injustice for a collection of discrete wrongs; it will ask how institutions foreseeably generate harms even when everyone inside them 'follows the rules'. That is why the operative legal lexicon must widen from liability (who wronged whom?) to design duties (what arrangements predictably produce which harms, and who must act upstream to prevent them?). It is why the social contract idiom must be re-tooled for non-ideal worlds, so that justice is not the hypothetical consent of equals, but the concrete obligations that follow from asymmetric histories. And it is why borders and memory must be treated as institutions rather than scenery: they are where a polity decides who may enter the circle of reciprocity, and how the past is curated so that present obligations either appear or vanish. Each chapter staged these claims at a different scale; the task of this closing chapter is to braid them into a single, forward-looking grammar of design, so that the book ends not with uplift, but with usable instructions.

The method began from domination in order to design for desubordination. Instead of imagining a people already free and equal, we began with the patterned subordinations that structure institutions and common sense. The point was not to deny dignity; it was to prevent dignity talk from floating above the histories that keep producing vulnerability. Read through Carole Pateman and Charles Mills, the social contract appears as a stack of domination contracts: fraternal patriarchy as the sexual contract that makes citizenship masculine; white supremacy as the racial contract that underwrites the social contract's 'neutral' institutions; and the settler contract that fuses property and sovereignty through dispossession. Once this is granted, two consequences orient this whole book: justice is the disciplined practice of redesign that redirects foreseeable harms away from those whom the domination contracts have trained the polity to neglect or control; and the contract idiom is re-tooled, so that obligations track benefits and injuries through time.

Our duties don't come from an imaginary promise, as if political obligation were settled by a one-off act of consent in a state of nature, or by a tacit agreement that we never meaningfully had the chance to refuse. They arise because we live inside institutional arrangements that distribute safety, mobility, recognition and exposure unevenly, and because many of us gain security or advantage from those distributions even when we didn't design them and don't individually intend their harms. The point is not to accuse every beneficiary of malice. It is to name a structure of implication: if our routines and protections are sustained by systems that render some people precarious, then obligation follows from participation and benefit, not from mythical authorship.

On this view, vulnerability isn't an unfortunate residue at the margins of an otherwise legitimate order. It is produced and maintained through ordinary policy choices, legal categories and administrative practices. Visa regimes and carrier sanctions do not merely regulate movement; they help manufacture clandestine travel. 'Safe third country' lists, accelerated procedures, detention thresholds and evidentiary demands do not just manage claims; they allocate credibility and risk, deciding whose uncertainty is tolerated and whose is treated as grounds for exclusion. Housing standards, labour markets, welfare conditionality and policing practices do not simply reflect inequality; they routinize it, shaping who can recover from shocks and who is left to absorb them. When those patterns are durable and predictable, they cease to look like accidents and start to look like design.

That is why the task shifts from consent to repair. The relevant moral question cannot be 'Did we agree to this order?' but 'What has this order done, for whom, and with what foreseeable effects?' Repair here means more than compensation after the fact. It means interrupting the pipelines that keep producing harm: expanding safe routes, ensuring timely identification and due process, making accountability traceable across outsourced contracts, and building enforceable duties of care at the border and in reception. It also means taking seriously harms that liberal stories often treat as external to politics, such as death at sea, family separation, destitution, or the slow violence of administrative delay.

And it shifts from justification to redesign. Contractarian argument tends to ask whether coercive institutions can be justified to free and equal persons in the abstract. A rectificatory lens asks what institutions must look like if they are to stop manufacturing vulnerability, and if they are to treat protection as a duty rather than a discretionary gift. The measure becomes practical and institutional: do the rules reduce exposure, make rights actionable and prevent predictable harms? In that register, legitimacy is earned not by an origin story, but by whether the ongoing architecture of law and policy is capable of repair, restraint and accountability.

Key here is the language of law and our institutional imagination, because legal reason is brilliant at allocating responsibility in discrete disputes, yet thin where harm is cumulative and structural. Reasonableness indexed to prevailing practice, causation narrowed to proximate triggers, remedies tailored to the parties before the tribunal: none of this is bad faith; it is how adjudication avoids paralysis. But it is why systems can be perfectly lawful and systematically unjust when the real action lies upstream in procurement frameworks, contractor incentives, eligibility thresholds and guidance that narrows discretion at the bottom while widening it at the top, and in the informational poverty of first-contact procedures. The legal argument here is not anti-law; it is anti-thinness. Widening the lexicon from ex-post liability to ex-ante duties of design follows: statutory requirements to publish disaggregated recognition rates; audits of algorithms that allocate attention; documentary burden-sharing that reflects real-world capacities; and independent oversight bodies empowered to compel compliance where private contractors perform public functions. Anyone who followed the reception conditions at Tug Haven or the lack of information employed in the screening of children will recognize why 'design' is a justice word: 'Unaccompanied children who had crossed the Channel by boat were being kept for days without access to beds or showers and, during 2020's curtailed screening, key trafficking-indicator questions were not asked until ordered by the High Court to be reinstated' (Bulman, 2020; *DA and Ors v. The Secretary of State for the Home Department*, 2020; UNHCR, 2021). These were not glitches in an otherwise decent system; they were what the system's design predicted. If domination is baseline, then reasonableness must be rekeyed from deference to redescription: the question is no longer whether the official acted as others would have done, but whether an avoidably harmful design choice was left uncorrected given what was knowable. That hinge concept is how law can name structural wrongs without abandoning its craft.

At the border, the domination contracts are most visible. Contemporary bordering is far from a neutral gate; rather, it is a choreography through which non-protection is manufactured upstream of adjudication: carrier sanctions and maritime interceptions that prevent claim-formation; 'safe third country' fictions that displace responsibility; guidance that marks entire cohorts inadmissible before their particulars can be heard; and reception systems that make rightlessness material. The UK Supreme Court's judgment on the proposed Rwanda removals crystallized the point by cutting through the legal fiction of safety where the evidential record showed a 'real risk of ill-treatment [and] refoulement' (UK Supreme Court, 2023). Parliament's subsequent attempt to legislate safety in the 2024 Safety of Rwanda Act, and the 27 June 2025 inadmissibility guidance recalibration, illustrated how discretion shifts to keep protection outside the circle of reciprocity even while the rhetoric remains procedural (UK Parliament, 2024; Home Office, 2025). Pateman's analysis makes the gendered mechanics explicit: when residence or status is tethered to a spouse, sponsor or employer, 'private' dependence is imported into the public category of the right-holder, disclosure of violence is chilled, exit options narrow and vulnerability is amplified in reception and accommodation (1988: 10–12). Justice at the border therefore turns on whether the safeguards set out earlier are treated as entitlements rather than discretionary 'support': timely legal advice and interpretation, trauma-informed procedures, accommodation not tethered to sponsors, clear work timelines, auditable statistics and oversight with enforcement powers. The point is simple: where foreseeable harms are built into the system, they are not accidents: they are design failures. The question is whether the system's design foreseeably reproduces racialized and gendered subordination under the cover of neutrality. Contemporary bordering is in this sense a pedagogy of organized irresponsibility; harms are foreseeable, but narrated as the regrettable by-product of order rather than the outcome of design choices. The Lampedusa wreck was not an isolated calamity, but the predictable endpoint of choices distributed across time and space externalization deals, interdiction practices, reception infrastructures that normalize crisis ordinariness. The decision by island clinicians to lay a young Eritrean mother and her premature infant in a single coffin, with the umbilical cord left uncut, is included here not to sentimentalize but to insist on the specificity of lives that abstract policy converts into flows, cohorts and backlogs.

If borders are where reciprocity is denied at the threshold, archives are where innocence is manufactured across time. Our chapters on nation and empire used the Windrush scandal to show how a liberal state can narrate a system of exclusions as an administrative anomaly, while the very design of citizenship and welfare had long been structured to downgrade colonial subjects' personhood. Linking Stuart Hall's (1980) observation about the 'trace' laid by imperialism in the nation-making process to the present day, we argued that the welfare state remains the principal site where that trace is either reproduced – through exclusionary meta-membership – or reworked towards inclusive belonging. Seen in this light, remaking the nation should not be read as a nostalgic retreat but as the contested site where welfare meta-membership is decided, foundational narratives are reopened and the entanglements of nation and empire are faced rather than ignored; it is also the level at which the political fictions that once naturalized dispossession can be named, refused and replaced (McCarthy, 2004; Hall, 1980). A memory architecture oriented to justice desegregates remembrance by connecting contemporary administrative practices (NRPF rules; data-matching with hostile environment logics; discretionary accommodation) to the older compacts that made such practices plausible. And, although it institutionalizes remembrance by linking acknowledgement to consequence, compensation and reinstatement of rights, this memory also makes presumptions in favour of applicants who cannot access paper trails because the state itself authored the gaps, indulges in documentary burden-sharing and creates shifts in standards of proof in cases where the state's own systems have made 'proof' scarce. This is memory as a lever, not as a balm.

One allegory threaded through the later chapters – Ursula K. Le Guin's 'The ones who walk away from Omelas'. Its power lies in refusing euphemism. The city's harmony is premised on a child's degradation; 'they all know that it has to be there' is the line that shows how moral indifference becomes civic common sense (Le Guin, 1975). We turned to Omelas not to stage individual virtue, but to clarify how institutions can be designed so that cruelty is useful to them and the sacrifice is justified as the condition of the good. If Omelas names the refusal to connect comfort to its price, the municipal practices of the Italian commune of Riace suggested, even under hostile national politics, a different ethic: reception as town-building, inclusion as material infrastructure (schools reopened, workshops restarted), belonging as an enforceable relation rather than discretionary charity. The parable and the municipal experiment were set side-by-side to make a concrete claim: complicity is a choice, but so is a design that makes decency ordinary. In that register, Benhabib's 'democratic iteration' (2009: 37–8) then shows how boundaries and norms can be renegotiated through reason-giving encounters with outsiders, so that presence generates voice, and voice, when institutionalized, grounds status.

With this in view, we can return to the question we asked at the start of this book. But, instead of asking 'What is justice?' we now ask 'Where does justice live, and how can it be made to live otherwise and longer?' It lives in concepts that refuse to launder domination as order, turning a sceptical diagnosis into a programme. To say that the social contract was always already sexual, racial and settler is not to despair; it is a design instruction to track benefits and injuries across time, and to build obligations accordingly (Pateman, 1988; Mills, 1997). The social contract lives in institutions that translate those concepts into guarantees, that widen the legal lexicon from liability to design duties, that re-key reasonableness from deference to avoidability, that give oversight bodies powers to compel compliance, that publish disaggregated recognition rates and that require algorithmic and procedural audits in high-stake decisions.

These are not technocratic add-ons. They are the form that rectificatory justice takes in administrative states, where harms are rarely inflicted by a single dramatic act, but more often produced by routine classifications, queues, risk scores, eligibility rules and outsourced chains of responsibility. In that setting, justice is more than mainly a posture or a declaration of values; it's a redesign problem. It lives in the mundane places where decisions are made and recorded, where discretion is narrowed or widened, and where the costs of error are assigned to some people rather than others.

This form of justice lives at borders because borders are where reciprocity is most easily denied while still being narrated as 'management'. They are the point at which the polity tests its own account of obligation. If reciprocity is treated as a boast, it becomes rhetorical cover. The state congratulates itself on being lawful and humane, while building procedures that predictably generate non-protection, through delay, disbelief, destitution and deportability. If reciprocity is treated as a discipline, it functions as a constraint on power. It forces institutions to act on the premise that those subject to border control are not merely risks to be sorted, but persons to whom duties are owed, including duties to hear, to identify, to protect from foreseeable harm and to justify coercion with reasons that can be challenged.

A justice-led border, then, is not simply a border that speaks the language of rights; it's one whose institutional architecture makes rights usable. That means the availability of safe and regular routes that reduce the need for clandestine travel. It means procedures that treat uncertainty as normal rather than suspicious, and that place the burden of administrative gaps on the state rather than on people with the least capacity to produce documents, narrate trauma coherently, or wait in precarity. It means standards for search and rescue that don't fluctuate with political convenience, and identification protocols that don't leave the dead or the disappeared as administrative residue. It means records that can be audited, decisions that can be appealed and outsourcing arrangements that do not dissolve responsibility into contractual fog. It also means designing against predictable failure modes. If we know that accelerated screening leads to missed trafficking indicators, then justice requires the staffing, training and time allowances that make safeguarding real. If we know that detention and poor reception conditions produce panic, retraumatization and self-harm, then justice demands enforceable minimum standards and independent monitoring with consequences. If we know that 'safe third country' designations can function as a legal fiction that exports risk, then justice requires transparent criteria, individualized assessment and effective remedies that suspend removal until risk is properly tested. In each case, the point is the same: institutions must be arranged so that the foreseeable outputs of the system are compatible with the duties the system claims to recognize. This includes early advice and communication support, procedures that do not punish disclosure, accommodation that is insulated from coercive dependencies and oversight that can compel remedial action. The test is whether the system is designed to prevent predictable harms, rather than to rationalize them after the fact. And it lives in memory architectures that link acknowledgement to consequence. The Windrush scandal taught that apology without transformation is anti-politics, that remembering is an institutional practice – concerning who curates, what is connected, which consequences follow – and that statutes and guidance should encode those connections rather than leave them to sentiment.

Scaling out, we resisted two temptations: a cosmopolitanism that generalizes from Euro-Atlantic premises while ignoring the histories that made the 'basic structure' it wants to regulate, and a nationalism that turns reciprocity inwards while treating external obligations as charity. The domination contract lens is relevant here too. Once you start from a domination baseline, rather than from idealized consent, the questions change. Climate loss-and-damage accounting is no longer an exercise in charity or discretionary aid, but a rectificatory practice that follows the path of benefit and the trail of imposed risk. Supply-chain due diligence stops resembling voluntary corporate ethics and starts to look like a jurisdictional problem, because corporate power governs lives across borders in ways that are functionally state-like. Migration responsibility-sharing is no longer keyed to mere proximity, but to capacity and contribution, because the burdens of protection are patterned by histories of extraction, labour demand, arms sales and climate impact. And widening authorship in norm-setting beyond the old metropoles becomes a condition of legitimacy, not a gesture of inclusion, because rules made by a narrow club predictably reproduce the partiality of their makers.

These are familiar settings once the method is kept honest, meaning that it refuses the comfort of abstraction that brackets empire, externalities and unequal life chances, and instead traces who benefits, who pays and which institutions stabilize that distribution over time. This must involve more than tacking on a 'global' chapter as an afterthought; it must insist that the same language remains in force at a higher scale. Domination is still the baseline to be identified. Rectificatory design is still the task. And enforceable guarantees are still the test of whether a regime is doing more than expressing moral concern.

Duties of design in law and administration require public authorities (and private actors performing public functions) to show evidence of how their arrangements avoid foreseeable structural harms, tie funding and licensing to compliance with design duties, publish disaggregated performance metrics to a statutory schedule, submit first-contact and credibility procedures to independent audit, complete algorithmic impact assessments where automated triage allocates attention, and provide enforceable remedies where design duties are breached. Proof must become a shared burden where the state's design choices make 'proof' scarce (as with the Windrush paper trails); it must presume in favour of the applicant, re-allocate documentary burdens, codify the presumption in guidance, train decision-makers to apply it, and monitor outcomes. Reception and recognition should be treated as one system: housing, income support, access to work, legal aid and appeal rights are elements of enforceable recognition, not dispensable add-ons. If you cannot live, you cannot give evidence; if you cannot give evidence, your 'right' is fictional. Gender-safe status formation must build routes to status independent of spouses, sponsors and employers; it must encode mandatory screening for gender-based violence with specialist interpreters, ensure safe housing without status jeopardy, and ring-fence legal aid. Pateman's words should be treated as compliance text – 'political right originates in sex-right or conjugal right' – and the task is to prevent that origin story from governing the present (Pateman, 1988: 11–12).

A word about hope belongs here, but not as ornament. The book opened under the shadow of cities turned to rubble and children buried in their pyjamas. It would be dishonest to end with uplift for its own sake. Yet it would be equally dishonest to ignore the ways in which a method already makes worlds, when a court refuses a legal fiction because the evidential record shows risk; when a council ties housing contracts to gender-safe design; when a ministry publishes disaggregated recognition data and changes guidance in response; when school boards are opened to those whom the border calls 'temporary'; when memory is tied to consequence rather than catharsis. To walk away from Omelas is not yet a plan; but the argument has been that the social life of justice is found precisely in those design choices that convert decency from discretion into enforceable routine, so that the moral imagination does not have to hope for good will from those least exposed to harm. The question thus shifts from 'What is justice?' to 'How does justice work? How is it invoked, mobilized, resisted and institutionalized? And how do our attempts to conceptualize it loop back into the world, altering the realities we seek to describe?' The measure of that work is plain enough to be unforgiving: do our arrangements predictably reduce avoidable harm for those most exposed? If they do not, we know what to change.

The remaining task is to find a new normal, and to hold to it, even when convenience and fatigue invite a return to familiar cruelties. The social life of justice is lived, contested and always under construction. It is the practice of answering, again and again, the question that opened this book. So, the answer doesn't arrive as a settled definition. It shows itself in the quality of our response: in the steadiness with which we name domination, in the seriousness with which we repair what we have inherited and in the ways we make reciprocity enforceable rather than aspirational.

Notes

1 UN analysts caution that these figures are conservative. Tonnage calculations exclude artillery shells and tank rounds, and bomb counts after January 2024 rely on incomplete public data. Even so, the evidence shows that tens of thousands of munitions, delivering roughly 30 kilotonnes of explosives, have made Gaza one of the most heavily bombarded urban areas in recent history, with unprecedented levels of rubble and ongoing humanitarian fallout.

2 I use Desmond Lee's (1987) translation and the Stephanus numbers that are printed in the margins of the paragraphs and consistent across reproductions of the ancient text. Stephanus numbers are the standard page and section references printed in the margins of Plato's works. Each citation gives the dialogue's page number plus a letter (a–e) for the marginal section (e.g., Republic 509d) and the numbering restarts with each dialogue.

3 In approaching what is often called the 'canon' of justice, this book proceeds with a deliberately sceptical, though not iconoclastic, stance. The familiar itinerary through Plato, Hobbes, Locke, Rousseau and Rawls is treated as a living archive of argumentative moves rather than as a syllabus to be venerated. Canonical texts are read alongside traditions that expose their omissions (feminist, critical race, decolonial and abolitionist work), not to stage a ritual

demolition but to test whether inherited categories can survive contact with the world they helped to shape. The method assumes a looping traffic between ideas and institutions: concepts migrate into budgets, rules and routines, and return as common sense. On that view, 'canon' becomes a diagnostic, not an honour roll: it names the architectures that stabilize hierarchy unless interrupted. Where those architectures prove resistant to repair, the book privileges redesign over deference, beginning from domination rather than ideal symmetry and widening the legal-political vocabulary from liability after the fact to duties of design before the harm.

4 Another way to stress this is to highlight instances where social contract thinkers were explicitly invoked or clearly operative in constitution making, legislation or legal reasoning. For example, Hobbes and Locke sit right behind Jefferson's justification of American independence: in his well-known letter to Henry Lee (8 May 1825), Jefferson says the Declaration of Independence aimed to capture the 'common sense of the subject' drawn from the 'elementary books of public right, as Aristotle, Cicero, Locke, Sidney, etc.' (Jefferson, 1904–5, vol. 12). That is a direct, first-hand acknowledgement that Lockean social contract ideas (natural rights and consent) framed a constitutional moment that still shapes political life, and they were also institutionalized in state constitutions even before Philadelphia. The Massachusetts Constitution (1780) opens by describing the body politic as a voluntary association formed by a 'social compact', and affirms the people's right to 'alter the government' if ends are not met; its Declaration of Rights sets out natural rights as the purpose of government). This is classic social contract vocabulary embedded in fundamental law. Rousseau's language surfaces (almost verbatim) in the French Revolution: the 1789 Déclaration des droits de l'homme et du citoyen defines law as 'the expression of the general will' (Declaration of the Rights of Man and of the Citizen, 1789, art. 6), and the 1958 Constitution of the Fifth Republic constitutionalizes that lineage by incorporating the 1789 Déclaration in its Preamble. Rousseau was also read as a practical constitutional

adviser: his 1772 essay, 'Considerations on the Government of Poland', counsels institutional devices to preserve freedom in a large state – frequent elections, tight deputy mandates, and curbs on the *liberum veto* – explicitly tying these proposals back to *The Social Contract* (Rousseau, 1997: 15–16, 26–7). Historians of the 3 May 1791 Polish–Lithuanian Constitution accordingly see the reformers drawing on Rousseau (alongside Montesquieu) to reconcile noble liberty with effective government (Lukowski, 1994). A striking post-revolutionary application of social contract language is Haiti's Imperial Constitution (1805): its Preliminary Declaration (arts. 1–4) proclaims the constitution to be 'the free spontaneous and invariable expression of our hearts, and the general will of our constituents', then founds the state on popular sovereignty and the abolition of slavery. Finally, social contract reasoning remains a live reference in contemporary adjudication: in *Toronto (City) v. Ontario [2021] 2 SCR 845*, the Supreme Court of Canada debated democracy and freedom of expression in elections, while expressly citing Rawls's political liberalism in support of the view that constitutional rights have both negative and positive dimensions (Rawls, 2005: 361–2).

5 Legal scholarship and jurisprudence furnish further corroboration. Hobbes's *Leviathan* underpins sovereignty arguments in early-modern constitutional litigation; Locke's *Second Treatise* remains a staple in property-rights cases; Rousseau's idea of the general will surfaces in Canadian federalism rulings; and Rawls's 'difference principle' saturates equal-protection commentary in US law reviews (Allen, 1999; Iacovino and Erk, 2012). Because court opinions cite works sparingly, the fact that these four works are still cited in contemporary judgments underscores their canonical status.

6 Does this not then limit the relevance of these conceptions of justice today? The answer is 'no', for the key reason within the body of the argument within *The Republic*, and the central theme of this book, can be expressed in the Greek word for justice: *dikaiosynē*. As Desmond Lee, who provided one of the most established and

commonly used translations of *The Republic*, details: the meaning of this word is used in the dialogues as 'a wide one and covers both individual and social morality, and from the start therefore the inquiry is concerned with both individual and community, both ethics and politics' (Plato, 1987: xxxii). Consequently, Lee continues, it becomes clear that the question being asked is: what is the basis of social and moral obligations? For even when rules, regulations or ethical codes are in place, the distribution of power and resources can determine who benefits and who is left vulnerable. Large-scale social failures, whether in housing, public safety or environmental policy, reveal that structural inequalities often persist beneath the surface of formal legal and moral systems.

7 By way of radical contrast with other European 'pioneers' of social thought, Marx pushes furthest towards a critique of legal justice, treating it as an ideology that can stabilize injustice by equating fairness with equivalence under conditions of pervasive inequality, the very move that Ó'Cinnéide worries about when legal vocabulary makes us search for a liable person rather than the responsible structure. Thus, in the first volume of *Capital*, Marx famously anatomizes the market's 'appearance form' in which law flourishes, ridiculing this as the 'very Eden of the innate rights of man. There alone rule Freedom, Equality, Property and Bentham' (Marx, 1990 [1867]: 280). That 'Eden', he insists, misleads, for the equality of exchange masks the appropriation of unpaid labour that occurs in production. Later, in the *Critique of the Gotha Programme*, he takes direct aim at distributive ideals that pretend to be egalitarian: 'equal right here is still – in principle – bourgeois right ... In spite of this advance, this equal right is still perpetually burdened with a bourgeois limitation ... This equal right is an unequal right for unequal labour ... Right by its very nature can consist only in the application of an equal standard', which ignores real differences in persons' circumstances (Marx, 2014 [1875]: 19–20). Only in a higher phase 'can the narrow horizon of bourgeois right be crossed in its entirety and society inscribe on its banners: From each according to his ability, to each according to his needs!' (ibid.:

20). Yet Marx's own positive lexicon of justice is underspecified. He gestures towards a need-based distributive principle, in a phase of communism, but leaves largely undeveloped the institutional forms that would prevent new hierarchies from crystallizing within the very apparatus designed to supersede bourgeois right. In contemporary terms, he shows why law's current lexicon cannot carry justice; he says less about how the grammar of a new one would not reproduce the non-economic characteristics of what preceded.

8 The key difference to note is that while social contract theorists used the idea of a state of nature to show what, in their view, makes political authority legitimate, older ideas of justice in *The Republic* did not rely on a pre-political moment where justice is absent, nor seek a deep break with 'nature' or wholly uncouple communities from individuals.

9 The next chapter will trace how injustices, past and present, have been integral to constitutional orders despite philosophical attempts to bracket them, and how that bracketing opens a gulf between the ideals projected by contract theory and the recognition cultivated by civil society.

10 Social contract approaches were arguably crowded out, first by utilitarians and later by Marxian critiques of ideology.

11 To stabilize such demanding norms in a pluralistic society, Rawls proposes the device of reflective equilibrium: 'a state reached after a person has weighed various proposed conceptions and … either revised his judgments to accord with one of them or held fast to his initial convictions' (1999 [1971]: 40). The model invites every citizen to compare her considered moral judgments with systematic principles and to adjust either until coherence is achieved.

12 IOM's subsequent global update for 2024 reports 2,452 deaths and disappearances on the Mediterranean that year (IOM, 2025a). Rolling totals on IOM's Mediterranean dashboard indicate that the cumulative number since 2014 now exceeds 32,000 (IOM, 2025b). All these figures are acknowledged minima; the Missing

Migrants Project explicitly cautions that the true toll is higher because many shipwrecks leave no survivors, many bodies are never recovered and reporting is uneven across routes (IOM, n.d., n.p.). Drowning is the predominant cause of death across migration routes, with the Mediterranean accounting for the vast majority of documented drownings in the past decade (IOM, 2024: 12)

13 Legally, this renationalization has run up against, and then been partially accommodated by, Schengen law. In *NW v. Landespolizeidirektion Steiermark* the Court of Justice held that internal border checks cannot be endlessly prolonged on the basis of the same threat (CJEU, 2022). Yet political pressure to keep 'temporary' controls in place helped to propel a reform of the Schengen Borders Code, adopted in May 2024, which gives governments more tools to respond to 'crises' while trying to preserve border-free travel (Council of the EU, 2024; Peers, 2024). The reform legitimizes practices previously regarded as incompatible with EU law, and risks making exceptional measures routine (CJEU, 2022; Council of the EU, 2024; Peers, 2024; Thym, 2024; PRAB Network, 2025).

14 Courts have both constrained and, at times, complicated this trend. The ECtHR's *M.S.S. v. Belgium and Greece* (2011) and *Hirsi Jamaa v. Italy* (2012) established key guardrails against transfers where reception conditions violate Article 3 ECHR and against 'push backs' on the high seas, respectively. Yet *N.D. and N.T. v. Spain* (2020) introduced a controversial carve-out for summary returns at the Melilla fence in narrow circumstances.

15 As of 22 September 2025, the most authoritative running totals collated by the UN from the Gaza Ministry of Health (MoH) indicated that about 65,000 Palestinians had been killed in the Gaza Strip since 7 October 2023 (65,062 as of 17 September). UN updates also record continuing famine- and malnutrition-related deaths within that total (the MoH reported 432 such deaths, including 146 children, by 17 September). In the occupied West Bank (including East Jerusalem), UN figures attribute around

1,000 Palestinian deaths in the same period (991 reported up to 8 September). Taken together, publicly reported Palestinian fatalities from Israeli military action across Gaza and the West Bank are therefore in the mid-60,000s, approaching the high-60,000s and still rising (OCHA, 2025a; 2025b; UNRWA, 2025; WHO, 2025a] On the civilian share of these deaths, there is no single, universally accepted percentage. However, UN human rights analyses of verified incidents (especially attacks on residential buildings) have repeatedly found that women and children constitute the majority of victims in those events, underscoring a predominantly civilian toll (OHCHR, 2024). In addition, independent reporting based on Israeli military data leaked to journalists suggested that only a small fraction of the dead were identified fighters, implying a civilian death share well above half (Graham-Harrison and Abraham, 2025). No other conflict has produced as many civilian deaths in so short a time period, in so small a territory as Gaza. Ukraine and Sudan show sustained, large-scale civilian harm but at markedly lower daily rates; Yemen's incident-verified direct civilian deaths are lower still (though indirect deaths are massive); Syria's long war remains unparalleled in cumulative civilian loss. Differences partly reflect method (verified incidents vs. statistical excess mortality) and access, but even on conservative, verified bases Gaza's recent civilian toll is exceptionally high. (OCHA, 2025a; OHCHR, 2022; 2025; OHCHR/HRMMU, 2025; Campaign Against Arms Trade, 2025).

16 A 'carbon sink' in climate science refers to how net greenhouse gas emission reductions represent the sum of reduced emissions. So, for example, plants, oceans, and soils absorb more carbon than they release (in contrast to a carbon source like fossil fuels which release more than they absorb). See also Brook and King's (2017) analysis of air pollution exposure in London, in which they conclude that 'for all ethnic groups except for Whites, there is a relatively higher concentration of highlighted LSOAs located within areas where the NO_2 concentrations exceeded the limit'.

17 As a legally binding international treaty, the 2016 Paris Agreement

recognized this multifinality and included a commitment by Global North countries to create a loss and damage fund for Global South countries to draw down, as a means of addressing the overwhelming role of high-income Global North countries in climate change and environmental degradation (Dehm, 2020). The remedial funds for this loss and damage have been called 'a major failure' (Kühn, 2021) when set against the expectation of Global South countries to refrain from economic development activities that would use fossil fuels and release further carbon into the atmosphere.

References

Achiume, E. T. (2022) *Report of the Special Rapporteur on Contemporary Forms of Racism, Racial Discrimination, Xenophobia and Related Intolerance on Ecological Crisis Climate Justice and Racial Justice.* United Nations General Assembly. A/77/2990.

African Union (1981) *African Charter on Human and Peoples' Rights.* https://au.int/en/treaties/african-charter-human-and-peoples-rights.

Agamben, G. (1998) *Homo Sacer: Sovereign Power and Bare Life.* Stanford: Stanford University Press.

Agger, B. (2006) *Critical Social Theories: An Introduction*, 2nd ed. Paradigm Publishers.

AIDA/ECRE (2025) *United Kingdom: Country Report*, April. Asylum Information Database, European Council on Refugees an Exiles.

Akhtar, S. (2021) 'The battle of Kenmure Street', The Identities Blog, 18 May. https://www.identitiesjournal.com/blog-collection/the-battle-of-kenmure-street.

Al Jazeera English (2023) 'Children of Gaza: Growing up amid war, starvation, and trauma'. https://www.youtube.com/watch?v=gGZRR1znkKk.

Al Jazeera English (2024) 'Gaza's children face long road to healing', 5 April. https://www.aljazeera.com/gallery/2024/4/5/gazas-children-face-long-road-to-healing.

Alcoff, L. M. (2015) *The Future of Whiteness*. Cambridge: Polity.

Allen, A. L. (1999) 'Social contract theory in American case law', *Florida Law Review*, 51(1), pp. 1–40.

Allen, D. S. (2004) *Talking to Strangers: Anxieties of Citizenship since Brown v. Board of Education*. Chicago: University of Chicago Press.

Alsaafin, L. (2025) 'Why we must keep talking about Gaza', *Middle East Eye*, 24 June. https://www.middleeasteye.net/opinion/dont-be-distracted-israels-war-iran-we-must-keep-talking-about-gaza.

Alsaafin, L. and Amer, R. (2023) 'So world knows: Gaza parents mark children's names on bodies amid bombing', *Al Jazeera English*, 28 October. https://www.aljazeera.com/news/2023/10/28/so-world-knows-gaza-parents-mark-childrens-names-on-bodies-amid-bombing.

Alsaafin, L. and Humaid, M. (2023) '"Death corridor": The al-Samounis recall terror of "safe passage" in Gaza', *Al Jazeera English*, 3 December. https://www.aljazeera.com/news/2023/12/3/death-corridor-the-al-samounis-recall-terror-of-safe-passage-in-gaza.

Alston, P. and Goodman, R. (2013) *International Human Rights*. Oxford: Oxford University Press.

Amnesty International (2015) 'Lampedusa's medic to the migrants', 15 May. https://www.amnesty.org/en/latest/news/2015/05/lampedusas-medic-to-the-migrants/.

Amnesty International (2023) 'EU/Tunisia: Agreement on migration "makes EU complicit" in abuses against asylum seekers, refugees and migrants', 17 July. https://www.amnesty.org/en/latest/news/2023/07/eu-tunisia-agreement-on-migration-makes-eu-complicit-in-abuses-against-asylum-seekers-refugees-and-migrants/.

Amnesty International (2025a) 'Italy: EU court ruling on "safe countries of origin" is a heavy blow to Italy–Albania migration deal', 1 August. https://www.amnesty.org/en/latest/news/2025/08/italy-eu-court-ruling-on-safe-countries-of-origin-is-a-heavy-blow-to-italy-albania-migration-deal/.

Amnesty International (2025b) 'Externalization of migration and the impact on the human rights of migrants', 11 June. https://www.amnesty.org/fr/documents/eur01/9485/2025/en/.

Anderson, B. (1991) *Imagined Communities: Reflections on the Origin and Spread of Nationalism*. London: Verso.

Anghie, A. (2004) *Imperialism, Sovereignty and the Making of International Law*. Cambridge: Cambridge University Press.

Anguelovski, I. and Connolly, J. J. T. (2021) *The Green City and Social Injustice: 21 Tales from North America and Europe*. London: Routledge.

Annas, J. (1981) *An Introduction to Plato's Republic*. Oxford: Clarendon Press.

Armitage, D. (2004) 'John Locke, Carolina, and the *Two Treatises of Government*', *Political Theory*, 32(5), pp. 602–627.

Arneil, B. (1996) *John Locke and America: The Defence of English Colonialism.* Oxford: Clarendon Press.

Asylum Aid (2025) 'Press release: Home Secretary informs Asylum Aid about her intentions to repeal the Safety of Rwanda Act 2024 in this Parliamentary session', *Asylum Aid*, 29 January. https://www.asylumaid.org.uk/resources/news-blogs/press-release-home-secretary-informs-asylum-aid-about-her-intentions-repeal.

Ayeb-Karlsson, S., Valiquette, T., Cockbain, E. and Durán, L. (2024) *A Storytelling Legal and Empirical Analysis of Human Trafficking and Exploitation Risks for Unaccompanied Children in Home Office-Operated Hotels in the UK.* London: UCL and ECPAT UK / Modern Slavery PEC.

Aziza, S. (2024) '"How many dead Palestinians are enough?" The unbearable prescience of the late poet Refaat Alareer', *Guardian*, 10 December.

Ba, O. (2020) *States of Justice: The Politics of the International Criminal Court*. Cambridge: Cambridge University Press.

Ba, O. (2021) 'Global justice and race', *International Politics Reviews*, 9, pp. 375–389.

Baldwin, J. (1962) *The Fire Next Time*. New York: Dial Press.

Balibar, É. and Wallerstein, I. (1991) *Race, Nation, Class: Ambiguous Identities*, trans. C. Turner. London: Verso.

Banner, S. (2005) *How the Indians Lost Their Land: Law and Power on the Frontier*. Cambridge, MA: Harvard University Press.

Bansak, K., Hainmueller, J. and Hangartner, D. (2016) 'How economic, humanitarian, and religious concerns shape European attitudes toward asylum seekers', *Science*, 354(6309), pp. 217–222.

Bansak, K., Hainmueller, J. and Hangartner, D. (2023) 'Europeans' support for refugees of varying background is stable over time', *Nature*, 620(7975), pp. 849–854.

Barnardo's (2025) *Let Children Be Children: The Impact of Age Assessments on Children Seeking Sanctuary & Asylum in the UK*. London: Barnardo's.

Barnes, M., Butt, S. and Tomaszewski, W. (2008). *The Dynamics of Bad Housing: The Impact of Bad Housing on the Living Standards of Children*. London: National Centre for Social Research.

Barney, R. (2006) 'Socrates' refutation of Thrasymachus', in G. Santas (ed.), *The Blackwell Guide to Plato's 'Republic'*. Oxford: Wiley-Blackwell, pp. 44–62.

Bauman, Z. (1989) *Modernity and the Holocaust*. Cambridge: Polity.

BBC News (2013) 'Dozens of African migrants die as boat sinks near Italy', 3 October. https://www.bbc.co.uk/newsround/24385117.

Beaumont, P. (2023) 'Israel launches major strikes on Gaza as violence flares up on Lebanon boundary', *Guardian*, 5 November.

Beck, U. (2009) 'Critical theory of world risk society', *Constellations*, 16(1), pp. 3–22.

BEIS/Defra (2022) *UK Climate Change Risk Assessment 2022: Technical Report*. London: HM Government. https://www.gov.uk/government/publications/uk-climate-change-risk-assessment-2022.

Benhabib, S. (2004) *The Rights of Others: Aliens, Residents, and Citizens*. Cambridge: Cambridge University Press.

Benhabib, S. (2009) 'Cosmopolitanism and democracy: Affinities and tensions', *The Hedgehog Review*, Fall 2009, pp. 30–40.

Benjamin, R. (2019) *Race after Technology*. Cambridge: Polity.

Benjamin, R. (2022) *Viral Justice: How We Grow the World*. Princeton: Princeton University Press.

Benjamin, W. (1968) *Illuminations*, trans. H. Zohn. New York: Harcourt Brace Jovanovich.

Bennani-Taylor, S. and Meer, N. (2024) 'Processing payments, enacting alterity: Financial technology in the everyday lives of asylum seekers', *Journal of Ethnic and Migration Studies*, 50(10), pp. 2384–2402.

Berardi, F. (2021) 'How an Italian mayor who turned his town into a haven for migrants wound up facing 13 years in jail', *Time*, 7 October. https://time.com/6104836/domenico-lucano-riace-mimmo-migrant-mayor/.

Berlant, L. (2011) *Cruel Optimism*. Durham: Duke University Press.

Berlin, I. (1969) *Four Essays on Liberty*. Oxford: Oxford University Press.

Berman, M. (1982) *All That Is Solid Melts Into Air: The Experience of Modernity*. New York: Simon and Schuster.

Berrang-Ford, L., Biesbroek, R., Ford, J. D., Lesnikowski, A. et al., (2019) 'Tracking global climate change adaptation among governments', *Nature Climate Change*, 9, pp. 440–449.

Bertram, C. (2004) *Rousseau and 'The Social Contract'*. London: Routledge.

Bhambra, G. K. (2014) *Connected Sociologies*. London: Bloomsbury.

Bhambra, G. K. and Holmwood, J. (2021) *Colonialism and Modern Social Theory*. Cambridge: Polity.

Bhattacharyya, G. (2015) *Crisis, Austerity, and Everyday Life: Living in a Time of Diminishing Expectations*. London: Palgrave Macmillan.

Bloom, A. (1991) 'Interpretive essay', in A. Bloom (ed.), *The Republic of Plato*, 2nd ed. New York: Basic Books, pp. 307–436.

Brewer, J. D. (1982) 'Racial politics and nationalism', *The British Journal of Sociology*, 33(3), pp. 369–392.

British Dental Association (2021) 'Child asylum seekers: Dental age check plan dropped, but key questions remain', *BDJ In Practice*, 34(6), 8 November. https://www.bda.org/media-centre/child-asylum-seekers-dental-age-check-plan-dropped-but-key-questions-remain/.

Brodine, V. (1972) 'Point of damage', *Environment*, 14, pp. 2–14.

Brook, R. and King, K. (2017) *Updated Analysis of Air Pollution Exposure in London*. Oxford: Oxford Centre for Innovation. https://www.london.gov.uk/sites/default/files/aether_updated_london_air_pollution_exposure_final_20-2-17.pdf.

Brooks, L. (2021) '"A special day": How a Glasgow community halted immigration raid', *Guardian*, 14 May.

Brown, W. (2001) *Politics Out of History*. Princeton: Princeton University Press.

Buchanan, A. (2004) *Justice, Legitimacy, and Self-Determination: Moral Foundations for International Law*. Oxford: Oxford University Press.

Buenting, J. M. (2010) 'Revisiting Thrasymachus' challenge: Another Socratic failure', *Aporia*, 14(2).

Bulman, M. (2020) '"Untenable": Child asylum seekers being held for days without access to beds or showers, watchdog warns', *Independent*, 19 October.

Burbidge, M., Smith Larsen, T., Feder, S. and Yan, S. (2022) 'Don't blame it on the sunshine! An exploration of the spatial distribution of heat injustice across districts in Antwerp, Belgium', *Local Environment*, 27(2), pp. 160–176.

Burke, R. (2006) *Decolonization and the Evolution of International Human Rights*. Philadelphia: University of Pennsylvania Press.

Burton, A. (1997) 'Who needs the nation? Interrogating "British" history', *Journal of Historical Sociology*, 10(3), pp. 227–248.

Butler, J. (2004) *Precarious Life: The Powers of Mourning and Violence*. London: Verso.

Butler, J. (2009) *Frames of War: When Is Life Grievable?* London: Verso.

Butler, J. (2011) 'Precarious life and the obligations of cohabitation'. Neale Wheeler Watson Lecture, Nobel Museum, Stockholm, May. https://www.terada.ca/discourse/wp-content/uploads/2012/06/Butler_Sweden2011.pdf.

Campaign Against Arms Trade (2025) 'Israel', 8 September. https://caat.org.uk/data/countries/israel/.

CaCHE (2024) *The Heat Is On: The Growing Problem of Overheating in Domestic Homes in England and the Need for a National Strategy*. Collaborative Centre for Housing Evidence. https://housingevidence.ac.uk/wp-content/uploads/2024/03/policy-brief-overheating-final.pdf.

Cantwell-Smith, W. (1996) *The Meaning and End of Religion*. Minneapolis: Fortress Press.

Care4Calais (2024) 'Government Inspector's damning report on Weathersfield', 9 February. https://Care4calais.org/Wethersfield-report/.

Carpenter, D. (2015) *Magna Carta*. London: Penguin.

Carrington, B. (2023) '"Remember me": Ella's law would be fitting legacy after London air pollution death, says mother', *Guardian*, 10 February.

CCC (2023) *Progress in Adapting to Climate Change: 2023 Report to Parliament*. London: HMSO.

Césaire, A. (2000 [1955]) *Discourse on Colonialism*, trans. J. Pinkham. New York: Monthly Review Press.

Chancel, L., Piketty, T., Saez, E. and Zucman, G. (2023) *Climate Inequality Report 2023: Fair Taxes for a Sustainable Future*. Paris: World Inequality Lab. https://wid.world/document/climate-inequality-report-2023.

Chaloner, J., Baggaley, R. F., Ryan, B., Nellums, L. B. and Pareek, M. (2022) 'Deter or dispose? A critique of the relocation of asylum applicants to Rwanda and its public health implications', *The Lancet Regional Health – Europe*, 18(100442).

Chauvin, S. and Garcés-Mascareñas, B. (2014) 'Becoming less illegal: Deservingness frames and undocumented migrant incorporation', *Sociology Compass*, 8(4), pp. 422–432.

Chemerinsky, E. (2014) *The Case Against the Supreme Court*. New York: Viking.

Chomsky, N. and Pappé, I. (2013) *Gaza in Crisis: Reflections on the US–Israeli War Against the Palestinians*, 2nd ed. Chicago: Haymarket Books.

Choo, A. L.-T. (2015) *Evidence*, 4th ed. Oxford: Oxford University Press.

Chowienczyk, P. et al. (2020) 'Inequalities in urban heat exposure: A spatial analysis for English cities', *Urban Climate*, 34(100702), p. 527.

Christman, J. (2022) 'Rousseau's silence on trans-Atlantic slavery: philosophical implications', *European Journal of Philosophy*, 30(4), pp. 1458–1472.

Cicchetti, D. and Rogosch, F. (1996). 'Equifinality and multifinality in developmental psychopathology', *Development and Psychopathology*, 8(4), pp. 597–600.

City of Sanctuary UK (n.d.) *About City of Sanctuary UK.* https://cityofsanctuary.org/.

CJEU (2022) Joined Cases C-368/20 and C-369/20, *NW v Landespolizeidirektion Steiermark*, Court of Justice of the European Union, Judgment of 26 April 2022. https://eur-lex.europa.eu/legal-content/EN/TXT/?uri=celex:62020CJ0368.

Clugston, H. and Walawalkar, A. (2024) 'Seven asylum seeker suicides recorded in Home Office housing in less than four months', *Liberty Investigates*, 27 June.

Cohen, J. (2010) *Philosophy, Politics, Democracy: Selected Essays.* Cambridge, MA: Harvard University Press.

Cohen, S. (2001) *States of Denial: Knowing About Atrocities and Suffering.* Cambridge: Polity.

Cole, R., Ferguson, L., Heaviside, C. et al., (2024) 'Systemic inequalities in heat risk for Greater London', *Environment International*, 190(10892).

Collier, B. (2019). 'Black absence in green spaces', *The Ecologist*, 10 October.

Collins, P. H. (2000) *Black Feminist Thought: Knowledge, Consciousness, and the Politics of Empowerment*, 2nd ed. New York: Routledge.

Committee on Home Affairs (2018) *Oral Evidence: Windrush Children*, HC 990, 25 April. London: House of Commons.

Couldry, N. and Mejias, U. A. (2019) *The Costs of Connection.* Stanford: Stanford University Press.

Council of Europe (2017) *Recommendation on Recognition of Qualifications Held by Refugees, Displaced Persons and Persons in a Refugee-Like Situation.* Strasbourg: CoE.

Council of the EU (2024) 'Schengen area: Council adopts update of Schengen Borders Code', Press release, 24 May. https://www.consilium.europa.eu/en/press/press-releases/2024/05/24/schengen-area-council-adopts-update-of-schengen-borders-code/.

Council of the EU (2025) 'EU member states agree to extend temporary protection for refugees from Ukraine', Press release, 13 June. https://www.consilium.europa.eu/en/press/press-releases/2025/06/13/eu-member-states-agree-to-extend-temporary-protection-for-refugees-from-ukraine/.

Courts and Tribunals Judiciary (2021) *Regulation 28: Report to Prevent Future Deaths – Ella Kissi-Debrah* (Ref. 2021-0113), 20 April. https://www.judiciary.uk/wp-content/uploads/2021/04/Ella-Kissi-Debrah-2021-0113-1.pdf.

Craig-Norton, J. (2019) *The Kindertransport: Contesting Memory*. Bloomington: Indiana University Press.

Curran, W. and Hamilton, T. (eds.) (2017) *Just Green Enough: Urban Development and Environmental Gentrification*. London: Routledge.

DA and Ors v. The Secretary of State for the Home Department (2020) EWHC 3080 (Admin) – High Court (Queen's Bench Div.), 13 November.

Dagger, R. (1981) 'Understanding the general will', *Western Political Quarterly*, 34(3), pp. 359–371.

Dannenbaum, T. (2018) *The Crime of Aggression, Humanity, and the Soldier*. Oxford: Oxford University Press.

David, A. Y. (1981) *Women, Race and Class*. New York: Random House.

Davis, A. Y. (2003) *Are Prisons Obsolete?* New York: Seven Stories Press.

de Bellis, M. (2023) 'Ten years since the Lampedusa shipwreck, what lessons have been learned?', *Amnesty International*, 3 October. https://www.amnesty.org/en/latest/news/2023/10/ten-years-since-the-lampedusa-shipwreck-what-lessons-have-been-learned/.

de Noronha, L. (2020) *Deporting Black Britons: Portraits of Deportation to Jamaica*. Manchester: Manchester University Press.

de Waal, A. (2025) 'How to measure famine', *London Review of Books*, 47(2), 6 February.

Debre, I. (2023) 'Fights in bread lines, despair in shelters: War threatens to unravel Gaza's close-knit society', AP News, 10 November. https://apnews.com/article/israel-hamas-war-palestinians-gaza-water-food-f225bf0723bb5b3ae1961ba6cdef1917.

Declaration of the Rights of Man and of the Citizen (1789) https://www.elysee.fr/en/french-presidency/the-declaration-of-the-rights-of-man-and-of-the-citizen.

Dehm, J. (2020) 'Carbon colonialism? The Paris Agreement, "fair shares" and decolonizing climate law', Legal Studies Research Paper No. 20/32, La Trobe Law School.

Denevan, W. M. (1983) 'Adaptation, variation and cultural geography', *The Professional Geographer*, 35(4), pp. 399–406.

Dennis, I. H. (2017) *The Law of Evidence*, 6th ed. London: Sweet & Maxwell.

Dobson, J., Malamud, J. and Whyatt, D. (2019). *Ethnic Inequalities in Access to Green Space: An Analysis for the UK.* Runnymede Trust.

Doctors of the World (2019) *Registration Refused: Patient Registration in General Practice.* London: DOTW UK.

Dodman, D., Hayward, B., Pelling, M., Castán Broto, V. et al. (2022) 'Cities, settlements and key infrastructure', in IPCC, *Climate Change 2022: Impacts, Adaptation and Vulnerability. Contribution of Working Group II to the Sixth Assessment Report of the Intergovernmental Panel on Climate Change.* Cambridge: Cambridge University Press, pp. 907–1040. https://www.ipcc.ch/report/ar6/wg2/downloads/report/IPCC_AR6_WGII_Chapter06.pdf.

Dorling, K. and Harris, M. (2023) *Ghettoised and Traumatised: The Experiences of Men Held in Quasi-Detention in Wethersfield.* London: Helen Bamber Foundation and Humans for Rights Network.

Dorling, K. and Harris, M. (2024) *At What Cost? The Ongoing Harm Caused to Men Seeking Asylum Held in Wethersfield.* London: Helen Bamber Foundation and Humans for Rights Network.

Dumbrava, C. (2022) 'Walls and fences at EU borders', EPRS Briefing, 13 October. https://www.europarl.europa.eu/thinktank/en/document/EPRS_BRI(2022)733692.

Dunlap, C. (2001) *Law and Military Interventions: Preserving Humanitarian Values in 21st Century Conflicts.* Washington, DC: Humanitarian Challenges in Military Intervention Conference.

Dunn, J. (1968) 'Justice and the interpretation of Locke's political theory', *Political Studies*, 16(1), pp. 68–87.

Durkheim, É. (1984 [1893]) *The Division of Labour in Society*, trans. W. D. Halls. Basingstoke: Macmillan.

Durkheim, É. (1992 [1950]) *Professional Ethics and Civic Morals*, trans. C. Brookfield. London: Routledge.

Edinburgh Evening Courant (1727) 'Run away on the 7th instant from Dr Gustavus Brown's Lodgings in Glasgow, a Negro Woman, named Ann ...', 13 February, p. 4. https://www.glasgowlife.org.uk/museums/glasgow-life-museums-blogs/legacies-of-slavery-and-empire/gustavus-brown-s-runaway-slave.

Edwards, J. (2023) 'A Gazan professor wrote a poem '"If I Must Die". He was killed in a bombing', *The Washington Post*, 14 December.

Ella Roberta Family Foundation (2023) *Ella's Life and her Legacy*. https://www.ellaroberta.org/about-ella.

Environment Agency (2021) *The State of the Environment: The Urban Environment*. Bristol: Environment Agency.

EPRS (2024) 'Fences at the EU's external borders', Think Tank, 15 March. https://epthinktank.eu/2024/03/15/eu-migration-and-borders-key-facts-and-figures/fences-at-the-eus-external-borders/.

EPRS (2025) 'Addressing pushbacks at the EU's external borders', Briefing, June. European Parliament Research Service. https://www.europarl.europa.eu/RegData/etudes/BRIE/2025/772882/EPRS_BRI(2025)772882_EN.pdf.

Eurocities (2025) 'Stronger cities, fairer Europe', Eurocities Annual Conference, 4–6 June.

European Commission (2023) 'The European Union and Tunisia: political agreement on a comprehensive partnership package', 16 July. https://enlargement.ec.europa.eu/news/european-union-and-tunisia-political-agreement-comprehensive-partnership-package-2023-07-16_en.

European Commission (2024a) 'Commission takes stock of key achievements on migration and asylum', Press release, 12 March. https://ec.europa.eu/commission/presscorner/detail/en/ip_24_1413.

European Commission (2024b) 'The EU continues to implement the Memorandum of Understanding with Tunisia with the disbursement of EUR 150 million in financial support', Press release, 4 March. https://ec.europa.eu/commission/presscorner/detail/en/ip_24_1301.

European Commission (2024c) 'Joint Declaration on the Strategic and Comprehensive Partnership between the Arab Republic of Egypt and the European Union', 17 March. https://enlargement.ec.europa.eu/news/joint-declaration-strategic-and-comprehensive-partnership-between-arab-Republic-egypt-and-european-2024-03-17_en.

European Parliament (n.d.) 'EU–Turkey Statement & Action Plan'. https://www.europarl.europa.eu/legislative-train/carriage/eu-turkey-statement-action-plan/report?sid=10001.

European Parliament and Council (2024a) Regulation (EU) 2024/1348 establishing a common procedure for international protection (Asylum Procedures Regulation). *Official Journal of the European Union*, 22 May. https://eur-lex.europa.eu/eli/reg/2024/1348/oj/eng.

European Parliament and Council (2024b) Regulation (EU) 2024/1349 establishing a return border procedure. *Official Journal of the European Union*, 22 May. https://eur-lex.europa.eu/eli/reg/2024/1349/oj/eng.

European Parliament and Council (2024c) Regulation (EU) 2024/1356 introducing the screening of third-country nationals at the external borders (Screening Regulation). *Official Journal of the European Union*, 22 May. https://eur-lex.europa.eu/eli/reg/2024/1356/oj/eng.

European Parliament and Council (2024d) Regulation (EU) 2024/1358 on the establishment of 'Eurodac' (recast). *Official Journal of the European Union*, 22 May. https://eur-lex.europa.eu/eli/reg/2024/1358/oj/eng.

European Parliament and Council (2024e) Regulation (EU) 2024/1359 addressing situations of crisis and force majeure in the field of migration and asylum. *Official Journal of the European Union*, 22 May. https://eur-lex.europa.eu/eli/reg/2024/1359/oj/eng.

European Union Agency for Fundamental Rights (2024) *Guidance on Investigating Alleged Ill-Treatment at Borders*. Luxembourg:

Publications Office of the European Union. https://fra.europa.eu/en/publication/2024/guidance-investigating-alleged-ill-treatment-borders.

Farris, S. R. (2017) *In the Name of Women's Rights: The Rise of Feminationalism*. Durham: Duke University Press.

Fecht, D., Fischer, P., Fortunato, L., Hoek, G., et al. (2015) 'Associations between air pollution and socioeconomic characteristics, ethnicity and age profile of neighbourhoods in England and the Netherlands', *Environmental Pollution*, 198, pp. 201–210.

Federman, J., Mroue, B. and Keath, L. (2023) 'Israel resists US pressure to pause war to allow more aid to Gaza, wants hostages back first', AP News, 4 November. https://apnews.com/article/israel-hamas-war-gaza-news-11-3-2023-94d5d0b58bc10a14be6ac191060e47e1.

Ferrari, G. R. F. (ed.) (2007) *The Cambridge Companion to Plato's 'Republic'*. Cambridge: Cambridge University Press.

Foster, S. (2021). *Rurality and Race: The Experiences of Black, Asian and Minority Ethnic People in the English Countryside*. London: Race Equality Foundation.

Foti, L. (2017) 'A global village', *OSCE Magazine*, 10 August.

Foucault, M. (1980) *Power/Knowledge: Selected Interviews and Other Writings 1972–1977*, ed. C. Gordon. Brighton: Harvester.

Fraser, A. and Gillon, C. (2023) 'Storytelling and policy change: The case of air pollution in London', *Environmental Politics*, 32(1), pp. 154–174.

Fraser, N. (1990) 'Rethinking the public sphere: A contribution to the critique of actually existing democracy', *Social Text*, 25/26, pp. 56–80.

Fraser, N. (2001) 'Recognition without ethics?', *Theory, Culture & Society*, 18(2–3), pp. 21–42.

Fraser, N. (2008) *Scales of Justice: Reimagining Political Space in a Globalizing World*. Cambridge: Polity.

Fraser, N. (2013) *Fortunes of Feminism: From State-Managed Capitalism to Neoliberal Crisis*. London: Verso.

Fraser, N. and Honneth, A. (2003) *Redistribution or Recognition? A Political-Philosophical Exchange*. London: Verso.

Freedman, R. (2022) *The United Nations Human Rights Council: A Critique*. Abingdon: Routledge.

Freeman, S. (2007) *Justice and the Social Contract: Essays on Rawlsian Political Philosophy*. Oxford: Oxford University Press.

Freeman, S. (2007) *Rawls*. London: Routledge.

Garling, S. (2013) *Wittgenstein and the Social Sciences*. Cambridge, MA: Academic Press.

Gauderman, W. J. et al., (2005) 'The effect of air pollution on lung development from 10 to 18 years of age', *New England Journal of Medicine*, 351(11), pp. 1057–1067.

Gazette of India (2019) *The Citizenship (Amendment) Act, 2019 (No. 47 of 2019)*. New Delhi: Ministry of Law and Justice (Legislative Department). https://indiancitizenshiponline.nic.in/Documents/UserGuide/E-gazette_2019_20122019.pdf.

Gellner, E. (2008) *Nations and Nationalism*, 2nd ed. Oxford: Blackwell.

Gentleman, A. (2019) *The Windrush Betrayal: Exposing the Hostile Environment*. London: Guardian Faber Publishing.

Geronimus, A. T., Hicken, M. T., Keene, D. and Bound, J. (2020) '"Weathering" and age patterns of allostatic load scores among Black and White Americans', *American Journal of Public Health*, 110(5), p. 5.

Getachew, A. (2019) *Worldmaking after Empire*. Princeton: Princeton University Press.

Giddens, A. (1993) *New Rules of Sociological Method*, 2nd ed. Cambridge: Polity.

Gilliland, F. D., Berhane, K., Rappaport, E. B., Thomas, D. C., Avol, E., Gauderman, W. J. and Peters, J. M. (2001). The effects of ambient air pollution on school absenteeism due to respiratory illnesses. *Epidemiology*, 12(1), pp. 3–54.

Gilroy, P. (1990) 'Nationalism, history and ethnic absolutism', *History Workshop Journal*, 30 (1), pp. 114–120.

Giuffrida, A. (2018) 'In Italy's "hospitality town", migrants fight to save mayor who gave them a new home', *Guardian*, 7 October.

GLIMER Project (2025) *Governance and the Local Integration of Migrants and Europe's Refugees*. www.glimer.eu.

Goldberg, D. T. (2021) *Dread: Facing Futureless Futures*. Cambridge: Polity.

Government of India (2024) *The Citizenship (Amendment) Rules, 2024*. New Delhi: Ministry of Home Affairs. https://sansad.in/getFile/BillsTexts/RSBillTexts/Asintroduced/16-Citizenship-E731202483628PM.pdf?source=legislation.

Government of Pakistan, Asian Development Bank, European Union, United Nations & World Bank (2022) *Pakistan Floods 2022: Post-Disaster Needs Assessment*. Islamabad: Government of Pakistan. https://www.undp.org/sites/g/files/zskgke326/files/2022-12/Pakistan%20PDNA%20Supplemental%20Report%20-%20Final.pdf.

Graham-Harrison, E. and Abraham, Y. (2025) 'Revealed: Israeli military's own data indicates civilian death rate of 83% in Gaza war', *Guardian*, 21 August.

Gramsci, A. (1971) *Selections from the Prison Notebooks*, ed. and trans. Q. Hoare and G. N. Smith. London: Lawrence & Wishart.

Grierson, J. (2021) 'Asylum seekers plea for help as COVID sweeps Kent former army barracks', *Guardian*, 22 January.

Groundwork UK (2022) *Making Up Ground: The Role of Green Infrastructure in Urban Regeneration*. London: Groundwork UK.

Hall, S. (1980) 'Race, articulation and societies structured in dominance', in UNESCO (ed.), *Sociological Theories: Race and Colonialism*. Paris: UNESCO, pp. 305–345.

Hammarskjöld, D. (1953) Address at dinner in his honour given by the American Association for the United Nations in cooperation with the New York University Institute for Review of United Nations Affairs, New York, 14 September, UN Press Release SG/336. https://digitallibrary.un.org/record/3946542?v=pdf.

Hampton, J. (1986) *Hobbes and the Social Contract Tradition*. Cambridge: Cambridge University Press.

Haraway, D. J. (2016) *Staying with the Trouble: Making Kin in the Chthulucene*. Durham: Duke University Press.

Harris, R. (1988). *Language, Saussure and Wittgenstein: How to Play Games with Words*. London: Routledge.

Hartman, S. (2007) *Lose Your Mother: A Journey Along the Atlantic Slave Route*. New York: Farrar, Straus and Giroux.

Haycox, H., Meer, N., Finney, N., Rhodes, J., Hill, E. and Leahy, S. (2025) '"The green areas are out of our reach": Racialisation, erasure and resistance in UK urban greening initiatives', *Sociology*, 59(1), pp. 161–179.

HEI/IHME (2024) *State of Global Air Report 2024*. Boston, MA: Health Effects Institute & Institute for Health Metrics and Evaluation. https://www.stateofglobalair.org/resources/archived/state-global-air-report-2024.

Heller, C. and Pezzani, L. (2016) *Death by Rescue: The Lethal Effects of the EU's Policies of Non-assistance at Sea*. Forensic Oceanography. Goldsmiths, University of London. https://content.forensic-architecture.org/wp-content/uploads/2023/04/2016_Report_Death-By-Rescue.pdf.

Henckaerts, J. M. and Doswald-Beck, L. (2005) *Customary International Humanitarian Law. Volume 1: Rules*. Cambridge: Cambridge University Press.

Higgins, R. W. (1993). Race and environmental equity: An overview of the environmental justice issue in the policy process. *Polity*, 26(2), pp. 281–300.

High Court of Australia (1992) *Mabo v. Queensland (No 2)* (1992) 175 CLR 1.

Hill, E., Meer, N. and Peace, T. (2021) 'The role of asylum in processes of urban regeneration', *The Sociological Review*, 69 (2), pp. 259–276.

Historic Environment Scotland (2018) 'Edinburgh's part in the slave trade', *HES Blog*, 15 November. https://blog.historicenvironment.scot/2018/11/edinburghs-part-slave-trade/.

HMIP (2021) *Detention of Migrants at Dover and Folkestone (Tug Haven, Kent Intake Unit and Frontier House): Report on an Unannounced Inspection, 8 October and 1–3 November 2021*. London: Her Majesty's Inspectorate of Prisons.

Hobbes, T. (1996 [1651]) *Leviathan*, ed. J. C. A. Gaskin. Oxford: Oxford University Press.

Hobsbawm, E. (1968) *Industry and Empire*. London: Weidenfeld & Nicolson.

Hochschild, A. (2005) *Bury the Chains*. London: Pan.

Home Office (2023) 'Safe and legal routes' (updated 20 July 2023). London: Home Office. https://www.gov.uk/government/publications/illegal-migration-bill-factsheets/safe-and-legal-routes.

Home Office (2024) *Permission to Work and Volunteering for Asylum Seekers* (updated 22 October). London: UK Government. https://www.gov.uk/government/publications/handling-applications-for-permission-to-take-employment-instruction/permission-to-work-and-volunteering-for-asylum-seekers-accessible.

Home Office (2025) *Inadmissibility: Safe Third Country Cases* (updated 27 June). London: UK Government. https://www.gov.uk/government/publications/inadmissibility-third-country-cases/inadmissibility-safe-third-country-cases-accessible.

Hopgood, S. (2013) *The Endtimes of Human Rights*. Ithaca: Cornell University Press.

House of Commons Library (2023a) 'Accommodation of asylum-seeking children in hotels', 31 May. Research Briefing. https://commonslibrary.parliament.uk/research-briefings/cdp-2023-0114/.

House of Commons Library (2023b) 'Asylum accommodation: Hotels, vessels and large-scale sites', 7 July. Research Briefing. London: UK Parliament. https://commonslibrary.parliament.uk/research-briefings/cbp-9831/.

House of Commons Library (2024) 'Asylum seekers: The permission to work policy', 26 July. Research Briefing. London: UK Parliament. https://commonslibrary.parliament.uk/research-briefings/sn01908/.

Houston, D. and Vasudevan, P. (2018) 'Storytelling environmental justice: Cultural studies approaches', in R. Holifield, J. Chakraborty and G. Walker (eds.), *The Routledge Handbook of Environmental Justice*. London: Taylor and Francis, pp. 241–251.

Humanitarian Outcomes (2022) *Floods in Pakistan: Rethinking the*

Humanitarian Role. London: Humanitarian Outcomes. https://humanitarianoutcomes.org/sites/default/files/publications/pakistan_floods_1122.pdf.

Iacovino, R. and Erk, J. (2012) 'The constitutional foundations of multinational federalism: Canada and Belgium', in M. Seymour and A.-G. Gagnon (eds.), *Multinational Federalism*. London: Palgrave Macmillan, pp. 205–230.

ICC (1998) *Rome Statute of the International Criminal Court*. The Hague: International Criminal Court. https://www.icc-cpi.int/sites/default/files/RS-Eng.pdf.

ICIBI (2022) *An Inspection of the Initial Processing of Migrants Arriving via Small Boats at Tug Haven and Western Jet Foil (December 2021–January 2022)*. London: Independent Chief Inspector of Borders and Immigration.

ICORN (2025) 'About ICORN'. https://icorn.org/.

IDMC (2023) *Global Report on Internal Displacement 2023*. Geneva: Internal Displacement Monitoring Centre. https://www.internal-displacement.org/global-report/grid2023/.

IDMC (2025) *Global Report on Internal Displacement 2025*. Geneva: Internal Displacement Monitoring Centre. https://www.internal-displacement.org/global-report/grid2025/.

IMF (2024) *World Economic Outlook Database*. Washington, DC: International Monetary Fund. https://www.imf.org/en/Publications/WEO.

IOI (2024) 'European Ombudsman criticises Commission failure to inform public how it assessed human rights risks in EU–Tunisia agreement', International Ombudsman Institute, 24 October. https://www.theioi.org/ioi-news/current-news/european-ombudsman-criticises-commission-failure-to-inform-public-how-it-assessed-human-rights-risks-in-eu-tunisia-agreement.

IOM (2024) *A Decade of Documenting Migrant Deaths: Data Analysis and Reflection on Deaths During Migration Documented by IOM's Missing Migrants Project, 2014–2023*. Geneva: International Organization for Migration Global Data Institute.

IOM (2025a) '2024 is deadliest year on record for migrants, new IOM data reveals', 21 March. https://www.iom.int/news/2024-deadliest-year-record-migrants-new-iom-data-reveals.

IOM (2025b) *Missing Migrants Project: Central Mediterranean Overview*. Geneva: International Organization for Migration.

IOM (n.d.) *Methodology | Missing Migrants Project*. https://missingmigrants.iom.int/methodology.

IPCC (2022a) *Climate Change 2022: Impacts, Adaptation and Vulnerability*. Cambridge: Cambridge University Press.

IPCC (2022b) 'Summary for policymakers', in *Climate Change 2022: Mitigation of Climate Change*. Cambridge: Cambridge University Press.

IPCC (2023) *Climate Change 2023: Synthesis Report*. Cambridge: Cambridge University Press.

Iqbal, B. K. and Asad, T. (2017) 'Thinking about method: A conversation with Talal Asad', *Qui Parle*, 26(1), pp. 195–218.

ITU (2024) *Measuring Digital Development: Facts and Figures 2024*. Geneva: International Telecommunication Union.

Jackson, Z. I. (2020) *Becoming Human: Matter and Meaning in an Antiblack World*. New York: NYU Press.

Jefferson, T (1904–5) *The Works, vol. 12 (Correspondence and Papers 1816–1826)*, ed. P. L. Ford. New York: Putnam's Sons.

Jerrett, M., Burnett, R. T., Kanaroglou, P., Eyles, J., Finkelstein, et al. (2001). 'A GIS-environmental justice analysis of particulate air pollution in Hamilton', Canada. *Environment and Planning A*, 33(6), pp. 955–973.

Jerrett, M., Buzzelli, M., Burnett, R. T. and DeLuca, P. F. (2004). 'Particulate air pollution, social confounders, and mortality in small areas of an industrial city', *Social Science & Medicine*, 58(3), pp. 517–529.

Jones, M. (1969 [1925]) *Autobiography of Mother Jones*, repr. New York: Arno Press.

Jones, M. D., McBeth, M. K. and Shanahan, E. A. (2014) 'Introducing the narrative policy framework', in M. D. Jones et al. (eds.), *The Science of Stories*. New York: Palgrave Macmillan, pp. 1–25.

Just World Books (2015) *Gaza Unsilenced*. Northampton, MA: Just World Books.

Just World Books (2024) *Gaza Writes Back, Memorial Edition.* Northampton, MA: Just World Books.

Just World Books (n.d.) 'About Refaat Alareer'. https://www.justworldbooks.com/authors/refaat-alareer/.

Kaviraj, S. (1993) 'The imaginary institution of India', in P. Chatterjee and G. Pandey (eds.), *Subaltern Studies VII: Writings on South Asian History and Society*. Delhi: Oxford University Press, pp. 1–39.

Kay, A. and Baker, P. (2015). 'What can causal process tracing offer to policy studies? A review of the literature', *Policy Studies Journal,* 43(1), pp. 1–21.

Keck, M. E. and Sikkink, K. (1998) *Activists Beyond Borders.* Ithaca: Cornell University Press.

Kellogg, W. W. (1987). 'Mankind's impact on climate: The evolution of an awareness', *Climatic Change*, 10, pp. 113–136.

Kelly, P. M. and Adger, W. N. (2000) 'Theory and practice in assessing vulnerability to climate change and facilitating adaptation', *Climatic Change*, 47, pp. 325–352.

Khawaja, B. (2025) 'The EU has simply abandoned human rights in Tunisia', Human Rights Watch, 12 May. https://www.hrw.org/news/2025/05/12/eu-has-simply-abandoned-human-rights-tunisia.

Knox, J. H. (2020) 'Constructing the human right to a healthy environment', *Annual Review of Law and Social Science*, 16, pp. 79–95.

Kothen, A. and Blais, K. (2013) *A City Says Yes! Reflections on the experiences of the Save Me campaign to promote refugee resettlement in Germany*. Brussels: ICMC Europe.

Kubin, E., Puryear, C., Schein, C. and Gray, K. (2021). 'Personal experiences bridge moral and political divides better than facts', *Proceedings of the National Academy of Sciences*, 118(6), e2008389118.

Kühn, M. (2021). 'COP 26: The climate conference that failed the South', Blog, 18 November. Welthungerhilfe.

LaCapra, D. (2001) *Writing History, Writing Trauma.* Baltimore: Johns Hopkins University Press.

La Repubblica (2013) 'La ragazza annegata mentre partoriva: L'ultimo orrore del barcone affondato', *La Repubblica*, 10 October.

Le Guin, U. K. (1975) 'The ones who walk away from Omelas', in *The Wind's Twelve Quarters*. New York: Harper & Row, pp. 275–284.

Lee, P. (2022) 'Why are air pollution levels in London so high?', *Impact on Urban Health*, 25 March. https://urbanhealth.org.uk/insights/data/why-is-air-pollution-so-high-in-london.

Lefebvre, H. (1996) *Writings on Cities*, trans. E. Kofman and E. Lebas. Oxford: Blackwell.

Lloyd, S. A. (2009) *Morality in the Philosophy of Thomas Hobbes: Cases in the Law of Nature*. Cambridge: Cambridge University Press.

Locke, J. (1988 [1689]) *Two Treatises of Government*, ed. P. Laslett. Cambridge: Cambridge University Press.

London, L. (2000) *Whitehall and the Jews, 1933–1948: British Immigration Policy, Jewish Refugees and the Holocaust*. Cambridge: Cambridge University Press.

Lukowski, J. (1994) 'Recasting Utopia: Montesquieu, Rousseau and the Polish Constitution of 3 May 1791', *The Historical Journal*, 37(1), pp. 65–87.

Macey, D. (2000) *The Penguin Dictionary of Critical Theory*. London: Penguin Books.

Madhok, S. (2024) 'Anti-imperial epistemic justice and re-making rights and justice 'after rights'', *The International Journal of Human Rights*, 28(8–9), pp. 1478–1500.

Marshall, C. (2020) 'Rosamund Adoo-Kissi-Debrah: Did air pollution kill my daughter?', BBC News, 29 October.

Marshall, J. D. (2008) 'Environmental inequality: Air pollution exposures in California's South Coast Air Basin', *Atmospheric Environment*, 42(21), pp. 5499–5503.

Marshall, T. H. (1950) *Citizenship and Social Class*. Cambridge: Cambridge University Press.

Marx, K. (1990 [1867]) *Capital: Critique of Political Economy, vol. 1*. London: Penguin.

Marx, K. (2014 [1875]) *Critique of the Gotha Programme*. Eastford: Martino Fine Books.

Maxmen, A. (2021). 'Famine in Tigray is world's worst crisis in a decade, says top official', *Nature*, 600(7890), pp. 575–576.

Mbembe, A. (2003) 'Necropolitics', *Public Culture*, 15(1), pp. 11–40.

McBeth, M. K., Jones, M. D. and Shanahan, E. A. (2014). 'The narrative policy framework', in P. A. Sabatier and C. M. Weible (eds.), *Theories of the Policy Process,* 3rd ed. Boulder: Westview Press, pp. 225–266.

McCarthy, T. (2004) 'Coming to terms with our past, Part II: On the morality and politics of reparations for slavery', *Political Theory*, 32(6), pp. 750–772.

McConnell, R., Berhane, K., Gilliland, F., London, S. J., Islam, T. et al. (2002). 'Asthma in exercising children exposed to ozone: a cohort study', *The Lancet*, 359(9304), pp. 386–391.

McLeod, A. M. (2015) 'Prison abolition and grounded justice', *UCLA Law Review*, 62, pp. 1156–1239.

Meer, N. (2018a) 'Race equality after Enoch Powell', *The Political Quarterly*, 89(3), pp. 417–433.

Meer, N. (2018b) 'Race and postcolonialism: Should one come before the other?', *Ethnic and Racial Studies*, 46(1), pp. 1163–1181.

Meer, N. (2022a) *The Cruel Optimism of Racial Justice.* Bristol: Bristol University Press.

Meer, N. (2022b) 'Who still needs the nation?', *The British Journal of Sociology*, 73(1), pp. 50–59.

Meer, N., Dimaio, C., Hill, E., Angeli, A., Oberg, K. and Emilsson, H. (2021) 'Governing displaced migration in Europe: Housing and the role of the "local"', *Comparative Migration Studies*, 9(2). https://link.springer.com/article/10.1186/s40878-020-00209-x.

Meer, N., Hill, E., Peace, T. and Villegas, L. (2021) 'Rethinking refuge in the time of COVID-19', *Ethnic and Racial Studies*, 44(5), pp. 864–876.

Melzer, N. (2008) *Targeted Killing in International Law*. Oxford: Oxford University Press.

Met Office (2022) 'A milestone in UK climate history', Met Office Press Office, 22 July. https://www.metoffice.gov.uk/about-us/news

-and-media/media-centre/weather-and-climate-news/2022/july-heat-review.

Mignolo, W. D. (2005) *The Idea of Latin America*. Oxford: Blackwell.

Mignolo, W. D. (2011) *The Darker Side of Western Modernity: Global Futures, Decolonial Options*. Durham: Duke University Press.

Mignolo, W. D. and Walsh, C. E. (2018) *On Decoloniality: Concepts, Analytics, Praxis*. Durham: Duke University Press.

Migration Observatory (2025a) 'Asylum and refugee resettlement in the UK', Briefing, 1 August. University of Oxford. https://migrationobservatory.ox.ac.uk/resources/briefings/migration-to-the-uk-asylum/.

Migration Observatory (2025b) 'The UK's asylum backlog', Briefing, 28 April. University of Oxford. https://migrationobservatory.ox.ac.uk/resources/briefings/the-uks-asylum-backlog/.

Miles, R. (1987. *Capitalism and Unfree Labour: Anomaly or Necessity?* London: Tavistock.

Milliken, D. (2021) 'Scottish police free men held by UK immigration force', 13 May. Reuters. https://www.reuters.com/world/uk/scottish-police-free-men-held-by-uk-immigration-force-2021-05-13/.

Mills, C. W. (1997) *The Racial Contract*. Ithaca: Cornell University Press.

Mills, C. W. (2007a) 'Contract of breach', in C. Pateman and C. Mills, *Contract and Domination*. Cambridge: Polity, pp. 106–133.

Mills, C. W. (2007b) 'The domination contract', in C. Pateman and C. Mills, *Contract and Domination*. Cambridge: Polity, pp. 79–105.

Mills, C. W. (2009) 'Rawls on race/race in Rawls?', *The Southern Journal of Philosophy*, 47(S1), pp. 161–184.

Mills, C. W. (2017) *Black Rights/White Wrongs: The Critique of Racial Liberalism*. Oxford: Oxford University Press.

Mills, C. Wright (2000 [1959]) *The Sociological Imagination.*, 40th anniv. ed. Oxford: Oxford University Press.

Modood. T. (2024) 'From then to now: Some friendly responses', in T. Sealy, V. Uberoi and N. Meer (eds.), *The Resilience of Multiculturalism, Essays in the Honour of Tariq Modood*. Edinburgh: Edinburgh University Press, pp. 272–298.

Mondon, A. and Winter, A. (2020) *Reactionary Democracy: How Racism and the Populist Far Right Became Mainstream*. London: Verso.

Mor, S., Aneja, R., Madan, S. and Ghimire, M. (2023). 'Kyoto protocol and Paris agreement: Transition from bindings to pledges – A review', *Millennial Asia*, 15(4). https://doi.org/10.1177/09763996221141546.

Morris, L., and Naz, F. (2021) *Net Zero City*. Independently Published.

Morsink, J. (1999) *The Universal Declaration of Human Rights: Origins, Drafting, and Intent*. Philadelphia: University of Pennsylvania Press.

Moses, A. D. (2002) 'Conceptual blockages and definitional dilemmas in the "racial century": Genocides of indigenous peoples and the Holocaust', *Journal of Genocide Research*, 36(4), pp. 7–36.

Moyn, S. (2010) *The Last Utopia: Human Rights in History*. Cambridge, MA: Harvard University Press.

Munro, A. (2025) 'General will', *Encyclopaedia Britannica*. https://www.britannica.com/topic/general-will.

Murakawa, N. and Gilmore, R. W. (2020) 'Covid 19, decarceration, and abolition', Department of African American Studies, Princeton University, 16 April. https://aas.princeton.edu/news/covid-19-decarceration-and-abolition.

Mutua, M. (2001) 'Savages, victims, and saviours: The metaphor of human rights', *Harvard International Law Journal*, 42(1), pp. 201–245.

NAO (2023) *The Asylum and Protection Transformation Programme*. London: National Audit Office.

NAO (2024a) *Investigation into Asylum Accommodation*. London: National Audit Office.

NAO (2024b) *Investigation into the Acquisition of the Northeye Site for Asylum Accommodation*. London: National Audit Office.

NAO (2025) *The Home Office's Asylum Accommodation Contracts*. London: National Audit Office.

National Toxicology Program (2019). *NTP Monograph on the Systematic Review of Traffic-Related Air Pollution and Hypertensive Disorders of Pregnancy*. National Institute of Environmental Health Sciences. NTP Monograph 07.

Ndlovu-Gatsheni, S. J. (2018) *Epistemic Freedom in Africa: Deprovincialization and Decolonization*. London: Routledge.

New York Times (2025) 'Read the Naval Academy's list of removed books', 4 April. https://www.nytimes.com/interactive/2025/04/04/us/250404-list-of-removed-books-from-nimitz-library.html.

Newman, S. P. (2018) 'Gustavus Brown's runaway slave', *Glasgow Life*, Legacies of Slavery and Empire blog, 14 August. https://www.glasgowlife.org.uk/museums/glasgow-life-museums-blogs/legacies-of-slavery-and-empire/gustavus-brown-s-runaway-slave.

Newman, S. P. (2023) 'Popularizing a database of resistance: Freedom seekers in eighteenth-century Britain', *Journal of Slavery and Data Preservation*, 4(5), pp. 18–29.

Nora, P. (1989) 'Between memory and history: Les lieux de mémoire', *Representations*, 26, pp. 7–24.

Nordstrom, C. (1998) *A Different Kind of War Story*. Philadelphia: University of Pennsylvania Press.

Nozick, R. (1974) *Anarchy, State, and Utopia*. New York: Basic Books.

Oakeshott, M. (1975) *Hobbes on Civil Association*. Oxford: Blackwell.

OCHA (2023) *Pakistan: 2022 Floods Response Plan*. Final Report, 15 December. Geneva: OCHA. https://reliefweb.int/attachments/a201e1d7-67ff-4d3c-9544-5762f4d62229/Pakistan%20Floods%20Response%20Plan%20Final%20Report%20October%202023.pdf.

OCHA (2024) 'Pakistan: Monsoon 2024 flash update #8', 9 September. https://reliefweb.int/report/pakistan/pakistan-monsoon-2024-flash-update-8-latest-monsoon-developments-and-response-efforts-09-september-2024.

OCHA (2025a) 'Humanitarian Situation Update #323 – Gaza Strip', 18 September. https://www.un.org/unispal/document/ocha-sitrep323-18sep25/.

OCHA (2025b) 'Reported impact snapshot – Gaza Strip', 17 September 2025. https://www.ochaopt.org/content/reported-impact-snapshot-gaza-strip-17-september-2025.

OCHA (2025c) 'Pakistan: Monsoon floods 2025 flash update #5', 2

September. https://reliefweb.int/report/pakistan/pakistan-monsoon-floods-2025-flash-update-5-02-september-2025.

Ó'Cinnéide, C. (2024) '"Cruel optimism": The limits of legal liability as a tool for engaging with structural injustice', in V. Mantouvalou and J. Wolff (eds.), *Structural Injustice and the Law*. London: UCL Press, pp. 32–58.

OHCHR (1949) *Geneva Convention Relative to the Protection of Civilian Persons in Time of War*. https://www.ohchr.org/en/instruments-mechanisms/instruments/geneva-convention-relative-protection-civilian-persons-time-war.

OHCHR (2022) 'UN Human Rights Office estimates more than 306,000 civilians were killed over 10 years in Syria', Press release, 28 June. https://www.ohchr.org/en/press-releases/2022/06/un-human-rights-office-estimates-more-306000-civilians-were-killed-over-10.

OHCHR (2024) *Update Report: Six-Month Update Report on the Human Rights Situation in Gaza*, 8 November. Geneva: OHCHR. https://www.ohchr.org/sites/default/files/documents/countries/opt/20241106-Gaza-Update-Report-OPT.pdf.

OHCHR (2025) 'Sudan crisis deepens amid rising civilian casualties and growing ethnic violence', Press release, 19 September. https://www.ohchr.org/en/press-releases/2025/09/sudan-crisis-deepens-amid-rising-civilian-casualties-growing-ethnic-violence.

OHCHR/HRMMU (2025) *Fact Sheet: Three Years since the Full-Scale Invasion of Ukraine*, 6 February. Kyiv: OHCHR/HRMMU.

O'Neil, C. (2016) *Weapons of Math Destruction: How Big Data Increases Inequality and Threatens Democracy*. New York: Crown.

ONS (2020) *One in Eight British Households Has No Garden*. 14 May. https://www.ons.gov.uk/economy/environmentalaccounts/articles/oneineightbritishhouseholdshasnogarden/2020-05-14.

ONS (2022a) *Ethnic Group, England and Wales: Census 2021*. https://www.ons.gov.uk/peoplepopulationandcommunity/culturalidentity/ethnicity/bulletins/ethnicgroupenglandandwales/census2021.

ONS (2022b) *Excess Mortality During Heat Periods: 1 June to 31 August 2022*. https://www.ons.gov.uk/peoplepopulationandcommunity

/birthsdeathsandmarriages/deaths/articles/excessmortalityduringheatperiods/englandandwales1juneto31august2022.

Open Syllabus (2025) *Open Syllabus Explorer / Galaxy*. https://galaxy.opensyllabus.org.

Organization of the Islamic Conference (1990) *Cairo Declaration on Human Rights in Islam*. UNHCR Refworld. refworld.org/legal/resolution/oic/1990/en/13797.

Orwell, G. (1949) *Nineteen Eighty-Four*. London: Secker and Warburg.

Owen, G. (2020). 'What makes climate change adaptation effective? A systematic review of the literature', *Global Environmental Change*, 62, 102071.

Oxfam (2020) *Confronting Carbon Inequality: Putting Climate Justice at the Heart of the COVID-19 Recovery*. Oxford: Oxfam. https://policy-practice.oxfam.org/resources/confronting-carbon-inequality-.

Oxfam (2023) *Climate Equality: A Planet for the 99%*. Oxford: Oxfam/SEI.

Pahuja, S. (2011) *Decolonizing International Law: Development, Economic Growth and the Politics of Universality*. Cambridge: Cambridge University Press.

Parekh, B. (2000). *Rethinking Multiculturalism*. London: Palgrave.

Pateman, C. (1983) 'Feminist critiques of the public/private dichotomy', in S. I. Benn and G. F. Gaus (eds.), *Public and Private in Social Life*. London: Croom Helm, pp. 281–303.

Pateman, C. (1985) *The Problem of Political Obligation: A Critique of Liberal Theory*, 2nd ed. Cambridge: Polity.

Pateman, C. (1988) *The Sexual Contract*. Cambridge: Polity.

Pateman, C. and Mills, C. W. (2007) *Contract and Domination*. Cambridge: Polity.

Paul, K. (1997) *Whitewashing Britain: Race and Citizenship in the Postwar Era*. Ithaca: Cornell University Press.

Pedersen, S. (2015) *The Guardians: The League of Nations and the Crisis of Empire*. Oxford: Oxford University Press.

Peers, S. (2024) 'Restoring the borderless Schengen Area: Mission impossible?' Swedish Institute for European Policy Studies. https://sieps.se/media/4ylfst2h/2024_12epa.pdf.

Pellow, D. N. and Brulle, R. J. (2005). *Power, Justice, and the Environment: A Critical Appraisal of the Environmental Justice Movement*. Cambridge, MA: MIT Press.

Perry, K. H. (2018) 'Undoing the work of the Windrush narrative', *History Workshop Online*, 22 April.

Pettit, P. (1997) *Republicanism: A Theory of Freedom and Government*. Oxford: Oxford University Press.

Phelan, J. and Link, B. G. (2015) 'Is racism a fundamental cause of inequalities in health?', *Annual Review of Sociology*, 41, pp. 311–330.

Phipps, A. (2019) 'Bearing witness: The burden of individual responsibility and the rule of law', in S. K. Kehoe, E. Alisic and J.-C. Heilinger (eds.). *Responsibility for Refugee and Migrant Integration*. Berlin: De Gruyter, pp. 9–24.

Pinho-Gomes, A. C., Roaf, E., Fuller, G., Fowler, D. et al. (2023) 'Air pollution and climate change', *The Lancet Planetary Health*, 7(9), pp. e727–e728.

Plato (1987) *The Republic*, 2nd rev. ed., trans. and with introduction by D. Lee. Harmondsworth: Penguin.

Plato (1989) *The Collected Dialogues of Plato: Including the Letters*, ed. E. Hamilton and H. Cairns. Princeton: Princeton University Press.

Polletta, F. (2006). *It Was Like a Fever: Storytelling in Protest and Politics*. Chicago: University of Chicago Press.

Porter, J. J., Dessai, S. and Tompkins, E. L. (2014). 'What do we know about UK household adaptation to climate change? A systematic review', *Climatic Change*, 127(3–4), pp. 371–379.

POST (2024) *Public Health Impacts of Heat (POSTnote 723)*. London: UK Parliament. https://post.parliament.uk/research-briefings/post-pn-0723/.

PRAB Network (2025) 'Reshaping Europe's space: Does the Schengen Border Code's Reform undermine people (on the move)'s fundamental rights?' Protect Rights At Borders, Policy Note IV. https://www.asgi.it/wp-content/uploads/2025/02/2025_SBC-Reform_ASGI_DRC.pdf.

Progressive International (2022) 'Italian pro-refugee mayor Mimmo

Lucano in his own words', 21 March. https://progressive.international/wire/2022-03-21-italian-pro-refugee-mayor-mimmo-lucano-in-his-own-words/en/.

Puar, J. K. (2017) *The Right to Maim: Debility, Capacity, Disability.* Durham: Duke University Press.

Pulido, L. (2017) 'Geographies of race and ethnicity II: Environmental racism, racial capitalism and state-sanctioned violence', *Progress in Human Geography*, 41(4), pp. 524–533.

Purcell, M. (2003) 'Citizenship and the right to the global city: Reimagining the capitalist world order', *International Journal of Urban and Regional Research*, 27(3), pp. 564–590.

Purcell, M. (2014) 'Possible worlds: Henri Lefebvre and the right to the city', *Journal of Urban Affairs*, 36(1), pp. 141–154.

Putnam, R. D. and Garrett, S. R. (2020) *The Upswing.* New York: Simon & Schuster.

Rappaport, E. D. (2000) *Shopping for Pleasure: Women in the Making of London's West End.* Princeton: Princeton University Press.

Ratzmann, N. (2021) 'Conceptualising the role of deservingness in migrants' access to social services', *Social Policy and Society*, 20(3), pp. 458–470.

Rawls, J. (1982) 'The basic liberties and their priority', *The Tanner Lectures on Human Values*, 3, pp. 1–87. https://tannerlectures.org/lectures/the-basic-liberties-and-their-priority/.

Rawls, J. (1993) *Political Liberalism.* New York: Columbia University Press.

Rawls, J. (1999 [1971]) *A Theory of Justice*, rev. ed. Cambridge, MA: Harvard University Press.

Rawls, J. (1999) *The Law of Peoples: With 'The Idea of Public Reason Revisited'*. Cambridge, MA: Harvard University Press.

Rawls, J. (2005) *Political Liberalism*, exp. ed. New York: Columbia University Press.

Razai, M. S., Kankam, H. K. N., Majeed, A., Esmail, A. and Williams, D. R. (2021). 'Mitigating ethnic disparities in covid-19 and beyond', *BMJ*, 372, n4921.

Reeve, C. D. C. (1988) *Philosopher-Kings: The Argument of Plato's 'Republic'.* Indianapolis: Hackett.

Refugee and Migrant Children's Consortium (2024) *Age Disputes: Briefing*. London: RMCC.

Refugee and Migrant Children's Consortium (2025) *Lost Childhoods: The Consequences of Flawed Age Assessments at the UK border*. London: RMCC.

Refugee Council (2024) 'Refugee Council response and top facts from the government's latest immigration statistics', 31 October. https://www.refugeecouncil.org.uk/press-office/media-centre/refugee-council-response-and-top-facts-from-the-governments-latest-immigration-statistics/.

Refugee Education UK (2025) *Higher Education FAQs: Asylum Seekers*. https://www.reuk.org/hefaq-asylumseeker.

Reuters (2024a) 'Baby saved from her dead mother's womb dies', 26 April. https://www.reuters.com/video/watch/idRW817026042024RP1/.

Reuters (2024b) 'Germany tightens controls at all borders in immigration crackdown', 10 September. https://www.reuters.com/world/europe/germany-put-temporary-controls-all-land-borders-source-says-2024-09-09/.

Reynolds, H. (1987) *The Law of the Land*. Ringwood: Penguin.

Richardson, E. A., Pearce, J., Mitchell, R. and Kingham, S. (2013). 'Role of physical activity in the relationship between urban green space and health', *Public Health*, 127(4), pp. 318–324.

Riley, P. (1986) *The General Will Before Rousseau: The Transformation of the Divine into the Civic*. Princeton: Princeton University Press.

Roberts, D. (1997) *Killing the Black Body: Race, Reproduction, and the Meaning of Liberty*. New York: Pantheon Books.

Romanello, M., Di Napoli, C. and Drummond, P. (2022). 'The 2022 report of the *Lancet* Countdown on health and climate change: Health at the mercy of fossil fuels', *The Lancet*, 400(10363), pp. 1619–1654.

Romanello, M., Di Napoli, C., Green, C. et al. (2023). 'The 2023 report of the *Lancet* Countdown on health and climate change: The imperative for a health-centred response in a world facing irreversible harms', *The Lancet*, 402(10419), pp. 2346–2394.

Rose, J. (2019) 'One long scream: Trauma and justice in South Africa', *London Review of Books*, 41(10), 23 May.

Rothberg, M. (2009) *Multidirectional Memory: Remembering the Holocaust in the Age of Decolonization*. Stanford: Stanford University Press.

Rousseau, J.-J. (1994 [1755]) *Discourse on the Origin of Inequality*, trans. M. Cranston. London: Penguin.

Rousseau, J.-J. (1994) *The Social Contract and Other Later Political Writings*, ed. and trans. V. Gourevitch. Cambridge: Cambridge University Press.

Rousseau, J.-J. (2010 [1762]) *The Social Contract*, trans. G. D. H. Cole. London: J. M. Dent.

Rubenstein, L. S. and Bittle, M. D. (2010) 'Responsibility for protection of medical workers and facilities in armed conflict', *The Lancet*, 375(9711), pp. 329–340.

Sampson, R. J. and Levy, B. L. (2022) 'The enduring neighborhood effect, everyday urban mobility, and violence in Chicago', *The University of Chicago Law Review*, 89(2), pp. 323–348.

Sandink, D. (2013). 'Reducing heat-wave risk through active and passive measures', *Municipal World*, 123(4), pp. 17–19.

Saussure, F. (2006 [1916]) *Course in General Linguistics*. Chicago: Open Court.

Sayers, P. B., Carr, S., Moss, C. and Didcock, A. (2020) *Flood Disadvantage: Socially Vulnerable and Ethnic Minorities*. London: Sayers and Partners. https://www.floodre.co.uk/wp-content/uploads/Sayers-Flood-disadvantage-Socially-vulnerable-and-ethnic-minorities.pdf.

Scarry, E. (2010) *Rule of Law, Misrule of Men*. Cambridge, MA: MIT Press.

Schlosberg, D., Collins, L. B. and Niemeyer, S. (2017) 'Adaptation policy and community discourse: risk, vulnerability, and just transformation', *Environmental Politics*, 26(3), pp. 413–437.

Scottish Government (2019) *Climate Ready Scotland: Second Scottish Climate Change Adaptation Programme 2019–2024*. Edinburgh: Scottish Government.

Seamster, L. and Ray, V. (2018) 'Against teleology in the study of race: Toward the abolition of the progress paradigm', *Sociological Theory*, 36(4), pp. 315–342.

Seeley, J. R. (1883) *The Expansion of England: Two Courses of Lectures*. London: Macmillan.

Sen, A. (1999) *Development as Freedom*. Oxford: Oxford University Press.

Sen, A. (2009) *The Idea of Justice*. London: Allen Lane.

Serhan, Y. (2023) 'The voice notes poet Refaat Alareer sent before his death', *TIME*, 14 December.

Shachar, A. (2011) 'Earned Citizenship: Property Lessons for Immigration Reform', *Yale Journal of Law & the Humanities*, 23, pp. 110–158.

Sharpe, C. (2016) *In the Wake: On Blackness and Being*. Durham: Duke University Press.

Shelton, D. (ed.) (2013) *The Oxford Handbook of International Human Rights Law*. Oxford: Oxford University Press.

Shilliam, R. (2018) *Race and the Undeserving Poor*. Newcastle upon Tyne: Agenda Publishing.

Shklar, J. N. (1969) *Men and Citizens: A Study of Rousseau's Social Theory*. Cambridge: Cambridge University Press.

Shklar, J. N. (1990) *The Faces of Injustice*. New Haven: Yale University Press.

Shurafa, W. and Kullab, S. (2023) 'Weary families trudge through Gaza streets, trying to flee the north before Israel's invasion', AP News, 15 October. https://apnews.com/article/israel-palestinians-gaza-hamas-war-evacuations-refugee-834a63b3ac48ce9230c649cddeafdf89.

Simmons, A. J. (1992) *The Lockean Theory of Rights*. Princeton: Princeton University Press.

Simpson, C. H., Brousse, O. and Heaviside, C. (2024) 'Estimated mortality attributable to the urban heat island during the record-breaking 2022 heatwave in London', *Environmental Research Letters*, 19(9), 094047.

Simpson, G. (2021) *The Sentimental Life of International Law: Literature, Language and Longing in World Politics*. Oxford: Oxford University Press.

Sinmaz, E. and Vinter, R. (2024) 'Rioters try to torch Rotherham asylum seeker hotel amid far-right violence', *Guardian*, 4 August.

Skinner, Q. (1996) *Reason and Rhetoric in the Philosophy of Hobbes.* Cambridge: Cambridge University Press.

Smith, K. (2010). 'Research, policy and funding', *The British Journal of Sociology*, 61(1), pp. 176–195.

Somerville, P. and Sprigings, N. (Eds.). (2005). *Housing and Social Policy Contemporary Themes and Critical Perspectives.* London: Routledge.

South Yorkshire Police (2024) 'Incidents of disorder in South Yorkshire', 4 August. https://www.southyorkshire.police.uk/police-forces/south-yorkshire-police/areas/IncidentsofdisorderinSouthYorkshire/.

Spillers, H. J. (1987) 'Mama's baby, papa's maybe: An American grammar book', *Diacritics*, 17(2), pp. 64–81.

Stanicek, B. (2024) *EU–Egypt Strategic and Comprehensive Partnership.* EPRS. https://www.europarl.europa.eu/RegData/etudes/ATAG/2024/760406/EPRS_ATA(2024)760406_EN.pdf.

Statewatch (2023) 'Schengen states make new call for border wall funds', *Statewatch News*, 19 June.

Stoler, A. L. (1995) *Race and the Education of Desire: Foucault's History of Sexuality and the Colonial Order of Things.* Durham: Duke University Press.

Summerfield, D. (2000) 'Childhood, war, refugeedom and "trauma": Three core questions for mental-health professionals', *Transcultural Psychiatry*, 37(3), pp. 417–433.

Táíwò, O. O. (2022) *Reconsidering Reparations.* Oxford: Oxford University Press.

Taylor, C. (1985) 'Atomism', in *Philosophical Papers, Vol. II: Philosophy and the Human Sciences.* Cambridge: Cambridge University Press, pp. 187–210.

Taylor, C. (1994) 'The politics of recognition', in Gutmann, A. (ed.) *Multiculturalism: Examining the Politics of Recognition.* Princeton, NJ: Princeton University Press, pp. 25–73.

Thym, D. (2024) 'Reinvigorating Schengen amid legal changes and secondary movements', Discussion Paper, European Migration and Diversity Programme, European Policy Centre. https://d1xp398qalq39s.cloudfront.net/content/Schengen_DPEMD1.pdf.

Tuana, N. (2019). 'Climate apartheid: the forgetting of race in the anthropocene', *Critical Philosophy of Race*, 7(1), pp. 1–31.

Tuck, E. and Yang, K. W. (2012) 'Decolonization is not a metaphor', *Decolonization: Indigeneity, Education & Society*, 1(1), pp. 1–40.

Tuck, R. (1989) *Hobbes*. Oxford: Oxford University Press.

Tully, J. (1999). 'To think and act differently: Foucault's four reciprocal objections to Habermas' theory', in S. Ashenden and D. Owen (eds.), *Foucault contra Habermas*. London: Sage Publications, pp. 90–142.

UCAS (2025) *Displaced Students: Asylum Seekers and Access to Student Finance*. Cheltenham: Universities and Colleges Admissions Service.

Uggen, C., Larson, R., Shannon, S., Stewart, R. and Hauf, M. (2024) *Locked Out 2024: Estimates of People Denied Voting Rights Due to a Felony Conviction*. Washington, DC: The Sentencing Project.

UK ENIC (2025) 'Qualification recognition support for refugees' (news and guidance pages). https://www.enic.org.uk/.

UK Government (2022). *UK Climate Change Risk Assessment*. London: HMSO.

UK Government (2023). *The Third National Adaptation Programme (NAP3) and the Fourth Strategy for Climate Adaptation Reporting*. London: HMSO.

UK Government (2024) *NHS Entitlements: Migrant Health Guide – Primary Care Registration*. London: Department of Health and Social Care.

UK Parliament (2024) *Safety of Rwanda (Asylum and Immigration) Act 2024*.

UK Supreme Court (2023) *R (AAA) v Secretary of State for the Home Department*. Press summary, 15 November. https://supremecourt.uk/cases/uksc-2023-0093#case-summary.

UK Visas & Immigration (2021) *Contingency Asylum Accommodation: Stakeholder Briefing Pack*. London: Home Office.

UKHSA (2022) 'UKHSA and ONS release estimates of excess deaths during summer of 2022', Press release, 7 October. https://www.gov.uk/government/news/ukhsa-and-ons-release-estimates-of-excess-deaths-during-summer-of-2022.

UKHSA (2025) *Heat-Mortality Monitoring Report: England, 2024*. London: UK Health Security Agency. https://www.gov.uk/government/statistics/heat-mortality-monitoring-report-england-2024.

UN Human Rights Council (2024). *Report of the Special Rapporteur on the Situation of Human Rights in the Palestinian Territories Occupied since 1967*. A/HRC/55/73. https://www.ohchr.org/en/documents/country-reports/ahrc5573-report-special-rapporteur-situation-human-rights-palestinian.

UN Special Committee (2024). 'UN special committee finds Israel's warfare methods in Gaza consistent with genocide, including use of starvation as weapon of war', Press release, 14 November. https://www.ohchr.org/en/press-releases/2024/11/un-special-committee-finds-israels-warfare-methods-gaza-consistent-genocide.

UNDP (2007) *Human Development Report 2007/2008: Fighting Climate Change – Human Solidarity in a Divided World*. London: Palgrave Macmillan.

UNHCR (2013) 'Rescue efforts focus on survivors of Lampedusa boat tragedy', 4 October. Geneva: UNHCR.

UNHCR (2021) 'UNHCR's Guide to Asylum Reform in the United Kingdom', 23 February. Geneva: UNHCR.

UNHCR (2023) 'Ten years since the Lampedusa shipwreck: what lessons have been learned?', 3 October. Geneva: UNHCR.

UNHCR (2024) *Pakistan Operational Update: Flood-affected Populations*. Geneva: UNHCR.

UNHCR (2025) 'Refugee family reunion: Why it matters', Briefing paper, 12 September.

UNICEF (n.d.) *State of Palestine Situation Reports*. https://www.unicef.org/appeals/state-of-palestine/situation-reports.

UNICEF (2025) 'Children drowning in the world's inaction', Geneva Palais briefing note https://www.unicef.org/eca/press-releases/children-drowning-worlds-inaction-unicef-geneva-palais-briefing-note-increase.

University of Glasgow (n.d.) *Runaway Slaves in Britain: Bondage, Freedom and Race in the Eighteenth Century*. runaways.gla.ac.uk.

UNRWA (2025) *Situation Report #188 on the Humanitarian Crisis in the Gaza Strip and the West Bank (including East Jerusalem)*, 12 September. https://www.unrwa.org/resources/reports/unrwa-situation-report-188-situation-gaza-strip-and-west-bank-including-east-jerusalem.

Unsgaard, O. F. (2017) 'The Riace model', *Eurozine*, 13 April.

van Krieken, R., Habibis, D., Smith, P., Hutchins, B., Martin, G. and Maton, K. (2014) *Sociology*, 5th ed. Frenchs Forest, NSW: Pearson.

Venturini, T., Baya Lafitte, N., Cointet, J.-P., Gray, I., Zabban, V. and De Pryck, K. (2019) 'Mitigation and adaptation in the UNFCCC debates'. http://climaps.eu/#!/narrative/mitigation-and-adaptation-in-the-unfccc-debates.

Victor, D. G. (2004). *The Collapse of the Kyoto Protocol and the Struggle to Slow Global Warming*. Princeton: Princeton University Press.

Vinter, R. (2024) '"They thought they were going to die": The asylum seekers who survived', *Guardian*, 29 December.

von Bertalanffy, L. (1968) *General System Theory: Foundations, Development, Applications*. New York: George Braziller.

Waldron, J. (2002) *God, Locke, and Equality: Christian Foundations in Locke's Political Thought*. Cambridge: Cambridge University Press.

Ward, L. (2021) 'Trust and distributive justice in John Locke's politics of money', *The Review of Politics*, 83(4), pp. 510–532.

Ward, L. (2022) *Recovering Classical Liberal Political Economy: Natural Rights and the Harmony of Interests*. Edinburgh: Edinburgh University Press.

We Are Not Numbers (n.d.) https://wearenotnumbers.org/tag/refaat-alareer/.

Weber, M. (1978 [1922]) *Economy and Society: An Outline of Interpretive Sociology*, ed. G. Roth and C. Wittich. Berkeley: University of California Press.

Weber, S., Stoop, N., van der Windt, P. and Zhai, H. (2024) 'A meta-analysis of attitudes towards migrants and displaced persons', IPL Working Paper Series, Immigration Policy Lab, Stanford/ETH Zurich.

Weheliye, A. G. (2014) *Habeas Viscus: Racializing Assemblages, Biopolitics, and Black Feminist Theories of the Human*. Durham: Duke University Press.

Weizman, E. (2011) *The Least of All Possible Evils: Humanitarian Violence from Arendt to Gaza*. London: Verso.

Wekker, G. (2016) *White Innocence: Paradoxes of Colonialism and Race*. Durham: Duke University Press.

WHO (2022) *State of the World's Drinking Water: An Urgent Call to Action to Accelerate Progress on Ensuring Safe Drinking Water for All*. Geneva: World Health Organization.

WHO (2024) 'Countries commit to recover lost progress in maternal, newborn and child survival', World Health Organization News Release, 30 May.

WHO (2025a) *Public Health Situation Analysis: Occupied Palestinian Territory*. Geneva: World Health Organization.

WHO (2025b) *Trends in Maternal Mortality 2000 to 2023*. Geneva: World Health Organization.

Williams, E. (1944) *Capitalism and Slavery*. Chapel Hill: University of North Carolina Press.

Williams, M. S. (2003) 'Citizenship as identity, citizenship as shared fate, and the functions of multicultural education', in McDonough, K. and Feinberg, W. (eds.), *Citizenship and Education in Liberal-Democratic Societies: Teaching for Cosmopolitan Values and Collective Identities*. Oxford: Oxford University Press, pp. 208–247.

Williams, W. (2020) *Windrush Lessons Learned Review*. London: HMSO.

Wise, P. H. and Darmstadt, G. L. (2015) 'The changing face of child mortality in war and conflict', *The Lancet*, 385(9976), pp. 1156–1158.

Wittgenstein, L. (1953) *Philosophical Investigations*. Oxford: Blackwell.

Wolfe, P. (2016) *Traces of History: Elementary Structures of Race*. London: Verso.

World Bank (2021) *Groundswell Part 2: Acting on Internal Climate Migration*. Washington, DC: World Bank. https://openknowledge.worldbank.org/handle/10986/36248.

World Bank (2022) 'Pakistan: Flood damages and economic losses over USD 30 billion and reconstruction needs over USD 16 billion', Press Release, 28 October. https://www.worldbank.org/en/news/press-release/2022/10/28/pakistan-flood-damages-and-economic-losses-over-usd-30-billion-and-reconstruction-needs-over-usd-16-billion-new-assessme.

World Bank (2023) *Poverty and Inequality Platform (PIP).* https://pip.worldbank.org/home.

World Conference on Human Rights (1993) Final Declaration of the Regional Meeting for Asia ('Bangkok Declaration'), UN Doc. A/CONF.157/ASRM/8 (with A/CONF.157/PC/59), 7 April.

WWA (2022) 'Without human-caused climate change, temperatures of 40°C in the UK would have been extremely unlikely'. https://www.worldweatherattribution.org/wp-content/uploads/UK-heat-scientific-report.pdf.

Young, I. M. (1990) *Justice and the Politics of Difference.* Princeton: Princeton University Press.

Young, I. M. (2011) *Responsibility for Justice.* Oxford: Oxford University Press.

Zagajewski, A. (2001) 'Try to praise the mutilated world', *The New Yorker*, 24 September. https://www.newyorker.com/magazine/2001/09/24/try-to-praise-the-mutilated-world.

Zolin, N. (2019) 'How refugees saved Riace, the tiny Italian town that could', *Adventure.com*, 21 January. https://adventure.com/how-refugees-saved-riace-the-tiny-italian-town-that-could/.

Index